Ends of the .

Ends of the Lyric

ह

Direction and Consequence
in Western Poetry

Timothy Bahti

The Johns Hopkins University Press
Baltimore and London

© 1996 The Johns Hopkins University Press
All rights reserved. Published 1996
Printed in the United States of America on acid-free paper
05 04 03 02 01 00 99 98 98 97 96   5 4 3 2 1

The Johns Hopkins University Press, 2715 North Charles Street
Baltimore, Maryland 21218-4319
The Johns Hopkins Press Ltd., London

ISBN 0-8018-5192-0
ISBN 0-8018-5193-9 (pbk.)

Library of Congress Cataloging-in-Publication Data will be found
at the end of this book.
A catalog record for this book is available from the British Library.

Contents

Acknowledgments

Earlier versions of chapters 3, 7, and the first part of 8 appeared in MLN (1981, 1990, 1995), and several pages of chapter 4 appeared in a first context in *Comparative Literature* (1986). I am grateful to the editors and publishers for permission to reprint.

A research fellowship from the Alexander von Humboldt Foundation, Bonn, Germany, for 1991 allowed me to work intensively on this project, and I am grateful for their generous support of international research in the humanities. The late Beda Allemann, who welcomed me as a German Academic Exchange Service scholar in 1973–74, when I began to work on Hölderlin, welcomed me again in his seminar at the University of Bonn, and I remember here his generosity and encouragement. My editor at the Johns Hopkins University Press, Eric Halpern, has been decisively supportive, as always, and he has my deep thanks.

The pleasure of working on poetry is added to by the kindness and sharing of others who care for it as well. I am grateful to the poets Robert Julian, William McCormick, Wilbert Snow, and Richard Wilbur, who have instructed me in the art. I am also grateful to my teachers in reading poetry, Paul de Man, John Freccero, and Geoffrey Hartman. Bernhard Böschenstein, Angus Fletcher, and Helen Vendler are distinguished scholars who have been especially helpful through their publications, conversation, and correspondence.

Many friends and colleagues have contributed to this book over the years through their knowledge and encouragement, and I thank Cynthia Chase, Jonathan Culler, Werner Hamacher, Neil Hertz, Greg Lucente, Richard Macksey, Rainer Nägele, Jim Porter, Claude Reichler, and Susan Wolfson. I am also very grateful to my students at the University of Michigan, who in seminars improved many of the readings included here.

Scarcely a page has not been shared with my friend Christiaan Hart Nibbrig. Through him I have been able to discuss the work while in progress with his students and colleagues at the University of Lausanne and elsewhere in Switzerland, a university culture especially encouraging of the study of poetry and long supportive of my own. Through his many generous conversations—his insights and his challenges—he has been responsive to the poems and readings in this book, and it could not have been written without his differential correspondence.

I dedicate this book to Amy Schuyler Harris, who supported the many absences when I worked, away, and who always in the end with her presence guided my directions toward the ends of the lyric.

Claviers, April 1995

Ends of the Lyric

Introduction

Poems end. They begin, and they end. In between beginnings and ends are the middles—the means—of getting from the one to the other. How poems get to their ends—the directions they take, and give, and the consequences of following them—is the topic of this study. That poems may not direct their readings to end, thus themselves not simply ending, is a finding I demonstrate, and I explore its consequences for both poetics and the reading of poetry.

The varieties of ends of poems are not just the contrasts of conclusions and stoppages or abandonments. They include as well exhortations to action—purposes and applications. The "end of the lyric" is a formulation I have avoided, because it offers the misunderstanding that one should think of the disappearance of a genre; it also sounds wrongly monolithic. "Endings of the lyric" I have also avoided, as I have reserved the term "ending" for a particular kind of end of a poem and a correspondingly particular kind of reading at such an end. But "ends of the lyric" is meant to

1

cover the formal, structural, and semantic domains of how poems end, as well as the question of goals and actions at and as the ends of poems. Poems can be used for many ends, wishfully by their authors—wishfully because they have so little control of the matter, virtually none outside of very special circumstances (private verse epistles, epithalamia, certain funeral and memorial poetry)—and willfully by their readers. Poems may be intended or taken to celebrate, grieve, console, instruct, delight, amuse, ridicule. They may be used and abused to impart wisdom, to encourage morality, to propagandize an ideology. I have scarcely anything to say in this study about such "ends"—applications and fates—of the lyric because I believe that conjoined to the specific features of how lyric poems end is one particular end in the sense of their purpose, goal, and consequence. And this is that poems end in their reading, and in offering the lesson of this special kind of construction and performance and reading—this special kind of *use*—of language at and as their end.

In this introduction I explain my selection and limitation of materials, my choice and understanding of key terms, my deployment of certain assumptions and methods, and my affinities and differences with some of my predecessors' theories and scholarship. But I also, in the course of treating these matters, both anticipate and justify the importance I have just granted to reading as the end and consequence at the ends of the lyric.

ᘒ▲

Ever since Plato, in the *Republic*, sketched a theory of literary genres by their "voice"—the poet speaking in his own voice (the dithyramb), the characters speaking in their own voices (drama), and a mixture of the two (Homer's epics)—theories of the lyric have been based, in part or in totality, upon a theory of its voice. (Linking lyric poetry to music is also recurrent, but is a red herring; scholars as different as Northrop Frye and W. R. Johnson convincingly argue the emphasis in lyric poetry, already in Greek lyric and to the present, on words as words, with "music"—which means many things, sometimes very little that is specific, in these discussions—distinctly secondary.) [1] The emphasis on lyric voice is the case all the way down to Paul de Man's effort to dismiss the genre aspect of lyric and its reading by way of the deconstruction of voice performed by (his understanding of) anthropomorphism and prosopopeia.[2] Examples along the way would include John Stuart Mill's famous "overheard" voice, T. S. Eliot's notorious "meditative voice" (which repeats and narrows Mill), Frye's endorsement of Mill's characterization, and W. R. Johnson's critique of Eliot (which turns out reinstating voice within discourse).[3] Eliot, it will be recalled, characterized one "voice of the poet" as that of "the poet talking to himself—or to nobody" (the other two were the poet talking to an audience and the poet talking through created dramatic characters—thus a version of Plato's triad). This became narrowed, in the course of his argument, to "writing, so to speak, in terms of one's own voice," which may be overheard but "is not primarily an attempt to communicate with anyone at all," and this is what he calls "meditative verse" in proposing this term to replace "lyric poetry."[4] Frye is very close to this when he calls the lyric "preeminently the utterance that is overheard." He adds, "The lyric poet normally pretends to be talking to himself or someone else," but the "someone else" is not there: "the concealment of the poet's audience from the poet" is the arrangement that distinguishes lyric from drama, *epos*, and written prose fiction, and, in a formulation he uses twice, Frye says "the poet turns his back on his listeners [audience]."[5]

From Plato onward, the theory of the lyric as a special kind of "voice" implicitly or explicitly includes a special relationship to an audience; this is true even in de Man's antitheory, where the "audience" is a structural reflex called "the defensive motion of understanding." Even Eliot, despite his exclusive narrowing of lyric (or "meditative") poetry, then has to allow the audience's reintroduction: "If the author never spoke to himself, the result would not be poetry, though it might be magnificent rhetoric; and part of our enjoyment of great poetry is the enjoyment of *overhearing* words which are not addressed to us. But if the poem were exclusively for the author, it would be a poem in a private and unknown language; and a poem which was a poem only for the author would not be a poem at all."[6] W. R. Johnson, in overturning Eliot's tendentious narrowing of the lyric away from an audience (which we have just seen he did not really maintain), says that lyric poetry primarily—historically, from Greek and Roman lyric to the nineteenth century—is "the I-You poem, in which the poet addresses or pretends to address his thoughts and feelings to another person [who] . . . (whether actual or fictional) is a metaphor for readers of the poem." Essentially, there is here "a speaker, or singer, talking to, singing to, another person or persons."[7] Audience is as central here as it was offstage in Eliot, and yet the poet's voice—"meditative" or pronominal—is the point from which the audience is conceived.

Mill's employment, and Eliot's repetition, of the image of "overhearing" the lyric voice is coy about the precise nature of the audience's experience, whereas Frye simply has the poet turning his back to the audience. Johnson, on the other hand, is unbothered about referring to "readers of the poem" even as he wants to keep the essence of the lyric in "the sung story that the singer and his audience share . . . this musical intimacy, this rhetorical, pronominal patterning, this dialectic of I and You, this lyrical discourse"; this is because he can begin with Catullus and Horace, already bookish poets, and can refer to Rome as "after the singer sang no more . . . and song lived primarily in books and in libraries."[8] I want now, with help from Frye, Johnson, and Helen Vendler, to bring our initial attention to the lyric "voice" and its audience to the consideration of the lyric's *readers*.

By a positive or a negative dialectic, the issue of the lyric's audience is always right behind or in front of its voice. The poet's voice alone (Eliot) has to get back to an audience somehow—"overhearing" is the sleight of ear—while a pronominal and silent voice (Johnson's I) is always in address to and communication with its grammatical or "shifting" other, a You (any You). "What is essential, then, to lyric," Johnson concludes his first chapter, "is rhetoric, and essential to this lyrical rhetoric . . . is the pronominal form and lyric identity, the dynamic configuration of lyrical pronouns that defines and vitalizes the situation of lyrical discourse." It is sufficient that rhetoric be construed grammatically—generative of an I-You discourse—for an audience to be constituted.[9]

Northrop Frye makes the audience central to genre theory, and also calls this rhetorical:

The origin of the words drama, epic, and lyric suggests that the central principle of genre is simple enough. The basis of generic distinctions in literature appears to be the radical of presentation. Words may be acted in front of a spectator; they may be spoken in front of a listener; they may be sung or chanted; or they may be written for a reader. . . . The basis of generic criticism in any case is rhetorical, in the sense that the genre is determined by the conditions established between the poet and his public.[10]

In Frye's list of four generic radicals of presentation, it is clear that "sung or chanted" refers to the lyric, and in his subchapter on "the rhythm of association" as lyric he amply acknowledges the "radical of lyrical *melos*" at its basis. But he both diminishes music properly so called, as I have already noted, and pairs this radical of *melos* with one of *opsis*. It is as if the "concealed audience" constitutive of the lyric poet's voice never really needed to be there, listening to anything sung, in the first place. The radical of *opsis* is boldly sketched by Frye as follows: "The radical of *opsis* in the lyric is *riddle*, which is characteristically a fusion of sensation and reflection, the use of an object of sense experience to stimulate a mental activity in connection with it. Riddle was originally the cognate object of read, and the riddle seems intimately involved with the whole process of reducing language to visible form, a process which runs through such by-forms of riddle as hieroglyphic and ideogram."[11]

I honor Frye's insight into the riddling, enigmatic, *read* character of the lyric, moving from sensation to reflection, throughout the chapters of this book. Here, I want just to note that Johnson's historical approach and Frye's speculative-conceptual one converge at the same point regarding the lyric's audience. Johnson laments the loss for the lyric of an audience's felt sense of address, and he believes this is a historical process threatening that clichéd "death of lyric," but it is emphatically more than a question of poets no longer singing or chanting before large audiences. That with the high romantic lyric "at best, the audience is extraneous to this poetry; at worst, all sense of audience has vanished," and that "modern lyric tends to be bereft of its singers and its audiences," is for Johnson more a matter of pronouns and their discourses than of singers, songs, and audience, and he can credit the later William Carlos Williams and Adrienne Rich with a "rebirth of lyric vitality" that is strictly discursive, that is, pronominal.[12] Frye's "singing or chanting" was, we might say, unheard except as overheard from the start; the audience was concealed (often literally absent), the chanting was to emphasize "words as words," and in the visual aspect of lyric poetry, the lyric is the occasion for intensely private, not public, reflection.

These two scholars' positions allow me to turn, with Helen Vendler, to my own position on the sense and use of the term "lyric" and the character of its audience as readers. The audience for lyric poetry was certainly once a literally listening audience, for Pindar and again for some, perhaps even most, medieval verse. It is no longer, and no one should waste any theoretical time or social-historical hand-wringing over this. The lyric has become a genre whose "public" or "audience" is readers. Vendler can thus refer to "written lyric" and not even need to specify that this covers almost all lyric poetry in modern, that is, postmedieval English. She can also state, with great clarity and verve, that *the voice of the lyric is, or is to be, the reader's voice:* "Lyric offers itself as a potential speech for its reader to utter, or *lied* for its hearer to sing. . . . A lyric is *a role offered to a reader;* the reader is to be the voice speaking the poem. . . . The poem is to be spoken in propria persona by anyone who reads it."[13] She offers these remarks in the course of her forcefully, and I think admirably, polemical argument about how lyric is not to be badly read—indeed, misread— as a "social genre" like drama, epic, or the novel: "Lyric, unlike the social genres, does not incorporate interaction with a 'collective'; it privileges the mind in its solitary and private moments. The poet does not have to make any special effort to place himself in solidarity with 'the collective'" (179). In agreeing with but also then freely adapting Vendler's positions, I want not so much to stick with her terms of "speech to be uttered" or the "voice speaking" by the reader of a poem, as to inflect her insights into the lyric offering a role to the reader and its interacting with its public not collectively, but individually and privately.

Silent reading is individual and private par excellence—even the most distracting public library cannot altogether deny one this truth—and the role of the silent reader that the lyric aims at is for him or her to be the recipient, the goal and end, of the lyric. Whatever once was the lyric's musicality and orality (and we must recall again how little is known about Greek "lyric"'s "musicality,"[14] and how long and rare it has been since modern lyric cared about an actually listening public), it has become an experience of private reading: this is how "the lyric," "lyric poetry," "Western poetry," and "the tradition of Western poetry"—all phrases I henceforth use without apology—are constituted and reconstituted.

Putting this slightly differently, I would say that there is no lyric without reading, and if this would become plausible for the case of, say, Pindar only with considerable qualification and redefining of terms (what is the text of Pindar? what do we know about how his poems were performed? what exactly *is* reading?), it ought to be almost self-evident for all the postmedieval poets I treat in this study. There is no lyric without reading because we cannot conceive of a poem that does not have at least the one reader who is its author; Eliot's formulation, we recall, allows and even necessitates this. In this view, the unconscious or trancelike composition of some surrealist's "automatic writing" is either fraudulent or deluded. And the reading of any single poem while (as, contemporaneously) it is written recalls to the author—and ought to recall to its readers and critics—the reading of other poems, by the same or any other author. This is what we call tradition. It has nothing to do with reading poems "as" their authors did, or might have. No more than we know who (or what) "Shakespeare" "was," do we know who all, or what all, "the lyric tradition" is, but it makes necessary sense to speak of it because it is impossible to read lyric poems—or any literature—without reading their tradition, their constitution and handing-down through writing, rewriting, reading, and rereading.

Lyric poetry as a private (but never singular) reading activity that is co-constitutive of the literary text itself, is what I take, then, to be its factual, historical condition—perhaps, following W. R. Johnson's account, already since Roman antiquity, certainly since the modern vernacular literatures. For the purposes of this study, the publication of Shakespeare's sonnets in 1609 as a bookish event and experience is a sufficient and self-evident and probably permanent marker of the *written and readerly* character of Western lyric poetry (permanent because popular music has taken over the oral aspect of lyric, rendering the tradition of the lyric a "high" one). One cannot imagine any access to or continuity with the depth and excellence of Shakespeare's sonnets except through their reading and rereading, and the conjunction of this constitutive nature of theirs with the subsequent Western lyric tradition may explain in part the selection and sequencing of the poets and poetry in this study.

Shakespeare's sonnets and 1609 are a point of departure, although this is Anglocentric, even as it is also, and for the same reason, facilitating. Literary history suggests no terminus a quo for the irreversible switch from "oral" to written and readerly lyric; it arguably might already have happened with the preservation of Pindar's poems and the adaptation of other Greek metric and strophic schemes, with Catullus, Propertius, and Horace, with Arnaut Daniel. The present study begins first with Shakespeare, then with the counterpoint of Leopardi to Dante. From these first steps, however, little further in the selection of poets studied or in their sequence was necessarily determined. My regret at not treating poems by Gaspara Stampa, John Donne, or Ben Jonson, by Mörike, Dickinson, Mallarmé, Rilke, or Yeats, will perhaps be accepted without further excuse. The selection as it did come to be made was partially suggested by a continuity of allusion and rereading and rewriting that I understood to stretch from Shakespeare to Keats and Stevens and Celan, but this continuity is not restrictive, and references to it are mostly in passing remarks and footnotes.

In writing about the very close reading of individual poems, it is best to choose those the excellence and interest of which (with perhaps an exception in one Shakespeare sonnet) are beyond question. Only with Celan, where the canon is still in formation, was my choice more free, or arbitrary. Fewer rather than more poems have to be concentrated upon with each author, for one cannot treat more and still respect sufficiently the degree of complexity in the poems' endings and the demands for patient analysis this puts upon their readers. Only Keats is an exception here, for his interweaving of the semantics and thematics and poetics of nonending (what I call his "'still' reading") requires attention—if necessarily partial and fleeting—to many more of his extraordinary poems. Hölderlin and Celan receive a largesse of analysis for two principal reasons: their poetry is so excellent, still so little understood in English, and so pertinent to the problems of poetics and reading that I address here, that their work justifies a great indulgence; and the quality and detail of readings their poems have sometimes received demand a correspondingly respectful and careful critique if they are to be surpassed in a possibly better understanding. Putting the chapter on Hölderlin after that on Keats, the chapter on Celan after that on Stevens, is a decision governed more by this greater luxury of attention than by any literary-historical reflection. For in any case, literary history in any causal or receptive sense plays no argumentative role in the selection or arrangement of the poets here studied, except that William Shakespeare and Paul Celan mark—including in Celan's own understanding—the extent of modern Western lyric poetry to our time.

The poets and poems, then, selected and ordered on these complex grounds, were further selected, of course, as they demonstrated themselves to be pertinent to and illuminating for a study of how poems and their readings both end and, in their special way, don't end, or at least don't end in any way this has conventionally been understood. A rereading of Barbara Herrnstein Smith's *Poetic Closure* has made it clear to me that closure—"the sense of finality, stability, and integrity"—is not what one finds in the poems treated here, nor in many others. (Nor was it what Herrnstein Smith claimed to find or be findable in all poems, and she also resisted any facile literary-historical account of this.)[15] What are the distinctive features and defining constituents of the "nonclosure" I instead find in Western lyric poetry? These can be introduced under three general rubrics, none of which is unique to the couple dozen poems in this study, but each of which is especially significant in them. The rubrics are direction, trope, and reflection.

We have already read several theorists and critics speaking of poems "addressed" (or not addressed) to their readers. I take it as axiomatic that all literary texts are addressed to their readers in the sense that the activity of reading is co-constitutive of what makes a text a text, and not just a jumble of black-and-white "alphabet soup" shaken over a page: for this is what texts would be, potentially significant but actually meaningless, under the merely *phenomenal* description of the unread. I further take it as axiomatic that all reading tries—it need not succeed, nor end with this, but it minimally tries—to understand the literary text: as Paul de Man declared, "Any text, as text, compels reading as its understanding."[16] Beyond these two positions, I adopt the further one that literary texts give *directions* to their readers for both the co-constitutive reading activity and the specific effort at reading as interpretation and understanding. This means something as basic as the fact that texts cannot be made to say anything a reader wants unless that reader is prepared to be reading wrongly or sillily: there are many (not an infinite number, but many) determinants that are restrictive, sometimes minimally, sometimes maximally, of our readings, and these are grammatical, rhetorical, lexical, sometimes stylistic, sometimes logical, and so forth. But the sense of "giving directions" also means something more specific with respect to reading texts—here, lyric poems—to their ends and endings. Literary texts direct us on our ways toward their understanding, and everyone can readily agree that characters' asides in drama, say, or a narrator's commentary upon characters and plot, are examples of such directions. In lyric poems, both their relative brevity and the intensity of their deployment of "speaking" and addressed personae (poets' "voices," discursive "pronouns," or however else construed) make these signals of directions especially dominant for the act of reading. Vendler's "a lyric is *a role offered to a reader*" seems very right here, if we understand the "role" to be the acting out or enacting of the poem's directions—moves—from beginning to end. Formal constraints in the cases of a strict form like the sonnet, or a triadic structure like a classical ode, only reinforce the sense of directions given and taken, and the formal and structural and semantic consequences for both the poem and its understanding.

Directions given by a text to its reader as each together makes its way toward ends—of texts and of understandings—are obviously as basic and unavoidable as grammatical forms, syntactic arrangements, formal schemes and structures, lexical and intuitive understandings. We shall see in this study a considerable variety of kinds of directions given by lyric poems, ranging from semantic gestures in titles, to the small prosodic and tropological features of rhyme, enjambment, caesura, and alliteration, to the larger formal and structural shapes of poems, to narrative and argumentative turns in their discourses. But in lyric poems, the directions are further embodied in and themselves directed by two specific textual features. I turn to the aspect of reflection and reflexivity later, after first giving attention to that of tropes.

Literature is made up of tropes. Anyone who resists this knowledge should not be in the business of professionally reading literature, any more than anyone who doesn't like wood should be in carpentry. (I leave in suspension the question of whether all language is made up of tropes. It is highly arguable that it is, but it is also highly arguable that it is not.) Lyric poems are especially tropologically constructed; to follow Paul Celan's formulation, "the poem would be the place where all tropes and metaphors want to be directed *ad absurdum*."[17] The absurdity aside, the special tropological construction of poetry is probably the case as much because of the density and continuity of the *intertext* in the tradition's handing-down of forms, themes, images, and allusions—I know of no other genre as continuous as the Western lyric—as because of the palpable *texture* provided to lyric tropes by the relative brevity of form and the density of sonorous and semantic interweave in each individual poem. Surely the fact that *verse, strophe,* and *trope* all return to the same sense of "turning" has much to do with the inconceivability of lyric poetry without tropes. There is nothing original in any of this: the centrality of tropes was universal knowledge for literate students in the West from antiquity through the nineteenth century, and many of the most influential readers of poetry in our century (when tropes fell out of primary and secondary instruction in literacy)—William Empson, Cleanth Brooks, Paul de Man, Joel Fineman among them—have taken it as a given.

We can resist the temptation of reading or arguing for one or more "master tropes" of the lyric with respect to the directions and consequences of its ends. One can rightly admire both Frye's insistence on metaphor and especially catachresis, and de Man's last speculations on prosopopeia and anthropomorphism, but these have seemed to me irrelevant or limiting, respectively, for the present study's interest in how specific poems end.[18] Empson's ambiguity—especially because it is so capaciously conceived, from grammar to semantics to logic, and so sensitively grounded in the actual reading of lines of verse—would probably have done better than the other candidates (paradox, descriptive image in the sense of the tropes of *mimesis* and *descriptio*, revisionary metalepsis, etc.) that have been periodically offered up.[19] But my concrete readings of individual poems, as they track their taking of directions given by the texts and their discovery of tropes as principal "signals" and "maps" of poetic and interpretive directionality, have nonetheless come upon one kind of trope too often, and in too many kinds of otherwise highly different circumstances (formal, thematic, historical) for it to escape our attention.

This is the trope of chiasmus, the inversion and crosswise arrangement of otherwise parallel pairs of verbal units (usually grammatical or semantic, but also phonetic), and it extends, as we shall see already in the Shakespeare chapter and then repeatedly thereafter, to include both a subset of technically separate lesser tropes (doubled epizeuxes or diacopes, antimetabole, etc.) and a range of formal, structural, narrative, argumentative, and discursive aspects of lyric poetry. Here again, there is no claim of originality; chiasmus had already been singled out by de Man as central to understanding the poetry of Rilke, and possibly central to much modern lyric from Baudelaire to Celan, some ten years before his unrelenting fascination with prosopopeia and anthropomorphism, and Joel Fineman's influential recent book on Shakespeare's sonnets built its argument around the understanding and deployment of chiasmus.[20] The attention this study draws to chiasmus is rather to its explanatory power for the practice of ending in the lyric poems at hand.

Lyric poems from Shakespeare to Celan do not move to their ends and direct their readers to them without inverting the end into its "other"—sometimes the beginning, sometimes a nonterminal activity I call "ending"—and also inverting themselves, qua texts, into their necessary readings which, however, are not just mimetic repetitions or reduplications, or dialectical fulfillments of the poems as, now, their interpretations or understandings. Lyric poems begin and end, but by their end they have inverted the end into its opposite, a nonend. Lyric poems are to be understood, and direct their reading toward understanding, but at the end of reading—reading lyric poems as far and as near (as closely) as one can—they have inverted the attempts at interpretation into discoveries of where reading has to rebegin, never end, or sometimes even realize its own threshold of unreadability.

Nonmimetic, nonreduplicative, nonparaphrastic, nonrepresentational: the reading at the end of the lyric and the lyric at the end of its reading are thus peculiarly recurrent and recursive without being repetitious and repeatable. It is no news to anybody that lyric verse and forms are built out of dozens of kinds of repetition. The recognition of a single metric foot, of a verse's metric length, of a caesura, of a rhyme, of alliteration and assonance and consonance, of anaphora and distichs and couplets, of an allusion and an imitation, of a multitude of lyric constituents would be impossible without the formal and structural principle of repetition.[21] All repetition presupposes the principle of difference, but it does *not* presuppose the principle of inversion, and this is what distinguishes the chiastic aspect of recurrence and recursiveness by way of inversion that I find from the widely recognized and important feature of repetition in the lyric. So, too, the cycles both of themes and forms within the lyric genre and of literary "modes" within all of literature that Northrop Frye argued for, are—if they exist— obviously (if slowly) repetitive and recurrent (cyclical) but not, so far as we yet know, inverting.

Why lyric poems should end with such stunning power and curious frequency in inverting their ends into nonends, and their readings into rebeginnings or not-yet-readings, is, within the limits of the present study, not to be accounted for other than by the structural, that is, tropological predominance of chiasmus in the lyric tradition, and the inadequacy of a hermeneutics of interpretation to explain the ends—the consequences—of the lyric.[22] The chiasmus is here not further explainable by or as a structure of Merleau-Pontyan self-consciousness or the Lacanian unconscious. Inversion as both a tropological means and a structural limitation of the knowledge provided by poetry is explored in my afterword by way of some "counter"-cases: *apotropos* and Pindar's Pythian 8 ode, and hysteron proteron and other tropes of inversion in passages of Dante's *Commedia*. The point there is to test the theoretical comprehensiveness and self-limitation of an understanding of lyric in terms of inversions at the ends of our understanding.

Chiasmi are unrecognizable, and a fortiori unreadable, without an awareness of inversion, minimally phonetic or visual inversions, frequently grammatical and syntactic inversions, and then maximally the semantic and logical inversions that chiasmi produce. The turning, twisting, crossing, and inverting force of the chiasmus thus yields inverted or reversed aspects that mirror one another precisely in their crossed "mirror imagery," and that produce reflection upon such mirror reflection. This brings us to the third textual feature to be introduced here. Reflection of a text in itself is called self-reflexivity, and this has long and widely been recognized as a constitutive feature of much Western literature, perhaps from the very beginning (the *Iliad* within its "shield of Achilles" passage). And if literary texts demand, direct, and produce their readings, then this direction-of-reading ought, in an extended understanding of self-reflexivity, also to be available for reflexion in the reading: self-reflexive reading, which reads itself reading. This, too, is nothing new.

Because this understanding of self-reflexivity has become almost canonical by now, and risks becoming tired (or repackaged as "postmodern"), a difference should be signaled here. Not only is the present study not at all historical in any claims it might make for the pervasiveness of self-reflexivity. Surely Dante and Shakespeare are incomprehensible without taking account of the constitutive and guiding functions of self-reflexivity in their texts, but Pindar's Pythian 1 and Pythian 8 odes, or Arnaut's sestina, can also be shown to be equally self-reflexive. The finding here, in these poets and these poems, is that the properly inverting character of reflection and reflexivity occurs by way of their recurrent deployment of mirrorings, scenes of reflection, and broader themes and narratives of reflexivity and remembrance. In other words, while it should surprise no one to find the imagery of mirrors, reflections (and obfuscations and shadings), eyes looking at eyes, and the like in Western literary texts, nor to find the explicit production of scenes of self-reflection and self-reflexivity in the texts' accounts of their personae and themselves, it *is* remarkable to find that re-presentational or mimetic models for such reflection, reflexivity, and its reading are repeatably inadequate to account for them as textual features, and that a model of lyric poetry and reading as chiastic inversion is more able to explain why poems reflect their readings in such a way that poems are always reflecting—reversely—the reading they are directing, and that readings likewise—but in reverse—reflect by inversion the directions they have been given and have taken. To freely adapt Helen Vendler one last time, that "the poem is to be spoken in propria persona by anyone who reads it," is a truth that needs to be understood not only by taking the "spoken" silently as silent reading, and not only by observing her own fine paradox that the "proper person" is "anyone who reads it," but finally by taking the "proper" character of reading lyric poems—the reading proper to them in the sense of a property of theirs—as the inverting reflection of their directions toward ends in their consequences of nonends.

In 1991 I visited a German museum exhibition that included writings by Marcel Duchamp. Duchamp was a highly serious player and student of chess, and he wrote on it as well. In a quotation I have subsequently been unable to track down, Duchamp wrote that he was interested in some endgames precisely because their construction was so improbable, so unlikely ever to occur in a game, that they were what he called "utopian endings." Apart from the beauty of this formulation, its collocation of ending with a nonplace has stayed with me in the years of finishing my study. My understanding of the ends of the lyric in some of its poetry's most interesting and powerful instances is that they are utopian not in that they do not occur—for they do—but in that they direct us to a place of language and thought the promised consequences of which are still, and always, and rightly elsewhere.

1

Shakespeare's Sonnets

Ends and Means of the Lyric

Shakespeare's sonnets are where English lyric poetry neither begins nor ends, certainly not where modern Western poetry either begins or ends, but they are where questions of poetic ending can still properly begin.

This book is not a historical study of a great tradition, nor is it a formal study of its great lyric forms, the sonnet among them. The figure of Shakespeare's sonnets nonetheless unmistakably lies across the path of a study that would mount its selective and comparative inquiry into how poems end while remaining unbound by historical causality and consequence on the one hand, by formal specificity and difference on the other. For one thing, the quality, but even more impressively the variety, of reading brought to the sonnets by others inevitably attracts and draws their next reader out of any single-minded pursuit. For another, the power of the Shakespearian sonnet form to end, such that the name and the distinctive closing couplet have become synonymous (even though the form was not invented by him), means that it cannot be bypassed in our series of analyses, especially because we shall look at another sonnet, by Baudelaire, as well. And the combination of recent scholarly readings of the sonnets with the questions of their endings and consequences yields a doubled interest in what can be learned from and claimed about them in a study that is both broadly (comparatively and nonhistorically) and specifically (poetically and hermeneutically) interested in how reading and poems guide one another to their shared but different ends.

More than twenty-five years ago, Barbara Herrnstein Smith's *Poetic Closure: A Study of How Poems End* grew out of what was originally a study of Shakespeare's sonnets.[1] In exceeding its origins it did not leave but contained them, and thus it recalls how the sonnets are central or at least basic to Anglo-American scholarship on poetic ending. With its combination of psychological and formal perspectives, and its far-reaching interests in communication and understanding, *Poetic Closure* also pointed toward many of the questions of structure and interpretation that would dominate the American university's study of poetry in the 1970s and 1980s. Herrnstein Smith's book got to its topic first—roughly contemporary with Frank Kermode's study of closure in prose, *The Sense of an Ending*—and it continues to provide lasting insight and guidance. For my part, I take a sentence from it as one of my points of departure in this chapter: "The sense of closure produced by a ['Shakespearian'] sonnet ending does not arise so much from the independent effectiveness of the rhymed couplet as from its effectiveness in relation to the formal structure that precedes it."[2] The formal and structural feature of a Shakespeare sonnet's ending couplet may or may not tell the story of the poem's end, and whether it does or does not is less a question of the presumed end—the question cannot begin at or presume the end—than of everything that tries to get one there: beginning, middle, and means. In linking "formal structure" and what she calls "effectiveness"—poetic efficacy, close to what German scholars were calling at the same time *Wirkung*, which then came to be translated as "response" (in "reader-response")—Herrnstein Smith here, as throughout her book, keeps the strictly formal and structural questions of poetics inseparable from those of the solicitation and guidance, the directions for reading, which the poetics give to interpretation and understanding.

The breadth of *Poetic Closure* exceeded the study of closure in Shakespeare's sonnets and even unabashedly strained the limits announced in its subtitle (speculating on closure in all literature, art, and experience), and despite the book's initial success and its author's continued renown as a critic and theorist, Herrnstein Smith's question of the end has not remained one about which scholars have much generalized, although it is of course always of interest to the individual sonnets' individual readers. Subsequent scholarly developments such as Stephen Booth's much-praised edition of the sonnets have certainly contributed to keep the poetry itself—as opposed to biographical fancy—a focus of critical interest.[3] Recently our best professional reader of poetry in the English language, Helen Vendler, has been guiding nonspecialist readers to the sonnets and through the particular poetic and figurative and semantic features of several of them in a pair of contributions to less scholarly editions of the poems.[4] But it is surely Joel Fineman's award-winning *Shakespeare's Perjured Eye* that brings recent scholarship and Shakespeare's sonnets most impressively together.[5]

Massively learned and tirelessly argued, Fineman's book will concern us in some detail, around one sonnet, in the second part of this chapter. Here, in introducing my question of Shakespeare's sonnets and their poetic ends, I want only to recall that for Fineman, the sonnets are paradoxically—one of his favorite words— an end, and a beginning, and something further and consequential without end. I refer to his historical, or pseudohistorical, argument, and by "pseudohistorical" no disrespect is intended. Rather, I would unmask the staged and mock-historical character of his book's pretensions—its pretense—to "literary history."[6] The sonnets, in his story, are supposed to be the end of a poetry of praise (marking a break from ancient epideictic poetry and poetics all the way to Dante and to Petrarch). They are supposed to be the beginning of the paradox of praise, a duplicitous praising of and damning by poetry as sheer differential language, in contrast to a poetics of visibility, and so they are to be the beginning of modern subjectivity as what is not seen but, invisible and endlessly interior, can only be spoken, and spoken as what it does not appear to be.[7] And they are consequential without end in that their shadow, cast over Shakespeare's plays with their dramas of character and plot, over subsequent poetry, and over our critical and theoretical terminologies of self, subject, and language, shades and envelops us still, so that we can no more read or think outside of the sonnets—so my slight exaggeration of Fineman's considerable hyperbole—than we can jump over "our" (Will Shakespeare's) "own" (poetically constructed and transacted) shadow.

This is not the place to document, criticize, and deconstruct Fineman's tendentious argument. Our honoring of his achievement would rather be visible and legible throughout.[8] It is instead worth recalling the rigorous and admirable honesty with which he is compelled, as he makes another of his many claims for the novelty and lasting originality of Shakespeare's sonnets, to glance to the left and the right and to acknowledge with variously fleeting asides, subtle qualifications, and extended footnotes that almost whatever he is claiming for the sonnets could be found, or claimed to be found, in English contemporaries, in Petrarch, in Dante, in medieval philosophy and transhistorical rhetoric and poetics.[9] In other words, these features of Fineman's text not only display his literary history for the pretense or mock-staging it is (including an institutional one, for only a professor of English would have made such world-historical claims for an English author—even Shakespeare—and only an English-language professional association would have honored it with its prize of the year); they also signal the autodeconstruction of the treatment of ends and beginnings in the book's argument. From the end— after the new beginning ostensibly marked by the sonnets—everything "back then" looks, which is to say *reads*, different(ly), but then again, knowing now—after Shakespeare and modern subjectivity—how to read, and not just look, we can read back and understand that already in Petrarch, in Dante, in the ancient poets and rhetoricians, things were written differently—otherwise and selfwise—than they looked or were seen to be. And so one can retell the story differently, with Shakespeare not at once an "end" and a "new beginning" at all, but a next step, a moment in the middle and means of a literary history of poetic writing and reading.

So, too, with Fineman's version of Shakespeare's sonnets' long shadow: Shakespeare's anticipation and "preinstruction" of us moderns (his lessons and *leçons*, his readings *for* us) is the half of the chiasmus—Fineman's favorite trope, to his great credit—that has as its inverted other the modern critical and theoretical (and especially Lacanian) reading tools and practices that, *après coup*, discover and authorize themselves as the "contemporary speculation about subjectivity," the subject subjected to representation, in Shakespeare's text.[10] The "historical" argument—if such it ever were, and it was not except as a narrative and argumentative ruse— is both its own self-justification and its own—inverted, other— self-undoing.

These brief and countertendentious rejoinders to Fineman's brilliant construction of Shakespeare's sonnets are at the head of this chapter not, as I said, to do critical and scholarly justice to the mass and detail of his argument, but to draw from it, first, the lesson that an inquiry into ends—poetic ending—will, just as Herrnstein Smith also showed, be unprotected from turning into an account of beginnings and middles and means: of everything that does or does not get one to an end. Second, Fineman teaches that to turn from anywhere else to Shakespeare, and from Shakespeare to anywhere else, is to turn in between visibility and language, between praise and its paradoxical others, between projections of the self in poems and their reflections, brilliant and far-reaching, in their readings. Finally—which is to say, in introducing our turn to the sonnets in turn—Fineman has indelibly made the turns of reflections and inversions and the trope of chiasmus the stock-in-trade of reading Shakespeare's sonnets, and we shall find him anything but wrong, unless it is in thinking that such turns and tropes are not also everywhere else in reading of poetic ends and means.

In her book Herrnstein Smith acknowledged I. A. Richards' brief essay "How Does a Poem Know When It Is Finished?" as, to her knowledge, "the only place in modern criticism where the question of poetic closure as such is raised," and she quoted his answer to what she called "this leading and loaded question" to the effect that "a poem begins by creating a linguistic problem whose solution by language will be the attainment of its end." A poetic beginning would create a problem, to which the poem's language would provide the solution in "the attainment of its end." What is slightly unclear in this formulation is whether all poems attain their end, and if not, how else they might end. In the same paragraph she quoted Richards being not so much unclear as cagily open-ended when he referred to a poem's "transactions between words" as deciding "what the poem may be and when and how (and whether) it is finished."[11]

Finished or ended: all poems end, they may or may not—from the perspective Richards sketches—all be finished. I begin looking at poems in this study, and at Shakespeare sonnets in this chapter, by first choosing two where a poetic *ending* is apparently an *end* in Richards' sense of an attainment or a finished thing. An achievement of a purpose or intention, an arrival at a goal or target, or a completion of a task might be serviceable synonyms for this sense of attainment of closure. And if we recall Richards' very exact pairing of beginning and end with problem and solution, we can see how what I call the *narrative* effort or dimension of poetry (including lyric poetry) would have its matching half or counterpart in the *interpretive* contribution of its reading. As reliably as poems move from their beginnings to ends in this version of their poetics—whether they move readily or resistantly is less an issue here—so would their reading move from the problem of their understanding (what do these strange language-acts mean?) to its solution, which is to say the delivery of the interpretations. You would know you were at the end of a poem—that it had ended—when you could say what it meant.

To call this model of lyric movement and understanding a "narrative" one is not to court a confusion of genres. Narrative, after all, is not a literary genre but an aspect and function of discourse. Northrop Frye wrote, in a passing but brilliant remark in his *Anatomy of Criticism,* that "the hypothetical core of literature" is "narrative and meaning in their literal aspects as word-order and word-pattern," and he perspicaciously associated this with the lyric genre.[12] The point of here designating the lyric as narrative is to illuminate how a correspondence of goal and end is both presupposed in a verbal artifact and reenacted in its reading. Narrative stories conventionally—that is, in their past tense—assume that the action (plot) to be told (represented) is already ended before the story begins, and so the telling returns to and rehearses the coming-to-an-end of the action, which the reading and understanding of the story repeat yet again. All the possible tensions between story and plot (or, in some formalisms, plot and story), between a narrator's knowledge and the characters' uncertainty, between suspense and predictability, do not necessarily alter the correspondence and *the reduplicability of correspondence* between goal and end. Indeed, such tension may be posited as constitutive of artistic production itself: the movement toward the correspondence of goal (arrival at an end) and end (the knowledge or confirmation, in the very act of doubling or repetition, that it is the end) would be, in this understanding, the extension and the experiencing and the release of such tension.

The axis of narrative in this sense, following Frye's, is the structure of constative language-acts construed according to the paradigm of the sentence, in that such acts have an incipient movement from predication to conclusion or grammatical closure: the sentence adds up, the grammatical relations and correctness of the parts become clear. Lyric poems as "sentences" (modeled on sentences, even the minimal ones of subject and verb) and statements, then, have this narrative axis along which their utterances and their corresponding understandings move. Even apparently non-narrative or performative lyric forms such as the apostrophe, or non-narrative and imagistic lyric forms such as description, could, in this extended definition, be understood as tending toward a narrative version of their illocutionary or representational character: as telling-and-listening, or communication; and seeing-and-reformulating, or comprehension.[13]

Between beginning somewhere other than an end—tautologically so—and having as its goal its end, a lyric poem moves across the middle and means of its lines' unfolding. (In a way that has been so obvious since Aristotle as to be easily overlooked, all the action in narrative is in what is between the beginning and the end, namely the middle in between.) The middle and means of a poem is its motion from beginning to end, which is in turn its direction and co-motion of its reading and understanding along the same trajectory. Shakespeare's sonnet 145 may serve as an illustration of this first model of the lyric. The only sonnet in tetrameters, it has been thought spurious by many scholars, and even its respectful editor Booth calls it "the slightest of the sonnets," and declares that "it is not a good poem," but I begin here out of respect for its considerable virtues of concision and clarity in displaying how a beginning can become an end via a middle and how this achievement (recall Richards' "attainment") may be the sonnet's very goal or aim.[14]

> Those lips that love's own hand did make
> Breathed forth the sound that said, I hate,
> To me that languished for her sake.
> But when she saw my woeful state
> Straight in her heart did mercy come,
> Chiding that tongue that ever sweet
> Was used in giving gentle doom;
> And taught it thus anew to greet:
> I hate she altered with an end,
> That followed it as gentle day
> Doth follow night, who like a fiend
> From heav'n to hell is flown away.
> > I hate from hate away she threw,
> > And saved my life saying, not you.

The narrative of a mouth giving voice to a phrase is the very enactment of the poem's own beginning: "the sound that said, I hate" is the first two lines, and as they leg-over to the next, the phrase skips its transitive object but instantly introduces or, better, substitutes an intransitive one: "said, I hate, / To me." Both the poem, and the story it tells, say, "I hate, / To me," with "me" being both the speaker and the reader, and with this beginning, the words' painful utterance introduces a tension—pathetic, semantic, and poetic—that no sooner will appear than it will become intolerable for the speaker, unsustained and altering for the reader.[15] For without respecting the formal division of a full quatrain (perhaps one reason critics suspect this sonnet), the poem turns at the beginning of its fourth line with the adversative "but" and thereby introduces another, eventually undoing twist of tension to the first, painful turn: "But when she saw my woeful state / Straight in her heart did mercy come." The "straight" means, of course, straightaway, but it already suggests the straightening or undoing turn introduced by the adversative (turning-against) "but." The story indeed undertakes the changing or undoing of its beginning. "I hate," once said "to me," must, after this "but" and the "straight" arrival of mercy, lead to another utterance than the painful one of the persona's "I" wounded by the tongue's hateful predication.

The eighth line has mercy teaching the tongue "anew to greet": it is worth noting that the change of utterance comes from an intervening utterance within, mercy "chiding" the tongue, and in teaching a lesson, this brings about an altered outward utterance. The poem's novelty of a new greeting, which is also the reader's greeting or reception of a novelty within the narrative now spun out over eight lines, gives way to the brilliant and beautifully cadenced ninth line that is also a new beginning and an anticipated, indeed, strictly prefigured goal and end: "I hate she altered with an end."[16] The effective beginning of the poem—"the sound that said, I hate, / To me"—is here, at the beginning of its end (the first line of the last quatrain), altered with the anticipation of its goal and end—the narrative undoing of its narrative pain and tension.

It is at this point that the poem's initial grammatical force (the enjambment "said, I hate, / To me") together with its sustained semantic force—the narrative tension of an act of predication moving toward its transitive or intransitive object—are brought together with the poem's form and sound to their mutual end. "I hate she altered with an end" states in a narrative past what happened in the persona's story, and in a lyric past/present what the sonnet, from its second line to its last, has been doing and does; and the remainder of the poem at once describes and enacts this ending alteration. The repetition of "follow" (in "That followed it as gentle day / Doth follow night")[17] flows into the alliterative f's of "fiend," "from," and "flown"; "following" the phrase "I hate" with an altered end means, effectively, to fling the phrase away, and so the twelfth line's "flown away" becomes, one line later, "threw away" (where the change in tense does not altogether erase the mediating assonance of "thrown away"): "I hate from hate away she threw." Such density of near self-contradiction or antiredundancy is in fact the penultimate moment of lyric achievement, of the attainment of an end that at once alters its beginning and thereby achieves its goal—in Richards' terms, "solves its problem."[18] To throw "hate" away from "hate"—to dismiss the semantics of the minimally predicative grammatical unit "I hate"—is to alter with an end: to end with the transitive object, and to alter or, indeed, to negate it at the same time; to turn a past, beginning event ("said") into its present, ending overcoming ("saying"), changing damnation ("doom") into salvation ("saved"). "I hate" becomes "I hate . . . not you." That this end *is* the poem's end and goal is exquisitely inscribed in the lingering, ongoing gerund of *"saying,* not you," another voice in contrast to the narrative one of its beginning and middle. The poem *was* always something else, but it *is* its end-"saying." Whatever it was that the partial features of the narrative's female personification (lips, tongue) "said," and then "altered," the whole poem closes "saying, not."

A second Shakespeare sonnet, unquestioned in its authenticity and also far more widely known and admired, may illustrate in a more abbreviated and condensed manner my same initial set of claims regarding the lyric's movement from a beginning, across its middle and means of grammatical and semantic tension, to the goal of ending. Sonnet 30, like the two modern examples Richards discussed in his article on poetic ending, also has the only apparently contrived terminus of "end" as its last word.[19]

> When to the sessions of sweet silent thought
> I summon up remembrance of things past,
> I sigh the lack of many a thing I sought,
> And with old woes new wail my dear time's waste.
> Then can I drown an eye, unused to flow,
> For precious friends hid in death's dateless night,
> And weep afresh love's long since cancelled woe,
> And moan th'expense of many a vanished sight.
> Then can I grieve at grievances foregone,
> And heavily from woe to woe tell o'er

The sad account of fore-bemoanèd moan,
Which I new pay as if not paid before.
    But if the while I think on thee, dear friend,
    All losses are restored, and sorrows end.

The poem's first twelve lines accelerate and accumulate toward an accounting of the "woe" that is at first perhaps surprisingly introduced after the deceptive innocence of "the sessions of
sweet silent thought" (deceptive because these are metaphorically
sessions of a court of law) and the "remembrance of things past"
(which Fineman finds also deceptively innocent, as always already
putting a praised present into the past "vanished sight" of now-
bypassed epideictic rhetoric).[20] It is with the mention of "past," at
the line-end position, that the real theme of "time's waste" is trig-
gered: the semantics of "sigh" and "lack," and the alliteration of
"woes," "wail," and "waste" conclude the first quatrain. The next
two quatrains, rhyming "Then" consequentially with the first quatrain's "When" in the first-word position, also raise the stakes of
the poem's newfound awareness of temporality, mortality, and
their ravages:[21] drown, death, weep, woe, moan, and vanished dominate the second quatrain, while the following four lines brilliantly
double this pain in each one: "I grieve at grievances," "from woe
to woe tell o'er," "fore-bemoanèd moan," and "I new pay as if not
paid before." This quatrain of doubled words of painful loss has
brought the poem from its innocent, "sweet" beginning across a
tumbling crescendo of grief, woe, and moans. But then this shifts
and ends with the strongly adversative "But if the while I think on
thee, dear friend." The "but" arrests the commotion and momentum of grief, the "while" draws out the instant of this arrest. More
specifically, the "but if" opposes and overcomes the immediately
preceding "as if" in which, in effect, each of the earlier lines had
to redouble mourning to "new pay as if not paid before." The sonnet begins to end where it began; unlike the commotion of the
intervening wailing and weeping and moaning and grieving, it is
returning to "sweet silent thought" with the phrase "I think." And
then the last line truly ends the poem, by which I mean its whole
commotion and trajectory are ended: "All losses are restored and
sorrows end." Indeed, the last two words condense the last cou-

plet, as well as the motion from the poem's beginning, across its anguished tension, to its conclusion: quite simply, enfolded in its single fold (*simplex*) upon itself, "sorrows end."

Sonnets 145 and 30 have been adduced for their exemplification of the technique of lyric ending as *closing* or *finishing*, as attaining an end and achieving a goal in such a manner that the poem's reading and understanding close upon and finish with the text's own ending. They do this in the straightforward and "straightforward" way of using their poetic middles to get, unilinearly, from beginnings to ends, following the arc or curve of a tension's mounting and dissolution, or a problem's appearance and solution. Shakespeare's sonnet form, whether in its use of its last six lines or of its closing couplet, seems especially adept at making a turn across or from its middle straight to its end.

Sonnet 30, which we have looked at so briefly this far, seems so straightforward with its alliterations, parallelisms, and doublings: all the *s*'s and *w*'s get one to the parallelism of "old woes new wail," and on to the doublings of lines 9–12, so that a momentum whereby repetition carries the reader forward appears to be the very grain of the poem. When it ends with "end," a faint rhyming echo of its first word "When" only serves to underscore the closure, while the encoded *envoi* of "*sorrows end*"—s-end—sends it definitively on its way.

But we should now, in preparing to turn to a very different kind of Shakespeare sonnet, and a very different technique with respect to ending, look back at sonnet 30, not to read it against the grain, but to notice the different grain, the cross-hatching within the grain of this text. The third line strikes an unmistakable balance between beginning and end in "I sigh . . . I sought," such that the "lack" that seems to travel away from the past, across the ravages of time, to its present mournful appreciation, seems also to travel back to relodge in a site in the past, in the "I sought": if "I sigh" is already within "I sought," then the lack—whence the sighing—is already there as well, a lack within or propelling desire itself. So, too, the moaning now is perhaps self-propelled and re-propelled if the "vanished sight" is, as Booth notes it possibly is, a "vanished sigh."[22] Sighing, when past or vanished, breeds sighing, like a sigh within the sought. The poem, in other words, for all its forward-moving momentum, seems triangulated in its middle among sigh, sigh, and sigh.

The parallelisms and repetitions are no less cross-grained in their actual textual functioning. Superficial phonetic tropes like alliteration give the impression of a unilinear shuttling, where one recalls (rehears) backward because one is steadily moving forward and encountering more of the same. But it cannot escape our attention that the same units in the alliterations and parallelisms function semantically and syntactically in another way. The parallelism "old woes new wail," with the parallel meanings *old* and *new* and the parallel sounds of the *w*'s, submits doubly not to parallel repetition but to chiastic inversion. First, "new wail" (taking "new" adverbially) is inverted in line 7's "weep afresh." Then the entire phrase is inverted in the entirety of line 7:

$$\ldots \text{old woes} \quad \text{new wail} \ldots$$
$$\times$$
$$\ldots \text{weep afresh} \ldots \text{long since cancelled woe}$$

This double chiasmus within the poem's middle, between lines 4 and 7, suggests that the middle is not just the means to the end, but a poetic nexus of its own interest, perhaps even of its own arrest, since the entanglement of old woes and new wailing, reinforced by the triangular suspension of sighing within the sought and the sight, makes the poem's sudden turn to ending sorrow that much more powerful, but also—paradoxically—that much less motivated by anything that went before, and therefore that much more suspect.

Not to arrive at an end and conclude with its understanding, but to suspect that ending, and that it ends at all, or rather suspends: this is another dimension of the achievement of Shakespeare's sonnets. I now look at one that also has been closely commented on by Stephen Booth and Joel Fineman, and through the lens of Fineman's interpretation we shall learn how reading a Shakespeare sonnet can confront that reading with what it means to be reading to and at a poetic ending. In a book full of subtle and dexterous readings, Fineman's commentary on sonnet 43 is distinguished by its amphibian ambidexterity—that is, it succeeds at being in two places at once, all the while also getting indifferently to one point, which is its end. The sonnet reads:

> When most I wink, then do my eyes best see,
> For all the day they view things unrespected,
> But when I sleep, in dreams they look on thee,
> And darkly bright, are bright in dark directed.
> Then thou, whose shadow shadows doth make bright—
> How would thy shadow's form form happy show
> To the clear day with thy much clearer light,
> When to unseeing eyes thy shade shines so!
> How would, I say, mine eyes be blessèd made,
> By looking on thee in the living day,
> When in dead night thy fair imperfect shade
> Through heavy sleep on sightless eyes doth stay!
>   All days are nights to see till I see thee,
>   And nights bright days when dreams do show thee me.

No less than five times does Fineman weave and alternate between the poles of conclusiveness and inconclusiveness in making his way to his own conclusion about this poem and its end. The context of his discussion is the young man subsequence and those sonnets among them in which "unifying continuities become doubly discontinuous, or . . . traditional mediations are . . . rendered ambiguous and then opposed to, or interposed between, the two terms they conjoin."[23] He first introduces sonnet 43 as if a counterexample to this characterization: "The young man's poet develops familiar Petrarchist antitheses and syntheses in an apparently straightforward and complementary way. . . . The traditional association of imagination and dreaming leads to a traditional conclusion." Development straightforwardly leads to a conclusion, traditional at that, in this first comment of Fineman. In his next paragraph, beginning with an adversative "Yet," we have the countergeneralization that "almost invariably even the most conventionally closed of Shakespeare's oxymoronic formulations are coded . . . with a formal reduplication that puts an edge on their most balanced resolutions." From conventional closure we have moved to an edgy and thus unbalanced resolution. But at the end

of his next paragraph, "this excess of rhetorical duplication"—
Fineman has followed Booth's learned commentary on the rhetorical devices of repetition—"also becomes— . . . it presents itself
as—the not at all confusing explanation of whatever confusions it
concurrently provokes." Confusion exists in the poem, but it leads
or overflows ("excess") into its opposite ("not at all confusing")
and becomes in fact a neat unfolding ("explanation"). From this
Finemanian paradox on a Shakespearian oxymoron—confusion
concurrent with nonconfusion—that nonetheless asserts "explanation," he then moves in his next paragraph back to an edgy un-
balancing: "It is only because we, in fact, register this unexpressed
rhetorical excess that we are prepared to see the poem undo, if
only very delicately, its own explicitly articulated black and white
assumptions." Fineman then returns a last time to a restabilizing
and conclusive comment on the poem—"both the movement and
the conclusion of the poem make fairly clear just what the poet
wants"—before returning to its final opposite:

> There is in the final line of the sonnet a noticeably trou-
> bling and irreducible uncertainty, an unambiguous am-
> biguity. . . . And it is precisely this kind of invidious ambi-
> guity, an ambiguity that is somehow more tellingly and
> disturbingly effective than any produced by more obvi-
> ous Petrarchist structures of sympathetic and antipathe-
> tic complementarity, that characteristically inflects even
> these young man sonnets that seem most deliberately de-
> termined to see the similarity between comparative dis-
> similars.

I return at the end of this chapter to the tactical service and
strategic stakes signaled in the turn and tone of Fineman's *"even
these young man sonnets."* Here, let us notice that in this fifth
change of tack in his commentary, Fineman noticeably wants to
raise the tone and temperature of our attention to Shakespeare's
rhetoric: far from having been led via rhetorical duplication to
traditional conclusions, explanations, or fair clarity, we are left
here with trouble that is invidious and disturbing. The "noticeably
troubling and irreducible uncertainty" of a Finemanian joining
and disjoining of similars and opposites—"an unambiguous am-

biguity," in which the ambiguity both is really ambiguous and is so not at all—is exemplary for him of what he more largely, and in a signal contribution to our knowledge of lyric poetry, calls "cross-coupling," the "chiastic doubling of unified doubles."[24]

We have already seen, in an entirely formalistic fashion, the double chiasmus in sonnet 30, and I remarked there on a suspension of means in the middle of the sonnet that is rather different from (and a difference within) its narrative trajectory to its end. Here, in surveying Fineman's masterfully nuanced interpretation of sonnet 43, the rhetoric of mirror inversions—for this is what a chiasmus visually represents—is everywhere explicit and, indeed, excessive, and the understanding of the poem carries the suspension and uncertainty of tropes from the very stuff of the poem's *means* to its very end, or lack thereof. Turning now to the sonnet itself, we can see how what Fineman has *seen* and converted to his *"reading"* also helps us *read* what cannot be thus *seen*.

While the sonnet plays in every line on seeing and looking, eyes and visual shapes, it displays with equal frequency an array of literary figures or tropes that move from the visual realm to the verbal. Stephen Booth's immensely helpful first note on the poem summarizes this basic feature and also, we shall see, abuts against the problem of its reading: "The recurring themes of this sonnet—things that are the opposite of what they would normally be expected to be, and the distinction between images or shadows of objects and the objects themselves—are played out stylistically in an intense display of antithesis and a range of rhetorical devices of repetition that make the language of the poem suggest mirror images." He goes on to name the rhetorical devices as antithesis, antistasis ("repetition of a word in a different or contrary sense"), epizeuxis ("repetition of a word with no other word between"), diacope ("repetition of a word with one or a few words in between"), polyptoton ("repetition of words from the same root but with different endings"), antimetabole ("inversion of the order of repeated words"), what he calls "a sort of fusion of antithesis and an antistasis of ideas," and of course oxymoron, and counts some two dozen uses of these devices in the sonnet.[25] Booth's opening sentence concludes that the highly rhetorical display "make[s] the language of the poem suggest mirror images," so that if we "see" in our mind's eye the themes of seeing, looking, eyes, shadows, and the like, and read the many tropes in the fourteen lines, the latter—language read—*looks* like the former in "suggesting" the visual realm and experience of "mirror images." Fineman, however, shrewdly counters that "it is because sonnet 43 thus deliberately overstylizes its Petrarchist style and overthematizes its conventionally oxymoronic themes that we do not really read the poem as a solemn inquiry into optical epistemology." I shall now argue that the chiastic reversal within Booth's protoargument (themes of the visual play themselves out in rhetorical language so that language suggests the visual) and Fineman's attempt to reverse Booth (we do not really read the poem as a discourse on or of the visual) get us deeply into sonnet 43, but only to the threshold of its reading and its reading at its end.

What Booth means most obviously and astutely is that many of the tropes he lists—epizeuxis, diacope, polyptoton, antimetabole, antistasis—take, in this sonnet, the *visual form* of mirror images: that is, quite independently of the tropes being *read*, or having any semantic content, they visually or iconically signify mirroring. This is most the case in lines 4–7: "bright, are bright," expanded to and surrounded as "darkly bright, are bright in dark"; "shadow shadows"; "form form," expanded to and surrounded as "*shadow*'s form form . . . show"; and "clear . . . clearer." So far, this is only seeing, not reading. The "double" mirror images in the brief list just provided are also, of course, chiasmi of a minimal, formal sort: "darkly bright . . . bright in dark," and "sh . . . ow form form . . . show." In the end couplet, another chiasmus can be spotted, seen, still without having to be read:

. . . days are nights . . .

×

. . . nights bright days . . .

Seeing chiasmi—the trope of specular or mirror inversion par excellence—may, then, lead to reading chiasmi. Notice, for example, the only readable chiasmus across lines 8 and 12, as "unseeing" is inverted into "sightless"—only readable because it involves the semantic decoding of the privative prefix becoming inverted into the (different but semantically identical) private suffix as well as the semantic identity of seeing with sight. Notice the only readable chiasmus in the first line, only readable because grammatical and homophonic (punning) in its encoding: "most I . . . eyes best," which constitutes the schematic inversion of "superlative–first person × first person–superlative." Notice, finally, the semantic chiasmus across the entire first two lines:

$$. . . \text{wink} \ (= \text{not see}) \ . . . \text{see}$$
$$\times$$
$$. . . \text{view} . . . \text{unrespected} \ (= \text{not seen})$$

To have seen mirror images (inversions) in words' various tropes has led to seeing chiasmi, which has led to reading their existence in the sonnet. The poem is indeed tropologically structured as a series of inversions, the most basic trope and structure of which is chiasmus. If we now actually read—and not just notice by reading—the chiasmus of the first two lines, we arrive at the problem of the entire poem's statement and the difficulty of its restatement in our interpreters' readings.

Booth remarked, in what is, it seems, an undernoticed observation, that the opening phrase is "curiously unidiomatic in its use of *most*. . . . This line first seems to continue the [sequence's] theme of studied refusal to recognize evil: 'to wink' meant 'to shut one's eyes to—connive at—a fault,'" and after a citation from *Macbeth* he cites the contemporary proverb, "Although I wink, I am not blind."[26] Hence I set up the chiasmus above as "not see . . . see × see . . . not see." If we take Booth's remark upon the curiously unidiomatic combination of "most" and "wink" seriously, we read that the first line is not literally about the sleep that the sonnet unfolds from lines 3 to 14, but is rather about *not seeing*, and willfully so: sleep, in other words, is metaphoric from the start, as "wink" first—idiomatically, literally—means not "not be awake," but "not see." "Unrespected" in turn, again following a note of Booth, may mean unseen as well as ignored and not prized. The paradoxical first two lines thus state that when I most do not see, I see best, and when I see (by day), I do not see. In this poem, from the start, not seeing at all is the best seeing, and daytime-seeing is already, and still to become, inverted into not-seeing, into "unrespecting."

The poem gives its readers directions toward a lesson—a

leçon, a reading—into not-seeing. If we no longer look at the visual shapes of the words (they look like mirror images), and also no longer imagine the plays of reversals in our minds' eyes (what Fineman called the sonnet's overthematization of its conventionally Neo-Platonic themes of substance and image, etc.), we are at the threshold of reading the chiasmus into not (no longer) seeing seeing. Sleep is the metaphor for this not-seeing, and thus so is dreaming. In this nocturnal, somnambulistic, and oniric world, language works by inversion, including the inversion of meanings via grammatical, syntactic, and semantic inversions. Thus, "thou, whose shadow shadows doth make bright" enacts what Fineman calls a "double reading," as "doth"—the singular verb commonly used in Renaissance English with both plural and singular subjects[27]—has "shadows" making the persona's "shadow" bright in one direction, the persona's "shadow" making "shadows" bright in the other: a grammatical inversion and a grammatical chiasmus, as it were. Thus, "thy shadow's form form happy show" has the formal (visual) inversion working along with or enacting a semantic inversion as well: as Booth says, "note the choice of *show*, a word that connotes illusion, to describe its opposite," namely "a joyous spectacle," "a pleasing sight," and he also notes the inverted meanings of "form" here, the model or reality of which the "shadow" is the mere image, and then the "mere external appearance."[28] The inversion of meanings—not visible but readable, grammatically and semantically—gets us further into the show, the play and display of this poem.

For the sonnet, in its several "exclamations," strains to say something about daytime "seeing" that cannot be seen and, on the evidence of the poem's best readers, can scarcely be read either. The 1609 Quarto prints question marks, and Booth edits them as exclamation marks;[29] in either case, apparently (if the questions are only "rhetorical" questions), the re-turning comparison from night to day would work to complement daytime's "clearer light" and "living day." But if instead of affirmative exclamations (or "rhetorical" questions meant to be affirmed: "How? . . . And how!") the questions really *are* questions, and if they may just possibly be answered in the negative, the contrast between the not-seeing that sees and the seeing that does not see is splayed further apart. "How would thy shadow's form form happy show / To the clear day with thy much clearer light / When to unseeing eyes thy shade shines so?" where an accent on "would" plausibly asks how this would be at all possible. "How would, I say,"—where the "I say" is emphatic, underscoring the repeated "How would"— "mine eyes be blessèd made, / By looking on thee in the living day, / When in dead night thy fair imperfect shade / Through heavy sleep on sightless eyes doth stay?" I allow that much in the senses of "thy much clearer light" or "imperfect shade" (which nonetheless, in the oxymoron, is also "fair") argues for these being affirmative exclamations on behalf of daytime sight, but the allowable sense that they are questions that raise the possibility of impossible sight ("How could I? . . . I could not.") is surely suggested as well.

The small but emphatic "I say," in parentheses in the Quarto and edited within commas, is the only place in the sonnet where the "I" speaks, in contrast to its several acts of not-seeing and seeing ("I wink," "I sleep," "I see"). An eye can see or not see, but only an I can say. We are, in other words, meant to hear and read that the "I" that is in "I say" is distinctly not an eye. The "I" asks and speaks about what perhaps cannot be seen in the clear light of living day. And the poem finally says something that cannot be seen either, but certainly can be read: Fineman's "noticeably troubling and irreducible uncertainty, an unambiguous ambiguity, as to just whose dreams are showing whom to whom, 'me' to 'thee' or 'thee' to 'me': 'All days are nights to see till I see thee, / And nights bright days when dreams do *show thee me*.'" (And Fineman here notes Booth's note on the conflict between the sense "show thee to me" and the rhythmic and idiomatic sense of "show me to thee.")

We cannot see with any clarity, let alone perfection, what the couplet says, but we are, at the end of this sonnet, obliged to read the repeated reversibility of direct and indirect objects that the word, phrase, sentence, and poem "show." If we continue to believe that what the sonnet "shows" can be seen, we are still not reading its show. Fineman is the best example of this threshold between still seeing, and still not seeing that one is not reading. The language that guided his interpretation of sonnet 43 was repeat-

edly and conventionally visual: the "excess of rhetorical duplication . . . *clouds and obscures* whatever mirroring or reciprocity it
stylistically and thematically suggests"; "both the movement and
the conclusion of the poem make *fairly clear* just what the poem
wants," where his critical language is clearly parodic of the
poem's. But it is in a set of his sentences explicitly about reading
that we may best understand Fineman's dilemma:

> Our appreciation of their [the poem's reversals] exagger-
> ation controls and also clarifies our reading of the poem's
> antitheses and complementarities. It is because "Then
> thou, whose shadow shadows doth make bright" ostenta-
> tiously invites a double reading that we, in fact, read the
> poem one way and not another. On the one hand, such
> displayed duplicity is what protects us from overreading
> the poem, for it is because sonnet 43 thus deliberately
> overstylizes its Petrarchist style and overthematizes its con-
> ventionally oxymoronic themes that we do not really read
> the poem as a solemn inquiry into optical epistemology.
> This is why sonnet 43, *as* we read through it, does not re-
> ally raise for a reader, at least not in any serious way, a
> question about the "precise distinction between image
> and actual object" [a quote from Booth's note on the turn
> from l. 5 to l. 6]. On the other hand, this is also what pre-
> vents us from underreading the poem, for it is only be-
> cause we, in fact, register this unexpressed rhetorical ex-
> cess that we are prepared to see the poem undo, if only
> very delicately, its own explicitly articulated black and
> white assumptions.

These remarkable sentences speak seven times of reading, to read,
and the reader, and not without more than a little self-confidence
about reading, for in their structure of "protection from over-
reading" and "prevention from underreading," it would seem that
one—Fineman—can only read just right. At the same time, they
employ a language not of reading but of seeing: "clarifies," "os-
tentatiously invites," "displayed duplicity," "to see the poem undo
. . . its own explicitly articulated black and white assumptions." We
may grant Fineman that all this language of seeing amidst his not

altogether modest claim of reading is, first, entirely conventional, and second, a gentle parody of the sonnet's language of the visual. But we may insist that, third, it marks the point where Fineman cannot see that he is not reading the sonnet. "*As* we read through it"—the italics are Fineman's, and thus call attention to his own language—is both temporal and, in the kind of double reading Fineman is here soliciting, expressive of manner, and in the latter sense, the way Fineman "reads through it" is as if seeing through it: as if the text were a lens, not a page of text—a visual instrument for seeing, not for reading.[30] This allows him to be exactly right that we do not read the poem "as a solemn inquiry into optical epistemology," nor question the "precise distinction between image and actual object," but also to be exactly wrong—that is, neglectful—about the significance of the precise distinction between senses and actual letters. For reading, as we shall be remembering in this book from here to Wallace Stevens and Paul Celan, necessitates the distinction of sense as meaning from sense as the sense-perception of vision, the precise distinction of actual letters seen and actual letters not seen (no longer seen) but read acting. This is why we cannot "see," with Fineman, "the poem undo, if only very delicately, its own explicitly articulated black and white assumptions," for when we *see* that the poem's explicitly articulated black-and-white is the text, the words and their letters, on the page, then we "see"—begin to read—that its undoing of vision is in action and in actuality from the first to the last lines, and is not something that can be visually seen.

For the "show" of the last line and the entire poem is a verbal and grammatical show that generates the counterintuitive semantics of not-seeing being seeing, and seeing being a nonseeing. The deictics of the last line point or refer to no visible realm where one could see the difference between, and thus separate, substance and shadow, "thee" and "me"; rather, they mark the difference within language's not-seeing, its "winking": now you see it (showing thee to me), now you don't (the inversion to showing me to thee). The entire poem "shows"—that is, it writes or inscribes for reading—the duplicity of showing, on the one hand for seeing, on the other for reading. For "show" means to display, to manifest, to make visible (Fineman's "displayed duplicity"), and it also, in this poem, means to display, to undo the "overstylized" and "overthematized" play of Neo-Platonic visualities: *to disguise* language as vision, in order then to hide vision away behind language. We read the poem as about seeing—this is its disguise, its "show"—in order to come to understand that not-seeing is reading. Thus, the poem's very first words: when we do not see, we see best, and this has nothing to do with quotidian, daytime seeing.

That the poem at the end shows us language, and shows us its best readers resisting reading in still trying to see, is a lesson that the poem provides, but it is not all that may yet be read at the poem's end. The chiasmus of the couplet (days . . . nights × nights . . . days) has within or between it a last near-mirroring of words in the phrase "to see till I see." Days are as good as nights, the line seems to say, until I get a chance to see you, where "nights to see" means ironically seeing very little at all. But when the final line returns to valorize night's nonvision ("nights bright days when dreams do show thee me"), we realize that the penultimate line had already turned out the lights on daytime and made it dark, dark enough for a nighttime nonvision: "All days are nights to see." How does one "see" in this reread penultimate line? One sees till one sees: "to see till I see." In this phrase, the first seeing includes duration, waiting, counting, and then, at a degree of intensification ("till"), it repeats, but with a difference: "I see," which is to say that one arrives at the metaphoric seeing of the last line ("nights [are] bright days") which was also, already, the reading metaphorically of the first line ("When most I wink" is the poem's metaphoric sleeping, and actual, literal not-seeing). From "unrespected" viewing, in the sense of viewing that knew little and saw less, this doubling of "see" is literally a "re-specting," a "re-seeing" of seeing that allows it be read as reading. "To see till I see" is to see the threshold where reading would "appear" if it were something one could see, but instead one can only read the vanishing of sight. The word where this occurs is "till," as it switches its sense from sustained waiting (until) to an instantaneous when (something happens), from passive to active, we could say.[31] At this switch-point, "see" inverts into "see," day and night chiastically invert, and the poem's inversion of seeing into reading is complete—except that its ongoing grammatical inversion in the last line is a last word that cannot be read to its grammatical or semantic ending.

ॐ

Fineman's brilliant book privileges the dark lady sonnets as the place where visibility gives way to language and the duplicity and difference within it, and within our subjectivity ever since. He has taken the lead—the direction for reading—of the sonnet sequence, such that the dark lady sonnets, coming later in the story, are a narrative development from and away from the preceding young man sonnets, and this narrative view of the sequence yields his own narrative argument about "the invention of poetic subjectivity in the sonnets." Fineman reads the invention of something at the end that was not there at the beginning, in mere poetry of praise, but that occurred across the middle and means of the sequence.

But we have also glimpsed (and an extended analysis of his book would find dozens of other passages) that Fineman must allow the "cross-coupling" and "chiastic doubling of unified doubles" that his argument reserves as the achievement of the dark lady sonnets to emerge in "even those young man sonnets that seem most deliberately determined to see the similarity between comparative dissimilars." Back in the middle and means of the sonnet sequence, is already what is—to be—at the end. But he would still have it be at the end of these "middle" poems: in the final line in Fineman's interpretation of sonnet 43, at what a page later he calls "a determinate place of first-person indeterminacy."[32] Fineman is always, even in the middle, pointing to and determining the end.

I have also, in this introductory chapter, been pointing to the end of sonnets, to see how they give directions for being read to their ends, and to see how they give directions for being read back to their means, their means of chiastic inversion and penultimate "seeing" of reading's difference from seeing. What Fineman exquisitely reads at the end of Shakespeare's sonnet sequence is there to be read in its middle, its means, in virtually any of the sonnets. Chiastic double-crossing; the inversion of deictics into indeterminacy; the emergence of the threshold of reading at the penultimate line of a poem, ending one mode of representation before the end, and thus *not* ending: we shall see these again in the course of this book's chapters, in a Leopardi poem, in a Hölderlin poem, in a Baudelaire sonnet. Shakespeare's "invention" is not poetic subjectivity, nor of course the sonnet—although it *is* the fount of much that is best in verse in English from the late eighteenth century to the Beatles. When we read Baudelaire's sonnet enacting the same chiastic structures of inversion and the same passage to a threshold where sight gives way to reading that we have seen in Shakespeare's sonnets—and we recall that Baudelaire almost certainly did not directly know Shakespeare's sonnets—we realize we are reading something not "Shakespearian" but "sonnetish," lyric, poetic. Reading to the end and understanding that lyric poems do not end but return to and retrope their means—which are the tropes that overcome sight in their figurations—is to read into the means of poetry.

2

This, That, and Something Else Again

The Loop and the Knot of
Leopardi's "L'Infinito"

In the non-Italianist circles of American literary scholarship, Leopardi is more often referred to than read as the great poet he is, and the same may be said for his "L'Infinito," a great European romantic lyric and a great Western lyric *tout court*. The problems of language, Leopardi's and his scholars', are considerable: his own Italian is fine and impeccably controlled, whereas that of his professional readers is massive.[1] For those with less-than-perfect Italian, there fortunately exist several noteworthy English-language contributions to making Leopardi and his best poem accessible and important to our understandings of poetry, including our interest in the techniques and structures of lyric ending.[2]

"L'Infinito" is unusual for being a fifteen-line poem (Leopardi called it an "idyll") with eight demonstrative pronouns or deictics; I begin with this grammatical feature and follow it into some other grammatical and semantic cruxes of the poem, all

with a view toward understanding how this remarkable lyric ends
and rebounds from ending.

> Sempre caro mi fu quest'ermo colle,
> E questa siepe, che da tanta parte
> Dell'ultimo orizzonte il guardo esclude.
> Ma sedendo et mirando, interminati
> Spazi di là da quella, e sovrumani
> Silenzi, e profondissima quiete
> Io nel pensier mi fingo; ove per poco
> Il cor non si spaura. E come il vento
> Odo stormir tra queste piante, io quello
> Infinito silenzio a questa voce
> Vo comparando: e mi sovvien l'eterno,
> E le morte stagioni, e la presente
> E viva, e il suon di lei. Così tra questa
> Immensità s'annega il pensier mio:
> E il naufragar m'è dolce in questo mare.[3]

(Always dear to me was this solitary hill, / And this
hedge, which from so great a part / Of the farthest
horizon excludes the gaze. / But sitting and gazing,
endless / Spaces beyond that, and superhuman /
Silences, and profoundest quiet / I in my thought
imagine (create); wherefore / The heart is almost
fearful. And as / I hear the wind rustle through
(between) these plants, that / Infinite silence to this
voice / I go on comparing: and I recall the eternal, /
And the dead seasons, and the present / And living one,
and the sound of it. So in this / Immensity my thought
is drowned: / And shipwreck is sweet to me in this sea.)[4]

The demonstrative pronouns or deictics are "*quest'*ermo colle, /
e *questa* siepe," "interminati / spazi di là da *quella*," "*queste* piante . . .
quello / infinito silenzio . . . *questa* voce," and "*questa* / immensità
. . . *questo* mare." As with all spatiotemporal demonstratives (like
their cousins, the pronomial shifters "I" and "you"), what they
mean depends on where the speaker stands, and in a poem, where
the speaker "stands" is an effect of the lines written and read lo-

cally above and below. It has never been hard for Leopardi's readers to visualize in their minds' eyes the landscape that begins the poem (even to give it specific geographical addresses and topography), and so also to imagine an understanding of *"this* solitary hill, and *this* hedge" in the first two uses of the deictics. The reader puts him- or herself—innocently, we may say—in the position of the lyric "I," imagines himself sitting on and gazing from or down along *this* hill, and then at *this* hedge that ultimately cuts off the view and the gaze.[5] But things get more interesting with the next demonstrative, which allows us to enter the poem's poetic argument and interpretive direction.

When the poem's speaker turns from "questa siepe" to the "interminati / spazi di là da quella," the interiority or imaginative nature (strictly speaking, the *fictive* nature: "io nel pensier mi *fingo*") of the new "objects" of attention—the endless spaces and so forth—obtrudes between him and what was previously "this," immediately before him. "This" ("questa siepe") becomes "that" (*quella* in "beyond that"), and yet when this "that" is, quite logically, beyond any former "this" in the poem, what is imagined "beyond that" ("di là da quella") is also posited, given its imagination *in* thought ("nel pensier"), as nearer—more proximate, intimate, actually interior to—the speaker, which action is what, the reader now realizes, displaced "this hedge" to "that."[6] This is, of course, the force of the vocabulary of the sublime at just this juncture, in which the "endless" and the "superhuman" and the "deepest" are felt so near to one—indeed, within one—as almost ("per poco") to threaten the heart, the seat of interiority, itself.[7] Here, as the nearer ("this") has been displaced farther away (becoming "that"), while the farthest away (the "endless," the "superhuman") has been brought inside one, we are, semantically and linguistically (deictically), in the face and the workings of a *poetic loop,* in which "this" is displaced to "that" and that which would be on the far side of "that" is also on its near side, closer than the former "this." The semantics and poetics of this loop will come to determine the poem and challenge us with its ending.

Failure to observe and account for this looping reversal of this and that, near and far, would yield not so much a semantic difficulty at this point—especially if one just reads oneself in the imagined sitting-and-imagining position of the lyric "I"—than an interpretive slackening with further consequences for a diminished understanding of the poem, for it weakens the force of the reintroduced demonstrative in line 9: "queste piante." The force of the phrase must be registered in its *re*turn of the greenery, that is, the hedge from its outward looping (into *quella*) to its more proximate, more immediate *queste*, as close as or closer than the *siepe* ever was. But once again, the paradoxical poetic structure appears in which what must at least initially be posited as beyond that greenery (like the "interminati / spazi di là da quella") is also instantly more proximate than the marker of the distinction between this and that, here and there: I mean "il vento," heard within "queste piante," instantly transformed into "questa voce."[8]

The transformation occurs in the midst of two exchanges, one described "naturalistically," the other explicitly poetic and tropological, and we should take each in its turn. Leopardi's "And when/as I hear the wind rustle among / through these plants" (the *come* must be understood as the Latin temporal *cum*, while the *tra* is faintly ambiguous, a point to which I shall return) is as intuitable and representational as anyone's experience of sitting outdoors amidst greenery; the present-tense *odo*, the temporally locating *come*, and the immediacy of the "queste piante" all collaborate to bring the afar near and present at hand in a naturalistic fashion. This, then, has as its immediate, contemporaneous consequence an action that is anything but intuitable, naturalistic, or representable as experienced: that "I go on comparing" "quello / infinito silenzio a questa voce." The "silence" that, in its plural form ("sovrumani / silenzi"), was—through the power of what I called a poetic loop—both thought beyond a "that" ("di là da quella") and felt within, near a heart, has now again been made distant, thrown back away from the speaker: "that / infinite silence." But it is also simultaneously brought, in a *re*turning, looping motion, *to* "this voice" in the act of comparing.[9] "This voice" in turn—in the turning of the verses' loop and trope—is the poetic product, the tropological and specifically catachretic (re)naming of "the wind . . . rustl[ing] among / through these plants" (already, in other words, very proximate, as indicated by the *queste*) but produced or renamed as more proximate and intimate than the nearby "queste piante." The wind has looped or passed through the marker, the greenery or hedgerow, which distinguishes outside from inside and this temporal event is recast—renamed, reposited, refigured—as the tropological comparison of outside with inside.

The naturalistically staged "event"—the wind, the rustling, the plants—appears to condition or contemporaneously accompany the comparison that brings in the voice, but the voice, in another turn of the loop we are discovering as the emergent structure of this poem, is itself a "comparison" or likeness produced and renamed from the wind, the plants, the hearing of them, and their nearness or "these"-ness (*queste*). (Of course it is another romantic retrieval of the Aeolian harp topos, but I am interested in how it works here, not in what it semantically has in common with the commonplace.) So much hinges on the productivity of the act of comparing. To put it formulaically, wind plus greenery—this is the formula of the romantic Aeolian harp—a near outside and a nearer, more proximate marker of the distinction between outside and inside ("queste piante"), *when heard* (*odo*), yield "questa voce." To which, then, "infinito silenzio" is being compared. The crucial marker for "infinito silenzio" is that it is—or, rather, was—*both* outside, beyond the hedge ("di là da quella"), and inside ("nel pensier . . . ove per poco / il cor non si spaura"). The voice is the product of the outside brought inside; the infinite silence is already the outside thought inside, and/or the inside thought outside, only then to be thought back inside. The nexus of the poem's constituents—outside and inside, far and near, wind and boundary and hearing and voice and silence—at this point of its poetics of comparison are an interlooped node and an interlaced knot.

The poetic consequence of the comparing is going to issue as the additive listing of consequences: "*e* mi sovvien l'eterno, / *E* le morte stagioni, *e* la presente / *E* viva, *e* il suon di lei."[10] This series of "ands" then becomes the addition or cumulation that piles up on or at least near the speaker as a penultimate, and singular, accumulated demonstrative: "questa / immensita." This recalls, of course, the language of the sublime in lines 4–6, but now apparently on the near side of any possible further distinctions between an act of thought first projected outward, then internalized as almost fearful to the heart. Here the categorical distinctions of "eternal" and "present," "dead" and "living," are added up and collapsed, and they "immensely" add up on and collapse, or subtract, negate "il pensier mio." The final echo of this *questa,* this "this," is the drowning in "questo mare."[11]

Although several specific words will be seen to carry their poetic weight in this ultimate series of consequences—*mi sovvien, tra, s'annega, naufragar*—it is the "vo comparando" that sets off the series, from its colon onward. I have already underscored the importance of specifically comparing "that silence" to "this voice," for it delineates the directionality of the poem's several loopings from inside to outside, or near to far, only to return from outside to inside, far to near: the direction, in other words, is always near, toward "this," even when it is outward and afar—all the way to the poem's last words, "questo mare." (This is, then, what several existing English translations miss in making the comparison go "to that infinite silence.") Equally important is the verbal form of the "vo comparando," and its powerful echo and allusion. The phrase is a gerund (Margaret Brose calls it an "aulic gerund," and notes the other, "intransitive gerunds" of "sedendo e mirando"),[12] thus indicating progressive, ongoing action. The "go[ing] on comparing" marks both the simultaneity of the comparison with the "come . . . / Odo," and the sustaining of the present of that "I hear" in the gerund's continuity: "I hear" becomes lengthened, maintained, and transformed into the comparison, which is itself the verbal version of the wind, rustling in the greenery, becoming "this voice." Hearing, voice, and "go[ing] on comparing" are in fact the tightly interlaced triangular knot at which the poem has gathered itself.

Hearing the wind in the plants is not just hearing nature and its inspirations, as some long-standing received ideas about "romanticism" would have it, and "this voice" is not an autonomous one that could be located already somewhere else in the lyric persona or the poem. The phrase "vo comparando" signals the further dimensions of the hearing and the production of the voice. It echoes and alludes to Dante's description—indeed, as it turned out, his canonical naming—of the "dolce stil novo" to Bonagiunta da Lucca in canto XXIV of *Purgatorio:*

"I' mi son un che, quando
Amor mi spira, noto, e a qual modo
ch'e' ditta dentro vo significando." (52–54)

("I am one who, when / Love inspires me, takes note,
and after the fashion / which he dictates within me,
goes setting it forth.")[13]

Dante's description of the sweet new style is also, of course, his
identification of the poetics of his *Commedia*. Love "breathes in"
him, inspires him, and—via the deft but explicit grammatological
exchange of "noto, et a qual modo / ch'e' ditta dentro"—he "goes
signifying," that is, creating and writing the poem we are reading.
The *Commedia* is then the sublation of the earlier "style"'s eroti-
cized and allegorized Love into the theological allegory of inspiration (from the Virgin Mary to Lucy to Beatrice), guidance
(from Virgil back to Beatrice, including her "dictation" of Dante's
confession at the top of Purgatory), and signifying repetition
(Dante-poet "repeating"—representing and narrating—the experience of Dante-pilgrim for the "signification," the teaching, of
Christian "everyman").

In recalling how Dante got his message and his voice—explicitly in the "vo comparando"'s recall of Dante's gerund "vo significando," implicitly in the wind's semantic recall of Dante's "mi
spira"—Leopardi's lines at this juncture of "L'Infinito" put all
their weight on the reader's hearing what the lyric "I" "hears"
in order to, *and to be already*, "go[ing] on comparing." In other
words, the lines are a moment and place of intense self-reflexivity
(or, more exactly, of listening to and hearing hearing) in which
the poem's "I hear"—the word *odo*—is heard or read by the reader
as what must be done to the "hearing" of the lyric persona, both
of whom then "hear" and "compare" Leopardi's "I"'s voice and
comparison with Dante's notation and signification.[14] Not identification but reflection and inversion, the semantic point of hearing the echo of Dante in Leopardi's phrases is the productive contrast thus enfolded and unfolded in the respective poetics. Dante
is explicit that his poetry follows Love: notation after (in)spira-
tion, signifying after interior dictation, "a quel modo." Leopardi's
comparing, we have noted, does not allow that silence to follow

this voice, nor this voice to follow that silence; rather, because this voice always already was, or was the catachretic naming of (this is the force of the gerund *"go on* comparing"), the wind flowing among this greenery, the comparing of "that" to "this" continues the conflating, not the sequencing, of outside and inside, far and near. Whence the additive, and finally negating "questa / Immensità."

Intertextual allusion and comparison allow us to "hear" the force of Leopardi's intratextual and tropological "go on comparing" of deictic opposites, of directional opposites, of semantic opposites such as "silence" and "voice." Like Dante's "vo significando," the progressive, gerund construction "vo comparando" sustains the efficacy and consequentiality—the force—of the poetic-textual act. In Dante's poem this consequentiality is what we read in its every line, its moving both from, in consequence of, its inspiration and guidance, and toward, toward the consequences of, its signification. In "L'Infinito," the "vo comparando"'s immediate consequence is "e mi sovvien l'eterno" and the following phrases, to their immense end. In other words, the present-tense ending of the poem, the very *presence* of its ending, is what comes from going on comparing, and specifically from the presence of remembering that immediately follows from the comparing.[15] And this ending is negation, and drowning. From this closing language and imagery, its further echoes and allusions and illusions, we shall be able to turn to the poem's ending and beginning.

The penultimate line's *s'annega* means "(my thought) is drowned," and it thus anticipates metaleptically—putting effect before or in cause of cause—the otherwise causal *naufragar* of the last line. Additionally, we should grant that the text of the skilled philologist Leopardi displays the *negare* within *annegare,* for to miss this would undercut at least three of the poem's ironies. The first irony lies in the meaning and function of the verb *mi sovvien.* The "I" that recalls or remembers the eternal and the dead seasons, and the present and living one and its sound, is of course re-called or taken back by them; more strictly speaking, that which would come up to one's mind, or come up to one's assistance (from the Latin *subvenio, subvenire*), ironically draws one under. Whence the second irony: the addition of the eternal and the dead seasons, and the present and living one and its sound, thus (consequentially) add up to "this immensity" subtracting or negating the "I" of thought.

Specifically, the adding up to negation occurs "*tra* questa / Immensità." With this penultimate reappearance of the demonstrative "this," how are we to understand the *intra* of *tra*? "Among" or "in" would appear to do well, but they blunt a precision made possible both by the paratactic pairs in the remembrance that brings about the consequential "thus" (*così*) and by the recall of the earlier *tra* ("tra queste piante"). "This"—most recently in "this voice"—is where this poem is always coming from and going to, including where its ongoing comparing is coming from and going to. The pairs of opposites that the remembrance collapses together (and all of our interpreters agree that the remembrance collapses opposites: Poggioli's eternity and time, Brose's absence and presence, infinite and finite, Oldcorn's present and "other" landscapes and times)[16] are themselves in, in the sense of *between*, the comparing and collapsing. Taken together, they constitute an "immensity"—nothing, no time or place, escapes them—and in between their collapsing, they evacuate and void any place that would be interior to an elsewhere or a someone else. "This" place, which is "this immensity" brought about by the comparison of "that infinite silence" and "this" specific, non-Dantesque poetic "voice," as well as this "betweenness" that negates any other place or voice: "this" is the knot tied and tightened *between* each of the half-loopings *between* "this" and "that," near and far, interiority and exteriority, wind and greenery. Such an understanding of the *tra*—as the betweenness of deictic opposites that collapses and reduces to a negating "this" as the same "this" expands to an "immensity"—sheds light back upon the *tra* of "tra queste piante" that, I remarked above, was underdetermined in its initial context. "Between these plants," rather than "among" or "through," is perhaps closer to what is the poetic productivity of the wind and the plants together yielding "this voice." As the plants, that is, the hedge, mark the place in the poem where "this" ("questa siepe") first became "that" ("di là da quella") and then looped back to "these plants," what one hears and then can give voice and ongoing comparison to in this poem is always *between a repeating, in-*

volving, and encompassing set of loops. Less a static place in or among which one could sit, gaze, imagine, hear, or give voice, "this" in this poem is between a dynamic of comparison, which is to say that between the dynamics of comparison are the dynamics and poetics of this poem.

If there is no place in the poem that is not dynamic, then after the drowning or negation of "my thought," where is the lyric "I" left? I mentioned a third irony that would be mitigated by a monodimensional anticipation of the last line's shipwreck in understanding the penultimate line's *s'annega* too literally as just "drowning," and it is the following: with the negation of the "I"'s thought in the penultimate line, the present-tense "m'è dolce" ("is sweet to me") in the ultimate one is, entirely consonant with the collapsing "between" at the end of the thirteenth line, an altogether and appropriately *vanishing* or near-virtual present. At the limit, there is no longer any "I" to *be*, in the verbal present, the present site of the sweetness of shipwreck in this line's "this sea." Which means there is no longer anyone to say or point to "this," and perhaps scarcely anyone to read this "this."

This point obliges us to return to the poem's opening line, to *its* verbal construction, and to the powerfully informing contrast and irony that structure the entire poem, its semantics as well as its poetics. "Sempre caro mi fu": the *passato remoto* indicates a past cut off from a present. The *sempre* may, of course, commonsensically refer to repeated actions or experiences within a time-bound past, and yet Brose is also on to the nascent irony of the line when she notes a "complex interplay" between "an indeterminate continuity and atemporality" of the *sempre* and what she describes as the "completed, time-bound distant action" indicated by the *fu*.[17] The "I" referred to in this line can hardly still be "always" when it *is* there no longer. Strictly speaking, he might as well be dead. Or drowned. In other words, the first line of the poem comes *after* the last, the absence of the connection between the presence of an "I" and a past experience in the "mi fu" coming *after* the negation and disappearance of the "I" in the vanishing present tense of the poem's last line of shipwreck.

The temporal and formal "loop" indicated at this scale—the last line looping back before the first, the first coming after the last—goes to the heart of the poem's difficulty for our comprehension as well as to the heart of its mastery of lyric ending. What I have been describing as its formal and structural loop—principally between its demonstratives and the semantic regions of opposites that they indicate, now between its formal end and beginning, and their semantic and verbal conditions of possibility (is an "I" there? is it "present"?)—is, as we shall be seeing throughout the chapters of this book, its version of its generic specificity as a Western lyric poem. That it begins after it ends, in an inverting and interlacing of opposites, and that it therefore cannot be read once without having been read twice, will be found in its various guises, always with quite specific tropological determinants (like the chiasmus that is the tropological and epistemological structure of the loops tied into a knot here),[18] to be the recurrent feature of reoccurrence that structures poetic ending in the Western lyric. In other words, the principle of ending, in "L'Infinito" but also in other lyrics we are here studying, is reoccurrence, and for it to end twice (both in its penultimate and—again—in its ultimate lines) and to have to have ended before it began (to explain, in its radicalness, the *fu*) means that it also begins repeatedly, once formally and yet again, semantically, in its beginning after the drowning by shipwreck at its ending. Its first and last statement is always something else *again*. Where the formal loop gives onto its semantic dimension may be glimpsed whenever one tries to paraphrase the formal relation of the first and last lines' verb tenses: the present tense of the ending (the negation, the drowning) of the "I" in the poem's last two lines is the precondition and predication of the "always" that "was"—and is no longer—for the "I" of the first line. And yet the "I," or a form thereof, *is* present in the line's "Sempre caro *mi* fu"; without that minimal presence, the *questo* and *questa* of the poem's beginning and their subsequent looping, interlacing, and tightening would make no sense at all.

At this semantic level of the thematics of shipwreck and drowning, and the presence or absence of an "I" with respect to a past of habitual experience, we are also again within the orbit of Leopardi's structural allusions to and echoes of Dante. Dante's *Commedia* is similarly predicated upon the survival of a shipwreck that, in the poem's very first simile, enables—impossibly—the poem's first canto and all that follows:

E come quei che con lena affannata,
uscito fuor del pelago a la riva,
si volge a l'acqua perigliosa e guata,
così l'animo mio, ch'ancor fuggiva,
si volse a retro a rimirar lo passo
che non lasciò già mai persona viva. (*Inf.* I, 22–27)

(And as he who with laboring breath / has escaped from the deep to the shore / turns to look back on the dangerous waters, / so my mind which was still fleeing / turned back to gaze upon the pass / that never left anyone alive.)

In Dante's poem, this shipwreck that is both submitted to and—miraculously—survived is, of course, Christian doctrine's death and resurrection, figured in Christian baptism's death of the old man and birth of the new. John Freccero's work has taught us that Dante's theology is nothing other than his poetics: the poem's condition of possibility is likewise its having already transpired as narrative so that it might come into being as the poetic creation of that narrative.[19]

There are, however, two other enabling fictions of Dante's *Commedia* that bear relevance to Leopardi's poem and, when taken together with the structure of resurrection, help explain the latter's particular achievement. One is a corollary of the resurrection motif, and this is the fiction that Dante-poet, outside or on the margin of his text, is always elsewhere than Dante-pilgrim, squarely in the narrative and its fiction of a past reality of experience. (It is this distinction that makes possible, and makes sense of, the *Commedia*'s powerful addresses to the reader: Dante-poet directs the reader to read Dante-pilgrim's situation and example, and thus often to avoid his error or temptation.) The second enabling fiction, itself a corollary of the first, is that the authority for the poem's writing is in its turn from outside and remains still outside the text: recall the "quando / Amor mir spira, noto, e a quel modo / ch'e' ditta dentro vo significando." Whether Beatrice, the Virgin Mary, or God himself and the intertextual authority hierarchically descending from Holy Scripture through the church fathers, the authority for a believing Christian is finally transcendental, not immanent, and it is also ultimately, if also only asymptotically, extratextual and theologocentric.

These three fictions of Dante's *Commedia*—that its author survives a fatal shipwreck; that "he," Dante-poet, is outside the narrative of "him," Dante-pilgrim; and that the poem's authority is transcendental—are resonant in "L'Infinito," but in their very differences from its own fictions, and so, like its deictics, they are also among its directions for its understanding. The fiction of death and resurrection via shipwreck is, as we have seen, potentially enabling of the poem to begin as it does "in the first place," with its *passato remoto* "after" its present but ego-negating ending. But with the structural condition and dilemma that this (re)beginning then poses—how is the "I" both absent and sufficiently present to be the point of reference for the two opening demonstratives, *questo* and *questa?*—the contrast with Dante's extranarrative poet becomes crucial. Leopardi's "I"—the *mi* of "mi fu"—is strictly textual and narrative;[20] he becomes the at-first-unspoken subject of the participial "sedendo e mirando" that are then revealed, three lines later, to modify the "I" of "io nel pensier mi fingo." In other words, Leopardi's "I" is always (*sempre*) in the process of textually—that is, here, grammatically—constructing itself as the force of various grammatical cases and voices, such that the ever-so-slight reflexivity and intransitivity detectable in "Io nel pensier mi fingo" suggest the poem's "I" thus "fabricating" itself. And the reader is obliged to mimic this very self-construction, imagining the opening lines' site, the sight and its obstruction, the indications of proximity and distance in the deictics, the very imagining itself ("I in my thought fabricate"). When the "I" hears (*odo*), it is at a juncture of "these plants," the wind ostensibly one instant outside, one instant among or between them, "that infinite silence" beyond the hedgerow, and "this voice," the latter of which is at once the product of all the preceding elements *and* an intratextual authority for their narration. Submitted to functioning as the fulcrum for the present-progressive comparison that is its own production, "this voice" is under- and overcome, negated and drowned, by its own textual conditions. Its present-tense activities, which are all the poem's actions that bear, reflexively, upon its own productivity—the "I" fictionalizes or fabricates, it listens, and it goes comparing—yield the narrative of its active self-absenting.

This last paraphrase of the poem's narrative may itself be restated, with a view less to its grammatical generation and evacuation of an "I" than to its modalities of action. In conjunction with the fiction of an "I" to whom *this* hill and *this* hedge always were (but no longer are, no longer grammatically can be) dear, but who must nonetheless still be "here" for the demonstratives to work, the poem invokes all that which a barely personal sight ("il guardo") could see—if so much were not instantly excluded. And that is all that a reader ever sees of this sight. The poem's ways of acting as if through a persona are then first a mode of vision marked as more inner than the *guardo* (*mirando*), followed by a correlative intellective fiction-making ("nel pensier mi fingo"). Next comes a hearing that is on the one hand within and to a received poetic topos (the Aeolian harp), yielding its own conventionally, romantically "inspired" voice, and on the other hand, is a listening to the *difference* between this inspiration by way of the crossing of deictically marked boundaries and the "inspiration" of Dante's text. Finally there is the hyperpoetic "vo comparando," which brings out both the looping and lacing together of spatial contrasts (the wind heard as this voice, that infinite silence then compared to the voice) that produces the poetry of this poem, and the contrast of such self-producing tropology with Dante's claim for authorized and instructive "going signifying." Restated in this schematic manner, the sequence of actions in the poem, even before its famous "drowning in (between) immensity" at its end, is entirely dissolving of outside perspectives or margins, as they are all absorbed, from the opening position of illusory presence and imposed blindness, into a single ongoing action of poetic comparison.

Dante's "vo significando" always still, at the limit, appeals to a semiotic end, be it as *arché* or *telos*, *Logos* or divine book folded upon itself (*Par.* XXXIII, 85–87). Leopardi's "vo comparando" remains intrapoetic in the sense that each term of the comparing—

the "quello / Infinito silenzio" and the "questa voce," that which is beyond an "I" and that which has been made, by the same comparing and tropological (catachretic) naming (wind = voice) internal to it and ostensibly issuing from it—is rigorously grammatically generated and grammatically untranscendental: *descendental*. This is a line of inquiry that allows us to understand all that does *not*, in any comparative or otherwise referential sense, bear upon the construction of "L'Infinito"'s poetics and meaning, any more than is the case with similar romantic lyrics by Wordsworth, Hölderlin, or Hugo. No God, no transcendental authority, no extratextual experience, not even—pace the still-widespread misunderstanding—any nature, for as we have seen, nature here ("quest'ermo colle," "questa siepe") is the extension of a demonstrative pronoun that itself extends an entirely intensive grammatical subject. But extending this interpretation of "L'Infinito" to the comparative study of the European romantic lyric would be beyond its means and ends. The aim of this chapter has been to show how a lyric generates itself from its looping and lacing together of its directions (its deictics and their semantic regions) and, from this chiastic knot, unfolds its beginning from its end and its end's sense from its rebeginning, thus looping more largely around again. The small formal trick that this fifteen-line poem is, from the beginning, one line longer than the sonnet's horizon of expectation is already a display that the poem ends one line after it might have and, viewed now from the other "end" of the loop, that it has already taken one line's step—death by drowning—before it takes the step of its first line.[21] Not ending without rebeginning, not beginning without already having ended, "L'Infinito" cannot be thought as any possible one-way journey to and arrival at a secure, authoritative site of meaning, original or derived, divine or Dantesque. The "carrying-over" that is the *metaphérein* and *translatio* of Leopardi's "vo comparando," and precisely in its *descendence*, is for his reader the remaining-within a loop from *questo* to *quello*, from this to that, from *fu* to *è* to *fu*, each always something else again.

3

Coleridge's "Kubla Khan"

❧

Fragmentation and Reflection

between Beginning and End

I wrote reflections that, in many ways,
were even stronger than their origin.
—Derek Walcott

The counterpart to poems that would end as they aim to, that
would direct and traject themselves unilinearly from beginning to
end—such as the first two Shakespeare sonnets we looked at, or
Dante's *Commedia* in its representational aspect—are poems that
would end as they begin, that would end at their very beginnings.
Less failed poems than poems of the failure to continue and end,
their achievement is their inachievement, their incompletion.[1]
These are poems that celebrate or lament but in either case *display*
their fragmentation; they are most recognizable in our modernity
as romantic fragment poems, and if Keats's two Hyperion poems
and Wordsworth's *Recluse* (and Blake's *Four Zoas* and Byron's *Don
Juan*) are the most famous long fragments of English romanti-

cism, Coleridge's "Kubla Khan" is surely its most famous lyric fragment.[2] I analyze "Kubla Khan" here from two vantage points and for two corresponding ends: how the poem insists upon its fragmentation in order to empower, synecdochally as it were, its partial status into a whole system of poetics and hermeneutics—thus negating, sublating, and overcoming its own fragmentation in the latter's totalization; and how the fragmentary in the poem nonetheless, against its first project, returns itself and its reader to a different form of nonending, not the completed and perfected incompletion of a fragment wholly understood, but the repeated fragmentation of the fragment in a chain of splinters metonymically continuing itself as a repetition that can never close upon or return to itself.

It is instructive to begin our approach to the poem by reviewing, however briefly and selectively, some of the terms of its reception. When Coleridge's "Kubla Khan" appeared in 1816, the contemporary reviewers spoke of the poem's "nonsense." This "nonsense" was immediately related to the ostensibly partial character of the poem: it was not wholly a meaningful *poem*, but only meaningless music; or else, Coleridge had dared too much, and therefore succeeded at only little, or even nothing at all, that was meaningful.[3] Even when the poem was soon judged very positively, the discussion remained within the confines of the question of partiality and meaning: "Kubla Khan" was so perfect because it was purely sensual music and imagery, and did not at all need to be more, or whole.[4] In both cases the poem was considered as a fragment, while the possibility of one's understanding it laid claim to totalization. Either one could wholly understand it—but unfortunately there was no whole to understand—or one *did* wholly understand it, and that meant that one understood it was not to be understood as a whole. The fragmentary and the totalized (or totalizable) were reciprocally codetermining. If the fragmentary reduced to the infinitesimal, its understanding increased to the totalizing, and if the understanding asserted its holism, it was in order to define and determine the fragmentary as such.

Nor do the later readings of "Kubla Khan" avoid this question of fragment and totality. One of the first great achievements of academic scholarship in romanticism, J. L. Lowes' *The Road to*

Xanadu (widely surpassed today and condemned as misinformed and misinterpretive, when not altogether ignored) investigated the poem from the perspective of "source-study" and valued it as a combination from parts of other texts, like a bricolage.[5] A more recent and literary-historically more persuasive study understands the poem as a part of Coleridge's project for a new kind of epic (to be called *The Fall of Jerusalem*), but which, as a part, had already cancelled the whole of the projected epic: the "symbolic" history encompassing all ages is reduced in the poem, so E. S. Shaffer argues, to a visionary instant, and the two classical genres of the drama and the epic are reduced to the lyric—whereby she nonetheless still calls "Kubla Khan" an "epic fragment."[6] The more readers know of this poem, of its sources and its author's intentions, the less they understand whether it is only a part or already a whole: to reemploy Shaffer's phrase in its double entendre, whether the poem is a fragment of something else (an epic) or a really big and unforgettable—an epic—fragment that inverts its partiality into a new kind of whole. The more we know, the less we understand: this is particularly the case with the meaning of the poem. If we understand it ever better in its parts, then we still wonder whether there is a wholeness of meaning to it at all. The critic George Watson once said, "The fact is that almost everything is known about the poem except what it is about."[7] The correlation of totality (knowledge) and fragmentation (understanding and meaning) continues to be sustained.

It is tempting to extend these soundings of the ratio of fragment and totality in the reception of "Kubla Khan" to the case of Coleridge himself, as a partial representation of the whole of romanticism,[8] and to the poem's constituents as the exemplary representation of romantic poetry as a whole. Let us linger for a moment at this latter observation. The poem's images, motifs, and ideas are indeed those held today to be typically romantic. The Oriental setting on the one hand, the emphasis on the sacred on the other ("the sacred river" repeated three times, and also the ending) are commonplaces of romanticism.[9] The phrase "caverns measureless to man" invokes late-eighteenth-century and then romantic theories of the sublime, as well as the suprahuman as that principle whereby romanticism distinguishes itself from an earlier, Renaissance standard of the human as "the measure of all things." The haunted, the Gothic, and the erotic (ll. 14 ff.) often appear, and indeed in that combination, at this time, as does an animation of the earth (17 ff.) that signifies not only romantic pantheism but also the renewed kind of lyric associated with romanticism: not the descriptive landscape poetry of the eighteenth century, but once again the apostrophizing nature poetry of personification (Wordsworth's *Prelude,* Shelley's odes, Hölderlin's river poems). The violence of the second strophe—an uncontrollable outburst—is easily correlated with the thematics of the French Revolution dear to the romantics, whereby Kubla Khan appears as the figure of a monarchical despot. At the end of the poem, the great estimation of the creative power of poetic "music" (45 ff.) and also the approximation of poetic speaking to imaginative seeing (48) are typical of romantic and modern poetry; the English romantics are, after Wordsworth and Harold Bloom, "the visionary company." The figure of the poet as inspired visionary does indeed close this highly romantic poem. If one adds to this the introductory note as well (we know now that its story of the poem's creation is false, but never mind; what is more important is first that the note belongs to the *text* of the poem, and then that its fiction presents itself for the reader as true), the representative character of "Kubla Khan" becomes even stronger: here one finds the motifs of the illness and solitude of the *poète maudit* and the poet-recluse; the "anodyne" as a narcotic, typifying a literary line from De Quincey and Baudelaire to Allen Ginsberg; the concept of "inner senses" associated by his friend Wordsworth with the imagination ("when the light of sense / Goes out," *The Prelude* 1805, VI, 534, 535); and lastly the image of composing poetry while in a trance or sleep, recognizable for us from claims by Rimbaud or by surrealism's *écriture automatique.*

Could one poem, one small part of a literary-historical period's production, actually have the whole of that time's themes within it? Of course not, but the facility (and, admittedly, the facileness) with which the word "romantic" could be applied as a label in the preceding paragraph to this theme or that image from "Kubla Khan" is an indication of the possibilities—expansive to the point of trivialization—of the extension of the ratio of part and whole that was first noted in the poem's reception. Let us turn our backs on such a catalogue of thematic commonplaces of European romanticism, for having demonstrated the possible thematic inversion of part into whole, it will now be the task to show a different match or "fit" between fragmented beginnings and the ends and endings of the poem's reading. For if working thematically with the question of fragment and totality in romanticism actually gets one nowhere,[10] we may correlatively see that in "Kubla Khan" the "theme" of the fragment is in no way understandable except as the thematization of its own reading. That is, there is no referent or semantic realm of "the fragment" other than in the textual implementation of its ends.

All questions of poetic fragmentation and its consequences (one of which is totalization) are questions of a poem's meaning and understanding; thus, to the extent that an image—say, a fragment as a shard or a ruin—becomes a theme in a poem, it will have structural and hermeneutic consequences. The presence of the word and image of "fragment" in the subtitle, the note, and the poem "Kubla Khan" itself challenges the reader to interpret and understand the whole poem and readings of it as fragmentary or total. The apparent reversibility of part into whole, fragment into totality (apparent in the poem's reception and thematization) is redisplayed and redeployed in the language and structure of the poem as the putting into play of the self-reflecting notions of part and whole, fragment and totality. But both the play and the reflection, in the end and in their ends, are anything but the circumscribable forms of aesthetic pleasure and hermeneutic closure that totalization has otherwise long promised and delivered.

Later I shall interpret the poem's note more extensively, but first two introductory observations are pertinent. Coleridge speaks there of the composition of the poem as "the images [rising up] as things, with a parallel production of the correspondent expressions." In this phrase, where the sequence of its words strains to assert a nonsequence or instantaneousness, first there are images as things, that is, images appearing and being taken as if they were things; then to this are added the expressions corresponding to the images, where "parallel" is taken to mean as much as "simultaneous"—although the "expressions" only appear afterwards in the syntax of Coleridge's formulation. The expressions—the words of the poem—correspond to images, which themselves appear as things. The "correspondent" and "as" would define a triadic relation of signification that is supposed to be simultaneous, but in the "composition" (albeit the fiction of the composition) there were only two elements, and in the poem itself only one: in Coleridge's alleged "sleep" there were only images and expressions, while the things were merely analogical, imagistic, or metaphorical ("as"); and now, in any present of the reader addressed by the note, one has only the words of the poem "here preserved." Although these words are supposed to correspond to originary images, and the images alleged to have appeared "as" things, there was and is no *reference* except for reference to the "fit" or joining of metaphoric correspondence. The appearance of images is the semblance of things, and the "parallel" appearance of words is the *correspondence* to this "first" appearance of (re)semblance.

This one phrase from the poem's note yields a direction for reading: a sequence of words that strains toward simultaneity and copresence of different dimensions (images, things, expressions) yields a chain—but less substantial than a chain, more like a dissolving line of flickering light—of metaphoric self-referentiality and self-reflection. In Coleridge's language, apparently clearly distinguished categories of identity and opposition (word and image, image and thing) first appear single, separate, and distinct, in order then to become comparable and substitutable in metaphors, although the "first" and the "then" of such a reformulation are in fact the reflections and references of the selfsame words "here preserved." In other words, the direction for reading is to understand sequence and its alleged dissolution into simultaneity as, in poetic fact and act, its own inversion: the simultaneity of a sequence of self-reflections that appears, but only appears, as a temporal series or extension.

The poem itself begins as if various oppositions, spatial and temporal, will be distinguished, maintained, and developed. Its strophic division clearly displays the three stages of a setting, an eventful narrative, and a retrospect together with a wishful prospect. The first strophe establishes a pair of oppositions out of which tension and dramatic action can be generated. On the one hand the setting of Xanadu is first described as infinite, where there is neither spatial ("caverns measureless to man") nor temporal ("a sunless sea") measure, but on the other hand the "pleasure-dome" is the place of the finite, with spatial boundaries ("twice five miles . . . were girdled round") and temporal categories ("blossomed" means seasonal change, and "forests ancient as the hills" introduces the past and time's continuity). The explicit opposition between "sunless" (l. 5) and "sunny" (11) indicates the broader categorical dichotomies that organize the opposition between Xanadu and the "pleasure-dome," and the first strophe as a whole: the dichotomy between the infinite and the finite, and more precisely, that between the outside and the inside ("girdled round" and "enfolding") as well as between the hyperbolic and the defined.

With its threefold sequence in the middle of the poem, the second strophe appears to represent in miniature the poem's tripartite strophic organization: the sequence of fragmentation (12–24), repetition and attempted closure (25–30), and paradoxical reflection (31–36). But this division is of a kind different from the formal stability of the three separate strophes. For what is fragmentation, and what "sequence" can issue from it? In this strophe, as a scene of fragmentation, oppositions and dichotomies such as those of the first strophe are also split apart. The clear distinctions and oppositions introduced in the note, and conditioning the whole poem, are here at stake, and none more than the opposition between fragment and totality.

After the "deep romantic chasm" has run aslant through the pleasure-dome and been personified ("As if this earth in fast thick pants were breathing"), this chasm becomes the place of an outburst: from this chasm, within the whole and the hole of the chasm, "A mighty fountain momently was forced." What follows from this is one of poetry's most curious representations of an origin as the result of fragmentations, and as such, one of its most diverting directions for reading. First, within this bursting-forth of the fountain ("Amid whose swift half-intermitted burst"), there is yet another outburst: "Huge fragments vaulted like rebounding hail." Like the fountain appearing as a part of the whole of the chasm, the relation between whole and part repeats itself here in the word "Amid," and indeed with the introduction of the word "fragment," as from the fountain—now construed as a whole—the "fragments" are thrown. We are at the fount of the fragments in the poem, or at their source and origin. With ever-increasing self-reflexivity of motion and direction, the poem makes this fount of fragments also the origin of the poem itself.

For as this "sequence" or process of division reduplicates itself—wherein a part within a whole becomes a whole for yet another part[11]—these very categories (of a part as something within or originating from a whole, a fragment as a part of a preexisting totality) invert themselves. With the repetition of the word "Amid" ("And 'mid," l. 23)—a repetition that, with its splitting of the word and with its addition of the letters *nd* still marked by the apostrophe's sign of ellision, is itself a further site of fragmentation and reproduction—the third fragmentation is not one of a part within a whole, but rather a chiastic inversion with the whole within the part: "And 'mid these dancing rocks at once and ever / It flung up momently the sacred river." What to this point has been a whole for the parts—the fountain for the fragments—is now, within these parts ("And 'mid these dancing rocks"), itself a part that at the same time produces and bursts a whole: the river. Or, more accurately, the river is produced in its bursting. And this happens precisely as the "fragments"—initially an undefined general concept—are identified as specific things ("rocks"): definitionally, as the whole of the word becomes a definite part. Thus, at the highest point of division and fragmentation, there is, in one meaning of "flung up," the production of what the beginning of the first strophe already assumed and spoke of: the sacred river. Finding thus a whole, or a beginning of a whole, within a fragment, the reader experiences that the poem and its first strophe begin "amid" the second strophe: they spring out of, take their origin from, the fragmented fountain. Thematically, the outer world of Xanadu arises within the fragmentation of the inner world of the pleasure-dome, while in the perspective of structural self-reflexivity the very possibility of the first strophe arises amid the second: only there, after its origin, does the condition of possibility for a narration of the course of the river obtain. This inverted temporality—the origin or the possibility of a beginning only after the beginning—is also inscribed in the strophe's temporal terms. The fragmentations are a series of instants ("Momently," ll. 19 and 24), but amid these instants there appears one ("at once") that suddenly becomes an infinity ("and ever," l. 23). Once again, the possibility of a continuous temporality of the river springs forth from out of a fragmentation. Or does this not, on the contrary, mean that this origin-as-fragmentation perpetually remains just that, fragmentation, never achieving a fluid continuity?

The lines of the second strophe immediately following (25 ff.) are characterized by a slower rhythm, and the calming repetitions of phrases from the first strophe and alliterations of *m* and *r*, as if the poem is now to "run onward" by way of a repetition of its beginning (cf. "ran," l. 26). But is this the beginning of a narrative of continuity and a narrative continuity? To the contrary, the river runs toward "tumult"; and with the reappearance of an "And 'mid" (29), this tumult is defined as a repeating present of the poem: the attempt at a whole comprehension or total representation of the narrative's time brings about its own destruction, as one hears that the past ("Ancestral voices") leads to a prophesied future of returning tumult (war).

As the last third of the second strophe sustains the attention to the running river, another representation of a middle appears: "The shadows of the dome of pleasure / Floated midway on the waves." This "midway" forms a centering between extremes—above ("dome") and below (under the "waves")—just as the following lines also represent a harmonizing ("the mingled measure") of extremes ("From the fountain and the cave": above and below, upwards and downwards). Even the "miracle" of the last couplet harmonizes extremes in the trope of paradox ("sunny" and "ice"). Such centering and harmonizing—a reestablished symmetry, even if also a narrative standstill—appear as an answer to the earlier splitting and fragmentation that were brought into the poem by the "slanting romantic chasm" and the several "Amids." Is fragmentation thus here annulled and elevated, sublated, into a new totality of symmetrical opposites?

The most interesting thing in these lines is the word "shadows." For shadows are the inversions of reflections; instead of light thrown back, they are the interruptions of light thrown forward. But as such shapes, they still refer back to their originals. Here the original is the pleasure-dome itself, but the centering and harmonizing of these lines is also the self-reflection of a figurative expression: the trope of the paradox. This self-reflection occurs in the middle of the statement, "It was a miracle of rare device," where "device" also means, in addition to invention, "devise" in the Renaissance sense of a rhetorical figure. The paradox itself— "A sunny pleasure-dome with caves of ice"—is a familiar, even tired figure, one of Petrarch's favorite paradoxes (fire and ice), then well-worn in later Petrarchism. The point here is that the shadow as representation has its counterpart in the sunny-icy device as rhetorical or tropological self-reflection; together, "midway" and offering symmetrical balance, the lines offer a pause and a dilemma. Is a possible narrative of the course of the river through the pleasure-dome brought to a standstill of rhetorical self-reflexivity, as if the poem would find itself in, "amid," a restored totality and symmetry of figurative language? These six beautiful and highly rhetorical lines nonetheless, and in spite of all their symmetries, repetitions, and apparently totalizing tendencies, yield a site of fragmentation.

In its subtitle the poem is called "a Vision," and according to this note it is a part of a recollected and re-presented vision. One notices immediately that the last strophe mirrors this structure of the poem's genesis: as the "I" of the narrator appears for the first time, it is said that he once "saw" something that he now wants to revive and re-present. More striking still is the parallel between the structures of the relations of signification in the note and in this last strophe. Like the poem that is supposed to produce the vision of "images as things" through its "correspondent" words, here a poetic re-presentation is intended to produce an image as a thing. Thematically, this refers to Xanadu—"That dome in air! those caves of ice!"—but in an entirely strict and literally self-reflexive sense it is also the poem "Kubla Khan": the line just quoted from the third strophe repeats and reflects quite closely line 36 from the second strophe. Thus, to recollect, revive, and re-present an image as a thing means to bring a previous image to consciousness—the paradox of the "miracle of rare device"—and to rewrite it again, or further. The figure of the narrator appears in this "I" as a figure of the poem's self-reflection of its reading; the "I" that has once seen a maid, and wants to revive and re-present her song of the pleasure-dome, here names the figure (poet and reader) who has "seen" (read) the words of the first two strophes of the poem and would now re-present them as the meaningful consequence, the meaning and end, of the poem's procedure.

The structural self-reflexivity of the poem casts light yet further into the thematics of this strophe. What the "I" saw and heard was "an Abyssinian maid, / And on her dulcimer she played, / Singing of Mount Abora." Abora is the river of Eden, thus the fount of mankind's beginning, or in the strict sense, the origin (as if "*ab-or*ginal"). Similarly, Abyssinia—at this time being explored as the place of origin of the Nile River—was frequently used as an image of an origin.[12] Furthermore, each name begins with *a* and *b*, so that these names of origins include the beginnings of the alphabet as well. Finally, *abba (a* plus *b)* is the Hebrew word for "father." Together, the two names and their significations refer to origins and founts, or more precisely, to a continuity between origins and beginnings, a successive, almost genealogical continuity, like that of the alphabet or a relationship between fathers and sons. These relations of signification are an attempted rewriting of the second strophe, where the origin arising from fragmentation only led to tumult and then to the standstill of the narrative. To remember, and to revive and repeat, the image of an Abyssinian maid singing of Abora, would mean to construct a double continuity between origin and image (what was there, and what is to be there again): like the maid's song of the origin, the third strophe's optative repetition of this poetic muse would represent the first, "original" images—those of the poem itself—as if they were real things ("I would build that dome in air / . . . And all who heard should see them there").

The names' play of allusion to the alphabet refers back to the first strophe. For there, too, the first three lines of the poem played with alphabetical order: "Xanadu" is pronounced as *z*, and the river *Alph*, in Greek (*alpha*) as well as Hebrew (*aleph*), signifies the first letter. Speaking of last things, one finds the first ones already included. Or, to put it another way, to write and read words (those of the poem according to the note; those of the first two strophes from the perspective of the third; those of the "Abyssinian maid" from the standpoint of the "I") means already to presuppose images (those of the vision and those of the "pleasure-dome" and the maid) and also images "as" things. Does this mean that the parts, like the letters, must already be understood within a delimited, finite whole (including, for example, the whole series of the alphabet)? Or does the appearance of the words of the poem in the first strophe already presuppose their "earlier" (narratively recounted) appearance in the image of the singing maid as well as their later (optatively projected) reappearance as actual, real images ("And all who heard should see them there")? Ultimately, does this correspondence of letters between the third and first strophes mean that fragments and fragmentation must again—or always already—be understood within a totality, so that "Kubla Khan" represents a Hegelian dialectic of the apparent totality of the first strophe, the productive fragmentation of the second, and the restored, re-collecting totality of the third? And might this dialectic of self-reflexive writing and reading be the actual, proper meaning of the poem's self-reflexivity: the poem directs the reading of its writing, such that the reading produces positively what the writing itself had negated?

To this series of questions that strain toward affirmation, two skeptical observations may first be appended. In one of the poem's manuscripts (the so-called Crewe MS.) there is "Amora" instead of "Abora." More significant than the play of love (*amor*) is probably the allusion to Amara, which in Milton's *Paradise Lost* (IV, 281) names a false Abyssinian Eden. As also in the note's fiction, the "original" can be untrue, and its further repetitions and representations a mirroring of the false instead of a production of the true from out of its "negative" source or origin. The second observation concerns the temporality of the repetition in the third strophe. It is indubitable, not that something was there before—be this Coleridge's vision, or the pleasure-dome, or the singing maid—but rather that the temporality has been determinable and determined up to this point: the whole poem up to line 41 is in the past tense, and indeed up to this point it is also self-reflexively past, that is, already written, and read by the narrative "I" that appears here and now. The remainder of the third strophe, on the other hand, is in the conditional or the imperative; it cannot rightly be said that anything is present, for there is no present without the indicative or the gerund, unless it be the performance of the "I"'s wishful projections. One can deduce the following from this distinction in temporalities. While the main part of the poem is in a narratable and readable temporal sequence—something was; now "I" am writing about it; "you" will then read it—the poem from line 42 onward is no longer narratable but only performable. The last thirteen lines are a matter of a *possible project* of writing and reading, wherein a first "reading" or recollecting— "Could I revive within me / Her symphony and song"—would be the condition of possibility for the further writing and reading. Up to line 41, the whole poem was scarcely anything but a superbly constructed and enacted set of directions for a perpetual self-reflexive self-reading and rewriting. Can the remainder now perform a further repetition? Only when a "reading" of the poetic "I"'s revival of the "song" is performed—even if only implicitly or virtually—would the "images" and "things" be there about which he could write narratively. But such a "reading" would already be the production or the writing. One can always read and write backwards from line 41—as that which is past, the meaning to be achieved always remains "behind" one—but from line 42 onward, one can only read and write forwards; which means that there is no meaning behind the lines that one could then represent or discover and interpret, but rather only a meaning that is still to be performed. The reversal of directions at lines 41 and 42, from behind to no-longer-behind or in front, is the watershed, the divide, and the crisis of meaning in the poem. Although the first five lines of the third strophe refer thematically to the preceding part of the poem, thereafter the "I" cannot read his own poem, but on the contrary, only the possibility of its writing its way toward a reading and a meaning. But this means not to read something, or to read a lack. How could such a poem as "Kubla Khan" finish, end, complete itself, at all? It is as if the "I" would only now come close to— come to the close of—writing a poem about the pleasure-dome, and find that it cannot be accomplished: "I would build that dome in air" presupposes that words could arise like images that are not yet there, and that is a question of the presuppositions of a reading that is also not yet there.

Our reading of the directions issuing from "Kubla Khan"'s structure of self-reflexivity has brought us to stand before an ever-inverting mirror symmetry of writing and reading—to write further presupposes a reading, but in order to read, something must first already be written—rather like the poem itself that first had to begin in order to arrive, in its second strophe, at the origin of its beginning. To play with a false etymology, is the "Abyssinian maid" the point in the poem where we came upon an abyss of sense? If we would understand this paradoxical symmetry, this standstill of self-reflection, we must avoid a totalizing allegorization of the poem's figurative rhetoric. For if the narrative self-reflexively led to the unreadable and therefore unnarratable structure of the poem, so that in the self-reflection of poetic rhetoric the possibility of narration was at once granted and taken back, the poem has still not arrived at a totality of its representation and meaning—even if as the representation of its non-sense.

This is the time to turn more closely to the poem's introductory note, where a more precise image of the allegory of this poem and its mirror symmetry appears. On the one hand there is the story of Coleridge's failed attempt to write down the "distinct recollection of the whole," on the other hand the counterimage of the self-restoration of the visions in the pool's mirror. After the interruption Coleridge retained only a "dim recollection of the general purport of the vision," which means he fell from the "distinct whole" into an allegorical, more exactly, an *enigmatic* part, for "dim" here indicates, almost like a technical term, the realm of the allegorical. (First Cor. 13:12 translates *aenigmate* as "darkly," and an enigma is called a "dark allegory" in the rhetorical handbooks.) The "lines and images" left behind indeed point to the destroyed whole, but the movement from parts to whole—from letters and words to purport or meaning—remains allegorically dimmed: Coleridge remains within a partial hermeneutic of the enigma with written fragments that are supposed to signify a "whole meaning." Writing within an enigma or allegory, the directions issued for reading can similarly aim and end only at and in the enigmatic or allegorical.

Opposed to this situation in the note, the counterimage in the other, adjoined bit of verse ("Then all the charm / Is broken . . .") at first appears as the temptation of a restoration of a whole understanding in the unifying of fragments into a renewed totality:

And soon the fragments dim of lovely forms
Come trembling back, unite, and now once more
The pool becomes a mirror.

But the allegorical fragments (again the word "dim") would reunite not just into a whole reflection of the meaning of the visions, but also—the allusion to Narcissus is unmistakable—into a mirroring of the observer as an image within the allegorical visions, thus, once again, an image (a part) among other images. This idyllic counterimage is therefore just as reflective of a partial character as was Coleridge's own experience in the first part of the note; the error of Narcissus was to take his image as an independent whole. When Coleridge writes in the note that some fragments were left behind for him, while the others passed away like disturbed mirror images on water, "without the after restoration of the latter," he indicates that the parts—including those of this recollection or understanding—remain forever fragmentary, without so much as the temptation of Narcissus's error.

The reference to "images on the surface of a stream" reminds one of lines 31 and 32, where the shadow of the pleasure-dome floated midway on the waves of the river. We are now in a better position to understand how this paradoxical centering remains in the middle of a fragmentation of attempted totalities. For as the shadow is an inversion of a reflection, its significance is here an inversion of its thematics: not the production of the pleasure-dome (as the meaning or referent of the shadow), but that of the figurative structure of the poem—an allegory of shadowy or dim mirrorings. And when a fragment is precisely to *mirror* a missing totality, this means, in this logic of inversion, that the "totality" is inverted into a fragment. For in the nature of the case, as well as in its employment as a figure, mirrorings are always inversions. Ultimately it is the same with our fragmentary understanding of the poem, for to interpret the fragments—the various words and images that aim to mirror a meaning—means to understand their inversions of meaning as totality into meaning as fragmentary, which then means forever to interpret their meaning in a fragmentary manner. As the adjoined bit of verse in the note says, the fragmented mirror images "each mis-shape the other": the conceptual pairs of fragment and totality, poem and meaning, text and interpretation, perpetually *misshape* one another, yielding not a symmetrical balance or equation between each other but rather an asymmetrical inversion of one into the other.

The figurative "content" of the poem includes such specific tropes as hyperbole, chiasmus, and paradox, but its figurative structure is more largely this misshaping or inverting organization of the fundamental categories of the true and the false, the original and the represented, the image and the meaning. The poem is structured in a temporal sequence according to which there was first a vision and its "distinct recollection," then the attempt at its representation: first came the images, then their verbal representation and narration. When this attempted representation and narration then fall into an allegory of figuration—from "distinct recollection" to "dim recollection" in the note, from "The shadow of the dome of pleasure" as referentiality (however attenuated) to "a miracle of rare device" as figuration in the poem—both Coleridge the author and a reader could perhaps still believe that the original would remain nonfigurative, literal, in the conditions of its possibility. This would then in turn serve as the condition of possibility for a literal understanding of the poem's allegory. But in the note, as the author falls ever further away from the original vision in the play of increasingly failing "recollection," it is said that "the Author has frequently purposed to finish for himself what had been originally, as it were, given to him." The important phrase here is the "originally, as it were," for the small proviso signifies that the allegory of figuration in the poem does not begin from a literal element, but rather takes its point of departure from an already metaphorical ("as it were" or "as if") "origin," or from the metaphor of origin as what precedes and leads to an end. As in the poem itself the origin of the river takes place only after the beginning, in a fragmentation and chiastic inversion, so in the note the origin of the poem has "from the beginning" already metaphorically or figuratively split or fragmented itself. Words are to be literal ("correspondent") images of the original images, but since these "originally" original images are already figurative ("as it were") expressions, the representational words of the poem are also always already unliteral, not wholly themselves, but rather figuratively doubled and divided. If a poem originates and begins from metaphoricity, it and its reader are already in a fragmented allegory of figuration.

This last inversion of literal and the figurative, according to which the "original" that one was "wholly" to represent is already brought forth as figuratively fragmented, also runs through the poem from the beginning onward. For when it is said, "In Xanadu did Kubla Khan / A stately pleasure-dome decree," the word "decree" is already similarly divided. In the third strophe, in the phrase "Could I revive within me," the performance of the narrative of the pleasure-dome and the narration of its performance came to a standstill together. Here, "decree" on the one hand means to pronounce and to perform a decision: for example, a pleasure-dome is be somewhere, and suddenly, by decree, it is there, already performed and produced. On the other hand, "decree" means to separate, to distinguish, and to decide: for example, the pleasure-dome should be itself and not something else. The two significations align themselves against one another as the possibility of a representation and the preceding judgment upon this possibility: if it were the case that a pleasure-dome is to be produced, then its representation and narration could also be performed; but this would also mean to decide what and whether a pleasure-dome would be at all. The crisis of the poem and its meaning, of its beginning meaningfully and ending in meaning, is contained in this. To decide between "decree" as performance and "decree" as judgment is the same as to decide between the literal and the figurative, the original and the restored, thematics and self-reflexivity, or the already-narratable and the only-performable. A "crisis" itself signifies such a separation and difference (Greek *krinein*), and the "device" of the poem—both the thematic as well as the figurative production of the pleasure-dome—itself already signifies "division." When one cannot distinguish and therefore cannot decide between two divided or fragmented significations, one then has or is in a crisis: that of the separation or differentiation (the "original-partition" in Hölderlin's sense) [13] between judgment and meaning.

When such a crisis is found in the attempt to read a poem to its end, it becomes the site of the *critique—krinein* once again—in the middle of literary criticism itself. Each time it would speak of the meaning of a fragment, criticism encounters a crisis of self-inversion: fragmentary poems, poems of fragments, like "Kubla Khan," refer to previous totalities that are to be reproduced in meaningful representations, both in the poetic writings themselves and in their critical analysis and interpretation, but at the same time the texts and their reading invert the ostensible previous totalities back into fragments through their mirrorings. Fragmentary poems never arrive at or end in a critical understanding without mirroring criticism in its own crisis of fragmented meaning and divided judgment, the still-divided parts of the text and understanding. Coleridge's paradoxical shadow floats midway on the waves, forever empowering itself in reflecting parts and images, but never arriving at the totality of a wholly self-mirroring meaning. This meaning of the fragmentary poem does not belong to any understanding of the matter that could stand at an end point, reach back, and narrate; rather, it is always underway, anticipating without completing or fulfilling. Endlessly self-inverting and self-empowering readings are projected by the poetry's self-reflection and remain the fragments of its meaning. The poem itself thereby becomes the fragment of the poem, and its reading the shadow or fragment of what reading to and in the end had "originally" aimed to be.

4

Reading Keats

ଛ⬤

"Still" Reading

If the English word "still" were studied in the manner and tradition of William Empson's *Structure of Complex Words,* this lean word would be found to inform and enrich some of the greatest of the language's poetry. In turn the poetry marks the word for its successive employers, above all for the consequent writing and reading of poetry. Shakespeare's sonnets, in my opinion, are the first and decisive mold for the word "still," shaping its duplicity and stretching out its tensions for a subsequent poetic tradition that runs at least to Wallace Stevens. As is readily imaginable and indeed memorable from their thematics of love, its loss, and the poetic promise of regain, the sonnets encounter and extend in the word "still" the antonymic senses of mortality's fatal end and of something poetic ever more to be. That is, "still" in its many grammatical forms (adjective, noun, verb, adverb), bearing the meaning of being or becoming without motion or sound, is brought into contrast with its other adverbial sense of constancy with a present or a future as with a past, of what is nevertheless, all the same, even or yet the case. Repeatedly, Shakespeare can locate in the pun of "still" the intersection of the lines of force of his sonnets' thematics, the attestation of life's decline into and arrest in stillness and the arrest and reversal of this decline in the affirmation of what will still remain and live on in memory, poetry, and love.[1]

Shakespeare's sonnets, we have seen, are instruments for and measures of time's reversals, such that their fourteen lines alternately move ineluctably forward and suspend, retract, and return this forward motion against themselves. This is why they are so difficult to read well, that is, in accord with their own duplicitous motions as opposed to our own, often impatient sense of just getting on with the reading, getting to the end of the short poem and the arrival at its understanding. It is perhaps less well known that Keats's poetry is informed by the same complex of sense, the same strains of tension, the same movements into opposition and reversal that issue from Shakespeare's word "still" and become part of Keats's poetic inheritance from his precursor. Beneath the richness of his themes, the lushness of his imagery, the daring of his tropes, and the surprising, often still unacknowledged complexity and tautness of his argumentation, Keats has embedded as a kind of structural spine the grammatical and semantic tension, the figurative punning potential, and the temporal plasticity that all inform the word and its Shakespearian legacy. For all their variety, Keats's poems—like Shakespeare's sonnets in their remarkable differences among their selfsame fourteen-line form, unlike them in their sheer formal variety—repeatedly direct their readers to reconfront the single issue that is also at the core of the present study of poetic ending: how does poetry move toward and into its end of, and as, its reading? How can motion across the time and space of verse come to its end when it also reverses the aim and direction of ending against its prior end? Keats's poetic technique of exploiting English's and Shakespeare's grammatical and semantic ambiguity yields what I call "'still' reading." Reading Keats's "still," we come to learn about still reading Keats—about the difficulty and density of reading Keats's words in their specific, material inscription, which leaves him frankly underread (with several exceptions, especially that of Helen Vendler's readings),[2] and about the kind of reading that is produced by lyric poetry when and as it resists the end of being read, the ending of reading.

Hyperion marks a point in Keats's oeuvre where he could not end, but only break off, return, and break off again: an "epic" about the battle between two generations of ancient gods—between the Titans, led by Saturn, and the Olympians—the poem was abandoned at a decisive moment, when Keats wrote his great odes, taken up again in its second version, "The Fall of Hyperion," and abandoned again in turn. In the face of this lack of ending, I begin with *Hyperion*'s striking beginning:

> Deep in the shady sadness of a vale
> Far sunken from the healthy breath of morn
> Far from the fiery noon, and eve's one star,
> Sat gray-hair'd Saturn, quiet as a stone,
> Still as the silence round about his lair;
> Forest on forest hung about his head
> Like cloud on cloud. No stir of air was there,
> Not so much life as on a summer's day
> Robs not one light seed from the feather'd grass,
> But where the dead leaf fell, there did it rest.
> A stream went voiceless by, still deadened more
> By reason of his fallen divinity
> Spreading a shade.[3]

These opening lines are a powerful spatialization wherein depth and distance indicate Saturn fallen into a fallen nature. But this is actually a periphrasis, a circumlocution for a spatialization of time, for time congealing or freezing toward a stasis; the poem some few lines later reinvokes this sense as one of "aching time," "moments big as years," where "unbelief has not a space to breathe" (ll. 64, 67). This opening periphrasis of time anticipates the passage's use of the word "still." "Saturn, quiet as a stone, still as the silence round about his lair" is an apparently unproblematic use of "still" as quiet or silent, unproblematic almost to the point of redundancy and tautology. But if it were truly redundant or tautological, then a problem would emerge that, indeed, frequently tempts the analyst of Keats with its apparent manifestation: why should something be gratuitously repeated? "Still as the silence" means quietude, and also stasis: "No stir . . . was there." But the privative sense of "still"—no noise, no stir or motion—which may be generalized as a sense of "no longer," also suggests as its counterpart a sense of "not yet," of an intensification toward a dynamic, as in the phrase "still waiting" rather than "waiting in a still manner." It is this second sense that is encountered a few lines farther into the opening passage. After the passage accents stillness— "where the dead leaf fell, there did it rest"—"still" reappears as an intensifying adverb, even if as an intensifier of deadening stillness: "A stream went voiceless by, still deadened more / By reason of his fallen divinity."[4] A stillness of "no longer" is matched or paired with a stillness of "not yet"—"Still as the silence" may mean something deadened, no longer lively, but it also means something not yet deadened, or not yet deadened enough: "A stream went voiceless by, still deadened more." Something is no longer going on, it is stilled or over, but it is still going on, not yet over.

This fulcrumlike balancing or teetering between a "no longer" and a "not yet" that is here introduced as a periphrasis of time may be familiar as a recurrent theme and dimension of Keats's writing. Recall, for example, how his "Ode to a Nightingale" begins with the phrase "One minute past . . . ," while the crucial moment in the initial drama of "The Fall of Hyperion" occurs "One minute before . . .": "One minute before death, my iced foot touch'd / The lowest stair; and as it touch'd, life seem'd / To pour in at the toes" (I, 132–34). One minute past, one minute before: no longer, not yet. Here, in the lines from *Hyperion* that we have been examining, Keats's sense of temporality is approached by way of his treatment of the imagery and activity of nature. With *Hyperion*'s opening imagery of a divinity fallen into a fallen nature, we would seem to be far away from the nature portrayed by the early Keats, far away from, say, *Endymion*'s "I will entice this crystal rill to trace / Love's silver name upon the meadow's face" (IV, 699, 700), where nature acts erotically with nature. But if we continue the contrast of the early and the later Keats, the treatment of nature gains in complexity. A very early claim about nature in Keats's sonnet "On the Grasshopper and Cricket" is that "The poetry of earth is never dead," for—the poem continues—the grasshopper "has never done / With his delights." In this poem, the opening line is memorable—genuine early Keats—and poetically uninteresting. "Never dead" means always alive, just as "never done" means always doing. But when the ninth line echoes the first—"The poetry of earth is ceasing never"—both the syntactic inversion and the participial form are significant, and lend considerable interest to the line and what it foreshadows of Keats's work. The privation or negation performed by the "never" in "ceasing never" comes only after the "ceasing": ceasing *not,* or ceasing never, nonetheless suggests and states ceasing, a ceasing that, as its participial form embodies, goes on without ending in a present indication, or in a perspective upon anything ceased, or over. It is, in other words, an "always," "not yet"; "ceasing never" extends or renders dynamic a nature "never dead" so that living might mean, however implicitly, a dying that never dies, as "never dead" is improved upon toward a ceasing that is never ceased or deceased.

Such a line from the early Keats, from an occasional, perhaps trivial sonnet, moves toward the most difficult late Keats: a phrase such as "ceasing never" moves toward what Keats calls "a constant change" in some lines from "The Fall of Hyperion":

> bright-blanch'd
> By an immortal sickness which kills not;
> It works a constant change, which happy death
> Can put no end to; deathwards progressing
> To no death was that visage. (I, 257–61)

"Ceasing never" aims toward a phrase such as "deathwards progressing / To no death." "Never dead," "ceasing never," "progressing / To no death": the movement, I am suggesting, is intrinsic to the poetic language, to its semantic range and syntactic and grammatical structures. Keats's language, we shall be able to claim, "works a constant change, which happy death / Can put no end to"—not even Keats's own death.

The lines just quoted from "The Fall of Hyperion" are anticipated in their statement, but with rather than without the appearance of the word "still," in the otherwise uninteresting lines about Glaucus's fate in *Endymion:* "Thou shalt not go the way of aged men; / But live and wither, cripple and still breathe / Ten hundred years" (III, 596–98). Several other passages, from the early to the late Keats, touch on Keats's language of change without end, and also will return us to the word "still." These lines from the early poem "Sleep and Poetry" combine and repeat what I have introduced as the senses of "still": something become static, "no longer" active, and something always continuing, "not yet" static:

> A drainless shower
> Of light is poesy; 'tis the supreme of power;
> 'Tis might half slumbering on its own right arm. (235–37)

The shower of light that is poetic language is not yet drained, and there will never be such a moment of drained, stilled, quieted, or static power—there is no longer to be a moment when or a perspective from which one would say "no longer." And yet this power, "supreme," is no longer at a height of activity or ongoing tension. It is "half slumbering," no longer fully wakeful, not yet asleep, and also not yet reawakened—draining, yet still drainless or undrained. A few lines later in the same poem, an image of nature awakening gives way to one that is at once erotic and meditative:

> let there nothing be
> More boisterous than a lover's bended knee;
> Nought more ungentle than the placid look
> Of one who leans upon a closed book. (259–62)

No longer boisterous, but bended or poised, the image of the lover conjoins with the double negative (rhetorically, the litotes) of "nought more ungentle"—nothing more ungentle meaning nothing more than a pose or look that is no longer active but not yet so gentle as to subside or disappear altogether. But there might be a hint of uncertainty, in the lines as well as in their context, whether this pose occurs one minute past, at the moment of no longer reading the closed book, or one minute before, when not yet having opened the still-closed volume. And so, too, there is uncertainty in the word "look": is it a gaze on the part "Of one who leans," or is it the outward appearance, the look, of the same persona? Is he looking or being looked upon; active or passive?

These several images, poised or posed between draining and drainlessness, power and slumber, boisterousness and bended, ungentle and placid, suggest as well a poetic poise and posture precisely but still indeterminately between reading and being read. That is, the problem of the activity of reading Keats's poetry is built, inscribed, into the poems themselves as passive, stilled objects nonetheless still directing the activity that passes over them. Keats suggests that the power of the poetry, the lover and the look, derives, perhaps in large part, from still being an image of activity, and yet inviting or giving way to another activity wherein the first one would become an *object* of a lingering gaze, no longer its own activity but not yet a mere or dead stasis. This transition from an activity to becoming an object for another activity (another's activity) describes quite precisely the situation of the two Hyperion poems. Saturn and Thea appear first, in *Hyperion*, before the impersonal gaze of the narrator and the reader; the action simply unfolds as a narrative. Then, in "The Fall of Hyperion," they appear before the personalized narrator/reader of the "I" who is the Keatsian persona. Two passages from these poems, the second a rewriting of the first, are also reworkings of the passages from "Sleep and Poetry" and they will help us extend the problem of reading poetry that the last passage has suggested. First from *Hyperion:*

> She [Thea, Saturn's sister] touch'd her fair large
> forehead to the ground,
> Just where her falling hair might be outspread
> A soft and silken mat for Saturn's feet.
> One moon, with alteration slow, had shed
> Her silver seasons four upon the night,
> And still these two were postured motionless,
> Like natural sculpture in cathedral cavern;
> The frozen God still couchant on the earth,
> And the sad Goddess weeping at his feet. (I, 80–88)

Like the lover's bended knee, halfway between stance and repose, Thea here has her head touched to the ground, while her hair is still falling, possibly not yet outspread, possibly no longer falling from above, but falling still. Time still moves, but it is slowed, where one time divides into four consecutive parts, and the number-game of time suggests the two are halfway between the one and four, "still . . . postured motionless," no longer moving, not yet moving again. To say that this posture is "like natural sculpture" is, of course, to recapitulate one of Keats's major themes and problems—the relations and differences between art and nature.[5] Saturn and Thea are like a stalagmite (a natural outspreading of mineral in a cave), but they are also like nature in that they still recall an unstilled capacity for motion and vitality ("a drainless shower"); and yet they are also like art in its very capacity to capture, pose, or still—render tranquil—such vital, animating power ("a drainless shower . . . is poesy," "like natural *sculpture*"). The two-way, ambivalent meaning of the phrase "natural sculpture" is halfway, sandwiched between "still . . . postured motionless" and "The frozen God still couchant"; if the first use of "still" moves semantically toward the sense of no motion, the second "still," in the phrase "The frozen God still couchant," reflects and repeats the first, the god frozen still, still motionless, but yet also still couchant, not yet altogether couched or collapsed—a gerundlike couching like Thea's "falling hair" that might still keep falling, whereas this couching might still be standing as well as falling.[6]

These lines submit their look of verbal activity-within-stasis to the look of reading. That is, the "I" of Keats's persona in "The Fall of Hyperion" looks placidly upon them; "The Fall," I can only baldly assert here, is the specific and sustained effort by Keats to write what it means to read one's own text and one's own textuality as the later version displays the splicing of the first text into the narrative of the second text as it unfolds before the "I" of the poet's persona. (But we shall see in close analysis rather than bald assertion the same state of affairs with respect to Keats's poem "This living hand.") Let us simply turn to "The Fall"'s version of the same passage we have just been reading:

> She prest her fair large forehead to the earth,
> Just where her fallen hair might spread in curls,
> A soft and silken mat for Saturn's feet.
> Long, long those two were postured motionless,
> Like sculpture builded-up upon the grave
> Of their own power. A long awful time
> I look'd upon them: still they were the same;
> The frozen God still bending to the earth,
> And the sad Goddess weeping at his feet. (I, 379–87)

Four changes are immediately evident. Thea's motion—if such it may be called—is intensified toward its end, an end to motion, or stasis: "touch'd" is now "prest," "falling" has (become) "fallen." As Thea congeals or freezes toward the static condition of sculpture, her animation—that is, *her* measure of temporality—is shed along with her naturalness, and so we have no longer the natural counting of time by the moon's "alteration slow" of "season's four"; rather, we have just the verbal redundancy of "long, long." Nor do we have "natural sculpture." Sculpture alone, not natural but builded-up or constructed, has absorbed "natural sculpture," or rather what was nature and is no longer (nor yet again) has become "the grave / Of [its] own power," just as "Sleep and Poetry"'s line about "might half slumbering on its right arm" has now become, finally, "sculpture builded-up upon the grave / Of their own power." From a plenitude of the "natural" and a still wakeful, still dynamic "might" (power), there has emerged a full grave of power, and the construction—the sculpture, or art—has emerged therefrom and thereupon. Finally, the passage signals a fourth change, perhaps the most dramatic one: "I," an "I," "look[s] upon" the figures, and this gaze absorbs and now embodies the passage of time, no longer counted off from the mutability of the moon, but absorbed from the "long, long" to "A long awful time / I look'd . . . : Still they were the same."

"Still they were the same." But what is "the same" when they, and this "still," are Keats's characters and words? On the one hand, they are the same as they were at the head of this passage or at the end of the preceding one, from *Hyperion,* for the final two lines are virtually unchanged and each couplet conveys the no longer/not yet sense that I have identified as Keats's use of the word "still"—frozen, no longer active, but still bending, and therefore not yet so static. On the other hand, the addition of "still they were the same" underscores the dissimilarity of the two passages, and heightens the sense of Keats's "still." The more one—"I"—look(s), the more the figures stay still, and are still the same, not yet changing or reanimating themselves. But to say this is not to look upon the apposite phrases that follow and gloss the "still they were the same": "The frozen God still bending," "the sad Goddess weeping." To look upon "those two . . . postured motionless, / Like sculpture builded-up upon the grave / Of their own power" and to see that "still they were the same," is to begin to *read* Keats's "still": the same word, "still they were still," in a grave of stasis yet also still upon it, still bending and weeping.[7]

Turning from the two Hyperion poems for the moment, I would observe that each remains unfinished, still a fragment, and each abandons its title figure, for each poem stands pierced or skewered on this key word "still." Saturn, in "The Fall," when he defends the threatened order of the Titans, calls for a recognition of constancy, of unchanged conditions, and yet he would use this recognition as an appeal for change that contradicts the very constancy and belies the initial claim for unchanging change; and he does all this through a persistent circling around the features of the word "still":

> the rebel spheres
> Spin round, the stars their ancient courses keep,
> Clouds still with shadowy moisture haunt the earth,
> Still suck their fill of light from sun and moon;
> Still buds the tree, and still the sea-shores murmur.
> There is no death in all the Universe,
> No smell of death—there shall be death—. (I, 418–24)

And if this is Saturn's fate, to appeal at once to what is still the same and yet still to come, it is also the lot of the Titanic calls for or descriptions of the god Hyperion (also a Titan), still unfallen, still ready to fall: "But one of the whole mammoth-brood still kept / His sov'reignty, and rule, and majesty;— / Blazing Hyperion on his orbed fire / Still sat, still snuff'd the incense, teeming up / From man to the sun's God; yet unsecure" (*Hyperion,* I, 164–68). Hyperion tries to accelerate the time of the sunrise, of *his* dawn (he is still the sun-god, to be replaced by the new god Apollo), but even as his sun is still his, still ready to do his bidding, it becomes stilled in the heavens—"While still the dazzling globe maintain'd eclipse, / Awaiting for Hyperion's command" (I, 288, 289)—and so the heavenly skies are eclipsed as something or someplace responsive to his call: "Hyperion arose, and on the stars / Lifted his curved lids, and kept them wide / . . . and still he kept them wide: / And still they were the same bright, patient stars" (I, 350–53).

These remarks must remain here only hints as to why the two long poems may not have been able to advance beyond the problems of the word "still." In turning to the odes, we remain still with the turn in the Hyperion poems from "natural sculpture" to "sculpture builded-up upon the grave / Of their own power," for when we read the Keatsian persona's "I" "look[ing] upon them: still they were the same," we see Keats's reading, reading the word "still"—and perhaps, more boldly, we see as nearly as we ever see (as in the great poems of Shakespeare, Hölderlin, Baudelaire, Stevens, Celan) that invisible activity that is reading. The turn from natural sculpture to sculpture built upon a grave might suggest a biographical curve to this reading of Keats's works, but the problem is rather the same one of nature and art in Keats briefly touched upon before. As Paul de Man and others have argued, any biographical reading of Keats lends a false coherence to his writing, and is actually regressive with respect to the direction of his work: his was a life "almost always oriented toward the future," lived by "a man whose experience is mainly literary . . . gained primarily from the act of writing,"[8] and such a life would in a biographical interpretation be misread back into the writing that is itself ahead of or guiding, directing, the life. The question of art and nature in Keats includes the question of his life: for him humanity is often being included within his sense of nature (sometimes it admittedly is not), whereas his sense of art is either seeking to include both nature and humanity or being questioned (as in the famous exchange with Moneta in "The Fall") in their name.

Keats's odes are forever bidding adieu. This thought, a paraphrase of a line and a half from the "Ode on Melancholy" (the lines actually read "And Joy, whose hand is ever at his lips / Bidding adieu"), is first encountered in the inaugural "Ode to Psyche," and it is already conjoined there to the word "still." There, in the vision feigned by the figure or personification of Fancy, the poetic persona sees Psyche and Cupid:

> Their lips touch'd not, but had not bade adieu,
> As if disjoined by soft-handed slumber,
> And ready still past kisses to outnumber.

Neither joining nor parting, achieving nor failing, the figures pose a moment still attached to a past in the sense that it may be reattached to or reenacted in a future. And yet it is also detached, "disjoined." Poised or balanced on the "still" of not yet, the readiness toward a superabundant future might remain in suspense just long enough to yield a "still" of no longer, a stillness of posed sculpture. This ode would still turn, in its last strophe, toward a fanciful art of natural and erotic bounty (its last strophe includes this image: "And there by zephyrs, streams, and birds, and bees, / The moss-lain Dryads shall be lull'd to sleep"). But the "Ode to a Nightingale" recalls this same scene within a more pointed tension between nature and art. There is a bittersweet, enthusiastic-melancholic inclination toward human death in the face of natural song:

> Now more than ever seems it rich to die,
>> To cease upon the midnight with no pain,
>>> While thou art pouring forth thy soul abroad
>>>> In such an ecstasy!

This first suggests a balance between an acknowledgment of the transitoriness that comes with human mortality and an avowal of the constancy of art and nature: "Still wouldst thou sing . . .", the ode continues. But this balance itself balances on the word "still," whose sense here of "not yet dead"—like the earlier "ceasing never"—might teeter or decline toward "no longer living," stilled. The last strophe does indeed tilt decisively in this direction:

> Adieu! adieu! thy plaintive anthem fades
>> Past the near meadows, over the still stream,
>>> Up the hill-side; and now 'tis buried deep
>>>> In the next valley-glades.

Natural song dies too, passes past a nearness of felt nature and into a past, a no-longer of this "still stream" no longer pouring forth a vital or reanimating source: this still stream leads to a burial ground, a grave of nature.

The burying of natural art, or of poetic song in nature, achieves its other face in the "Ode on a Grecian Urn." This is to say that the wishful combination of art, human eroticism, and nature, all to be endowed with staying power or even immortality, turns into yet another gaze upon a stillness of a grave. The urn's representation of a "flowery tale" or "leaf-fring'd legend," which is shown to include the "Fair youth, beneath the trees, [who] canst not leave / [His] song, nor ever can those trees be bare," is preceded by an initial address to the objet d'art as "Thou still unravish'd bride of quietness." "Thou still . . .": you, urn, are still here to be addressed, viewed, appreciated. And yet "still," the word, is also still here. The "still unravish'd bride," like the maiden who is "the goal" described upon the urn, is in the condition of not yet, not yet an object of sexual consummation, and this leads to the heightened claims of "cannot fade" and "for ever" that dominate the second half of the second strophe and the first half of the third. But the line-end position of "quietness" retrospectively reaccents "still" as of a quietude, a no-longer; in this two-way reading that the line gives to the word, "still" is reaccented as if followed by a comma, as if with a lengthened pause that extends to the stillness of the stilled. And dead-center in the poem, where an ode might classically or conventionally turn, the word reappears:

> More happy love! more happy, happy love!
>> For ever warm and still to be enjoyed,
>>> For ever panting, and for ever young;
> All breathing human passion far above.

The claim for a "still" of not yet produces a statement of no longer. The lines are an extolling of youthful passion poised in a suspended present, following upon a similarly glorified nature and art (the immediately preceding lines are "Ah, happy, happy boughs! that cannot shed / Your leaves, nor ever bid the Spring adieu; / And, happy melodist, unwearied, / For ever piping songs for ever new"). But this very praise elevates the suspended moment right out of time and into a pseudotranscendent stasis. Far above the human, "still to be enjoyed," the urn yields, in its next strophe, its well-known counterdescription as a place of sacrifice, an altar, emptied, silent, desolate; and by the last strophe, "ever piping" and "ever warm" have become "silent form" and "Cold Pastoral!"

With the shift from warm to cold within a single poem, we are already turning toward Keats's late, perhaps his last poem, "This living hand." But a pair of matters in the ode "To Autumn" must first draw our attention, albeit in passing and in a way that does not do justice to a poem that is difficult not to read as an apotheosis of English poetry, even as it is also surprisingly difficult to read *as* an apotheosis of Keats's verse, or even of his odes; and this is because, in its absorption of humanity and the human voice into an address to and presentation of nature, where art would be natural and nature art, it is so exceptional in Keats's oeuvre. Whether the poem can be both exceptional in and exemplary of Keats at the same time, is the question at which, perhaps, our understanding of "To Autumn" is still without consensus.[9] Nonetheless, two sets of matters in the poem are directly relevant to our interests in this chapter. The end of the first stanza, filled as it is participially and infinitively to overflowing with natural ripening, reads:

> to set budding more,
> And still more, later flowers for the bees,
> Until they think warm days will never cease,
> For Summer has o'er-brimm'd their clammy cells.

This "budding more, / And still more" is of a something evermore about to be, as Wordsworth put it (*The Prelude*, 1805, VI, 542), of an eternally—always "later"—active, gerund-present: it is the quintessential "still . . . not yet over." The "never cease" echoes the "ceasing never" of the early sonnet in the apparently truest manner. But the "until they think" of these poor bees recalls the seduction of the Grecian urn ode's "Thou, silent form, dost tease us out of thought / As doth eternity: Cold Pastoral!" The bees are deluded, thinking in error. And perhaps the word "still," budding more, and still more, overflows one of its registers and into another, cooler one—that of no longer. We know the third stanza turns to the cooler "soft-dying day" of "rosy hue":

> Then in a wailful choir the small gnats mourn
>   Among the river sallows, borne aloft
>   Or sinking as the light wind lives or dies;
> And full-grown lambs loud bleat from hilly bourn;
>   Hedge-crickets sing; and now with treble soft
>   The red-breast whistles from a garden-croft;
>   And gathering swallows twitter in the skies.

The beginning of this last stanza announced to autumn, "Thou has thy music too." In this remarkable, remarkably beautiful passage, bits of natural life absorb and embody the music, usually in terms appropriate to human artistry: the gnats' choir, the crickets' singing, the red-breasts' treble. But what about the lambs' bleat and the swallows' twitter? Two other patterns in the passage seem to move in the direction of this same question of discordance, or of a possible *concordia oppositorum*. One is the image of balancing, between rising and sinking, living and dying, an image sustained and extended by the near-oxymoron of the full-grown lambs, balanced between lamb and sheep, or lamb and lambchop. The other pattern is, in this passage, a progressive marking of the humanized limits of nature, from "river sallows," to "hilly bourn," to "hedge" and "garden-croft": a movement toward a nature of human, cultivated dimensions.[10] I suggest that, on the far side of the passage's incomparable balancing act, and its apparent consolidation of humanity and poetic song together with natural activity, the seemingly transcendent move to "in the skies" that closes the poem only hints at something supernatural; it also very naturally, mortally, even fatally brings in the understated finality of the gnats' mourning and the full-grown lambs' bleating, for swallows gather and twitter to feed, to eat off of nature, mixing their celebration with the insects' swift ends. The liminal balancing of celestial soaring and subhuman descent in this last line is answered to, displayed and echoed, in the superbly articulated yet inarticulate twitter, like the bleat that balances on "lives or dies": a balance still, between not yet over and no longer.

In turning now to "This living hand," we can be less merely descriptive of a recurrent feature and problem of Keats's poetry, and more engaged in how such a feature enters into any sustained attempt at "'still' reading" Keats. The feature is no longer the word "still" itself,[11] and so much the better, for the brief text offers the opportunity to test and display the kind of reading that Keats's poems direct far beyond their deployment of this single word.

> This living hand, now warm and capable
> Of earnest grasping, would, if it were cold
> And in the icy silence of the tomb,

So haunt thy days and chill thy dreaming nights
That thou would wish thine own heart dry of blood,
So in my veins red life might stream again
And thou be conscience-calm'd. See here it is—
I hold it towards you.

These verses were found on a manuscript page of Keats's unfinished verse tale "The Cap and Bells," and it is not known whether
they are a piece of dramatic speech sketched for this poem or
some other drama. If they were, then the "I" and the "you" (and
the "hand") would be visible before one another—or at least
imaginatively so—as a speaker before an interlocutor or audience
while the discourse is spoken, provoking the imagination to see
proleptically a dead hand. Lawrence Lipking, who considers this
text "one of the best examples in literature of a radical ambiguity
or 'rabbit-duck'—an artifact that can be read in two fully cogent
yet mutually exclusive ways"[12]—tilts toward this dramatic understanding, suggesting that a response to the broken last line might
be implied: the spoken and living response, "But you are not
dead." But Lipking also makes the best possible case for the opposite reading: that the text is a poem addressed to a reader, in
which instance he imagines what is obviously *not* there to be seen,
namely, a living hand. He also argues convincingly that a "com-
promise" between these two understandings (say, that the text is
addressed privately to Fanny Brawne) is untenable: each interpretation is weakened; "the two versions tend to cancel each other
out when combined."

But they also do when left uncombined, for they are radically
contradictory. A living hand turning into a dead one, or an absent
one turning into a present one—which is it to be? Faced with this
dilemma, Lipking, for example, tends toward combining them:
"Both versions . . . do obey, at least in one respect, the same artistic principle: the power of a speaker to control and manipulate
our imaginations." In naming the persona a "speaker"—rather
than, say, a "writer"—Lipking shows his cards, and he even draws
the possible signification of a hand *writing* into his understanding
of the text as an essentially dramatic situation: "the very act of
writing might be thought to confirm that a warm and capable

hand is moving toward the reader." (In fact, this experience need not be so: were I seated to the left of a writer of English, his or her hand would write away from me.) But Lipking's image of a hand *writing*, along with his reference to Keats's line "When this warm scribe my hand is in the grave" (from "The Fall of Hyperion"), serves to point toward a different understanding of the Keats poem, which would not resolve the ambiguity but deepen it still further. In the line from "The Fall of Hyperion," "this warm scribe my hand" inscribes itself in the grave at the moment it *writes,* and that is the point Keats introduces in the opening eighteen lines. The "fanatics' dreams" and "savage's guesses" are distinguished by Keats through their being designated as *un*written ("pity these have not / Trac'd upon vellum or wild Indian leaf / The shadows of melodious utterance. / But bare of laurel they live, dream, and die" [I, 1–7]), while "Poesy alone can tell her dreams," "can save / Imagination from the sable charm and dumb enchantment" (I, 8–11) by dying into script: "Whether the dream now purpos'd to rehearse / Be poet's or fanatic's will be known / When this warm scribe my hand is in the grave" (I, 16–18). At this instant, the end of line 18, the "hand" must be read as "in the grave," that is, in its other legitimate sense, as already written, as *handwriting*—in contrast to those untraced utterances—and thus the semantic effect is that the line declares—directs and performs—itself to be "poetry," a shadow that lives in and beyond the grave.[13]

Now it is this motion, whereby the "warm scribe my hand" writes itself into "hand" as *handwriting,* that the poem "This living hand" rehearses, and to more haunting effect. The poem insists that "hand" be read initially as "living," "warm and capable / Of earnest grasping," against which sense the lines then pose an opposite instance that the reader is invited to imagine: the cold, dead hand, "in the icy silence of the tomb." But then it closes with "See here it is— / I hold it towards you." Is "it" the living hand, or the dead one? It is, in this reading, the living hand turned dead, written as dead in the poem's proleptic narrative, and "it"—the two letters of the neuter pronoun—is the *handwriting,* or "hand," of the "living hand": "it," and the whole text of "This living hand." This dead or written hand, then, comes before us declaring itself "living" in the first line, and from our necessity of reading it as living it enacts its proleptic wish: that the reader(s) pour life into the "entomed" tomb of text so that it might live "again," as meaningful representation. The "living hand" thus *appears* as living, writes itself into death or script, to reemerge as the *handwriting* it always already was, only reanimated now as the *figure* of the hand: not a real hand, but a representation of a hand via handwriting.

But now, if one reads the poem through "again"—and this poem, like Keats's word "still," is not properly read once until it is read at least twice—the opening "living hand" is understood as an entombed script or text that is "living" only to the extent that it is animated by the reader's understanding, in accordance with the poem's narrative and directions. But from this "second" perspective, the poem yields a "See here it is—I hold it towards you" in which the problem is not the "it" (we know it is the written word, the two letters) but the "I." The first time through, the "I" could be thought to be Keats or at least some persona writing itself into its disconnected or dead mode: handwriting. But this time around, however, "This living hand" is handwriting alive and warm only because it is read—it is "capable / Of earnest grasping" only because the reading seeks to "grasp" or com-prehend it. So, too, "*my* veins" are already the text's lines, reanimated with the blood of meaningfulness. The "I" is therefore also arrived upon as dead, as script, and yet the text "speaks" here: "I." From this dead hand and its vamping "speech," precisely because it is still being read, the reader is enjoined to read still, and this time he "gives blood"— meaning—to the textually productive persona ("I") through a necessary misreading: the "I" is revived as living, as capable of writing the beginning, "This living hand," in the "first" place. Thus the reader returns to the beginning of the "first" reading, to the *living* hand "living" (again) to write itself into death (handwriting), to be read as such, and then to be misread back into life. Unlike the living Keats (in his letter to Charles Brown of 30 November 1820), his "hand" never wearies of its posthumous existence.

From the ambiguity of the "it" one reads one's way to the ambiguity of the "hand" and the "living" (a real living hand, and yet a handwriting alive only when read), and there one reads the "I" as ambiguous in the strongest sense: is there no "I" at all except for the letter "I," or is there a living "I"? But here the former must be read and misread as the latter, as "I, the Keatsian persona," so that the word "it" might live again, so that the poem and its reading might continue as meaningful. In other words, the poem's meaning and its reader move not in a circular pas de deux, nor perhaps in a figure eight, as much as in the figure—rightly privileged by recent literary theory—of a Möbius strip (privileged because, like a text, it is a spatial representation that is meaningful only when considered temporally): one always begins on one "side" (the "living hand") to find it is really the "other" ("it" as handwriting) and then to find further that this "other" must also be the "first," opposing "side" as well. What is indeterminate here is that one can never really know where or when one is beginning the reading, since it must necessarily have already begun; and one does not know where or when the reading ends, because the only alternative to reading one's way into and through the misreading is simply no hermeneutic alternative at all (nor an end any poetics has any interest in)—it would be to stop reading altogether, with the poem (its script of letters of "it" and "I") dissolving into a meaningless death. This would be a different kind of "'still' reading": not the "still life" that captures the inanimate, nor the photographic "still" that can capture everything visible but its motion, but *stillborn* reading, a no-longer-reading, instead of a reading not yet stopped, finished, or ended.

This commentary may be considered complete in at least one sense, which is that it would gain nothing by considering the poem as a fragment: although, like Coleridge's "Kubla Khan," it writes itself into an ongoing continuation beyond which any actual continuation or completion of the text would only cancel the considerable meaningfulness at which it has arrived, it is unlike the Coleridge poem in doing this without the threefold employment of the term "fragment." Beyond or beneath the thematics of Coleridge's poem of the fragment and its reflections, Keats's poem is of the structure of the writing of letters that still need their reading. At this "still" of ongoing need and, therefore, ongoing lack, there can be no talk of completion, however *determinate* my reading has tried to be. It is determinate perhaps precisely to the extent that it remains a description—a description of how the poem directs and works with its reader—more than an interpretation. To say what the poem *means* would be to interpret the very juncture of text and interpretation that this poem enacts or writes: "This living hand"—see here it is—I hold it towards you.

The existence and function, in Keats and in other poetry, of words like "it" and "I" and "still" yield a kind of reading that reads toward and against the threshold of reading as interpretation: reading as an activity or process that might produce a thematic representation of meaning. To say that reading Keats's "still"— "'still' reading"—resists, or bumps up against an obstacle to a reading of meaning is not the same as to say that reading poetry reaches something like Jakobson's view concerning the reflection of the poetic utterance upon its own sign and signifying procedures.[14] Nor is it to say, as some wildly subjective positions (or their deliberate and polemical misrepresentations) would perhaps hold, that if words do not assume or reach an end in some stable representation of meaning, then "anything goes" (a position against which all of my attention to and respect for the *directions* of a poetic text is directed). Rather, "'still' reading" as I have sketched it here, locating it in Keats and sensing it in poetry *tout court,* is part of a logical and tropological—a discursive—activity, on the far side of Hegel and his dialectic, which may be called the indeterminate negation of determination. That is, if something very special goes by the wayside, namely the determination of the sign, or of poetry and its poetics, as meaning, or interpretation and hermeneutics, then it is not that "anything goes," that anything is allowed, but rather that some, perhaps many, perhaps *every* thing(s) goes— slips, becomes difficult to grasp as before, to retrieve as common, in the face of what Keats calls the "grave" of poetic verse and Hölderlin calls "the fixed letter" ("der feste Buchstab'").

Keats wrote himself into this dilemma across the course of his career. Two last passages, from "The Fall of Hyperion," may serve to suggest the tentative, still lingering ending where he left himself, and leaves us, still reading.

> Then Moneta's voice
> Came brief upon mine ear—'So Saturn sat

When he had lost his Realms—' whereon there grew
A power within me of enormous ken
To see as a god sees, and take the depth
Of things as nimbly as the outward eye
Can size and shape pervade. The lofty theme
At those few words hung vast before my mind,
With half-unravel'd web. I set myself
Upon an eagle's watch, that I might see
And seeing ne'er forget. No stir of life
Was in this shrouded vale. (I, 300–311)

The "depth of things" that Keats would *see* and take or possess
is explicitly (because of the contrast built into the wishful analogy
"as nimbly as the outward eye / Can size and shape pervade") not
a perceptual seeing of real, substantial objects; contextually, it is
reading his earlier *Hyperion,* as the narrative of that poem begins
to unfold at this point in "The Fall of Hyperion." It would also be
the unveiling or revealing of that "shrouded vale" of the poetry,
just as the immediately preceding lines appeared to display a literal unveiling or revelation of Moneta's face from behind her veils
of linen and gauze, curtains and smoke, shade and shadow. But
this seeing—reading—arrives not at a "depth of *things*" substantial, not at a long buried, now finally disentombed "deep meaning" that an interpretation might then represent "in clear light" of
understanding as a thing to be seen, evaluated, measured ("size
and shape"), and judged. Rather,

> Now in clear light I stood,
> Reliev'd from the dusk vale. Mnemosyne
> Was sitting on a square-edg'd polish'd stone,
> That in its lucid depth reflected pure
> Her priestess-garments.—My quick eyes ran on. (II,
> 49–53)

The depth is of polished surface, an illusory depth, reflecting
above as if below—while seemingly reflecting one *in* the other—
the figure of a shape (Mnemosyne) and her "garments," her veils
or figures (themselves recalling their context of "shrouded vale"
and "dusk vale"), through which the reading persona moved and

at which it again, still, finds itself arrested: and yet still seeing and reading ("My quick eyes ran on . . ."). Which is where Keats's text broke off, eight lines later, and all our subsequent reading reads still. To see depth as surface inscribed and reinscribed is perhaps, as Keats's most Keatsian successor put it, to behold "this shallow spectacle, this invisible activity, this sense." Polished stone and lucid depth are reflected, inversely, as shallow and specular. From Keats's seeing of reading, as I have understood the lines from "The Fall of Hyperion," to Stevens' reading of Keats's sight of reading, "invisible" but "seen" as "active": this activity, which is Stevens' reading of Keats, yields the doubled sense(s) of "this sense" that never just ends at and in a meaning—to see reading, and to be still reading.

5

Lightning Bolts, Arrows, Weather Vanes, and the Crux of Soullessness

Directions and Ends of the Poetic Image
in Three Hölderlin Poems

Friedrich Hölderlin's poems have almost always been read under the image of Hölderlin the poet, and this has not always been to their advantage. Initially his poetry suffered repeated periods of neglect corresponding to the abandonment of the poet himself, abandoned first by friends and supporters such as Hegel and Schiller (and undervalued and then neglected by Goethe), abandoned in the end to madness, custody, and a few patronizing visitors (with important and insightful exceptions such as Mörike), ignored after that by several generations of (non)readers. When, a century later, the neglect was inverted into attention and then adulation, the concern was certainly for Hölderlin's poems—this is the period, during and after World War I, of the first two critical editions of his writings, and few editors and scholars could have shown their subsequent devotion to detail without the example of his first great editor, Norbert von Hellingrath—but it was a concern very much directed by one or another image of the author: Hölderlin the Hellenophile (especially of a Dionysian strain), Hölderlin the nationalist poet ("Der Tod fürs Vaterland," etc.), Hölderlin the poet-thinker. These may have replaced Hölderlin "the beautiful soul" ("die schöne Seele") or Hölderlin the madman, but they were still the covering images that surrounded his poetry like bookboards.

If the attention to the poetry remained under the shadow of the imagery attached to the poet himself—especially Hölderlin the nationalist and Hölderlin the philosopher's companion—through World War II, the following decades saw an improvement of Hölderlin's fortunes, but one that nonetheless kept his poems confined to a certain, and ultimately limiting, image of poetry and its custodianship. This improvement began with two developments: the momentum and prestige and autonomy acquired by the massive critical Grosse Stuttgarter edition (1943–85), and the corresponding rise of a Hölderlin "philology industry" that slowly worked its way out from under the wings of biographical hagiography, nationalist ideology, and Heideggerian philosophy. Although Friedrich Beissner, the principal editor of the Grosse Stuttgarter Ausgabe, started both as a classicist steeped in the Hellenophilic image of Hölderlin and as a young man participating in wartime celebrations of Hölderlin the poet of Germany, his project of the critical edition evolved into a monumental effort at reconstruction and scrutiny that freed itself from crude caricatures of the author, and created and preserved the space in which philological tact and rigor could replace wishful ideological projections. At the same time, the revival of German universities and their German literature departments in the postwar decades, and the parallel rise in Hölderlin's stature such that he received full scholarly honors, together allowed for comprehensive interpretive debate around the poems, their poetics (or "poetology," as it came to be called), their philosophy, even their politics. Although Martin Heidegger's commentaries remained for a long time the arch through which Hölderlin readers still had to pass, and the arch that still put his image into a perspective and against a background, a scholarship based on philological respect, philosophic neutrality or learned interest, and historical-critical acumen came, by the 1960s, to define Hölderlin's literary-scholarly image. Peter Szondi's and Dieter Henrich's works best exemplify this considerable achievement.

And yet. The very turn toward a philologically scrupulous and critically rigorous appreciation of his poetry developed from under the authority of Hölderlin the great author, an authorization that actually allowed for a limited kind of reading of his texts. What I mean is that if it took rather much longer for Hölderlin to join his contemporaries Schiller, Goethe, and Kleist as one of the undisputed great writers of classical German literature, when he did emerge, his poems took on a monumental and achieved quality that demanded of their readers a corresponding mix of veneration and seriousness: a readiness for interpretive labor that would be as awe-inspiring as inspired by awe. Hölderlin became and now is a great German poet, and great poets write magnificently accomplished poems, they make—especially when they are German—serious statements, they may even have systems and worldviews. In the face of—but perhaps precisely because of—the fragmentary character of so many of Hölderlin's manuscript versions of his poems, a compensatory drive for their completion in interpretive understanding and critical appreciation is everywhere visible in the scholarly literature. Even when the Hölderlin industry was rocked in the late 1960s by the argument, first from Pierre Bertaux and then by many younger scholars, that Hölderlin was a Jacobin, a partisan of the French Revolution, a political radical through and through, this destabilization of what one expected from a great German author quickly led to an equivalent and thoroughgoing restabilization of a view of Hölderlin, as revolutionary political signs and statements were predictably sought—and found—in virtually every text. Beissner's critical edition similarly read partial manuscripts, draft versions, and fragments toward their coherence in a single, achieved, definitive masterpiece of a poem, and many critical studies undertook to understand one poem in terms of its coherence with others in their statements, their enactments of a poetic project or trajectory, their place in this or that stage of a career or in this or that systematic version of its whole.

Hölderlin, in other words, has been massively studied as perhaps only the Germans can do to their national literary treasures, and he has been massively found to have achieved such mastery of language, form, statement, and philosophic understanding that readers can only retrace and then celebrate his accomplishment. Only two recent and still underempowered tendencies have worked against this image of the poet and his poetry. Deconstructive readings have noted the fissures in the formal excellence, the contradictions in the systematized thematics, the irony behind the pathos, the inefficacy and despair behind the political wishfulness, the difference within the competing versions of Hölderlin's philosophy of origins or of dialectical idealism. But deconstruction has never entered the mainstream of Hölderlin scholarship, as it has not anywhere else in the German university, and so there has been nothing like the enlarged and irreversibly altered understanding of English romanticism that occurred in the wake of American deconstructions of Wordsworth, Keats, and Shelley.[1] The other tendency against the dominant image of Hölderlin and his poems is paradoxically both more promising and more tenuous than his deconstruction has been to date: this is the effort of the current historical-critical edition (begun in 1975), the fourth critical edition of the century, the Frankfurter Ausgabe, which proceeds with principles and emerges with results thoroughly different from those of the long-standard Grosse Stuttgarter Ausgabe.[2] Editing and reading the Hölderlin manuscripts not toward a best and last "definitive" or "final" version of a poem, but seeking instead to acknowledge, preserve, and make somehow readable their palimpsestic, intertextual, processual, and workshoplike status, where many texts rewrite or overwrite one another in the same notebook and even on the same page, the editors have produced a version of Hölderlin that calls for a new kind of reading that we have scarcely invented. But therein lies the tenuousness of this countertendency: not only is the challenge so novel and so considerable to prevailing practices of reading and writing about Hölderlin, but the project has become ever more slow, and is now stalled (the publisher has foundered and another is awaited), so that, faute de mieux, the texts of the Grosse Stuttgarter Ausgabe are still the standard for our readings.

I recall all of this here—embarrassing as it is in its generality, its elementary sketchiness, its institutionally determined banality—not so that we might continue in this vein, but that we might jump from it to an analysis of some of Hölderlin's techniques of poetic ending with a better understanding of what we are getting into and what we are trying to get out of. A whole long book has been written about trends in Hölderlin scholarship and their representative value, and that was only in 1965;[3] it would be much longer, and perhaps more interesting, if it were updated or rewritten today. Our point cannot be to contribute to this kind of understanding of Hölderlin's larger reception, nor to prolong an abbreviated representation of it to an English-language audience. The point has rather been that reading Hölderlin's poems—individual, irreducibly brilliant, intractably resistant to generalization yet ineluctably drawing their readers toward that temptation—has so often meant reading them from and to a prior and final image of what Hölderlin the poet is "all about." Issuing from their source or origin in him, aiming toward their own accomplishment in their contribution to the achievement of his total oeuvre, itself wholly understandable as our image of their author, their origin: this hermeneutic circularity has guided and limited our specific interpretive readings of Hölderlin's poetic texts and intertexts. We will not be able to do without the powerful lessons (leçons, readings) of some of Hölderlin's best readers. Indeed, unlike my procedure in most of this book's chapters, I feel obliged to follow several of them closely—less for the intrinsic interest of what they both reveal and miss (although, as Paul de Man's Blindness and Insight showed, there is much to be learned from this, both about literary reading and about literary language itself) than because the complexity of Hölderlin's poems and the stakes of their reading mean an economy of demonstration can be derived from his earlier and most productive interpreters. As we try to follow the directions the poems themselves take and give, the ends they project and deflect, the endings they return to and leave us with, we will doubtless remain within the orbit of all the readings— their assumptions and practices—which surround Hölderlin's texts with his image, but perhaps we will succeed in reading against the gravity and the grain of a circularly self-propelling system of understanding Hölderlin as the one who leads to our understanding.

આ

Readings of Hölderlin's poetry, already under his image as "the poet of poets," have always taken their point of departure from his stunning, inimitable images. The images, once they have been noticed, appear to initiate and direct the readings toward their mutual unfoldings: the unfolding or explicative labor of the readings is directed toward and along the direction of the images' own unfolding into poems. The images initiate a mediation between the texts and their reading, and the readings mediate between images and achieved poetic statements. The given, almost *immediate* textual status of the image in Hölderlin (and the "almost" of this immediacy will come to command our attention) has demanded and appeared to command the performance of its reading.

The image may also be said to claim a second mediation, or to show a second face of *its* mediation: not only does it direct its reading, but it specifically directs the mediation of its representation and representationality. This is to say that the imagery of Hölderlin appeals to, and appears to depart from, a given, visual reality; it appears to re-present or reproduce a sight, a site, an element of a landscape or scene. This perhaps most conventional sense of the poetic (or literary) image—a verbal re-presentation or reproduction of the visual—would permit a ready mediation from the powerfully *unfamiliar* language of Hölderlin's poetry to the possibility of its leading its reading to its understanding as the poetic restatement, the rendering verbal, of a visual scene or an otherwise experientially or imaginatively *present* moment.

Such double mediation of Hölderlin's images, from the words of imagery to the wholes of poems and from the visual donnée to the fait accompli of the read, may be noticed in two readings of Hölderlin that represent, respectively, what was once the most influential interpretation of the poet in this century and what is still a standard for his philological reinterpretation. Martin Heidegger's commentary on "Wie wenn am Feiertage" was the first of his exegeses of Hölderlin, which together, as I have noted, overshadowed all other approaches to Hölderlin for some thirty years. Peter Szondi's "Der andere Pfeil" marks a moment of turning from the philosophic to the philological understanding of Hölderlin—or at least of insisting and establishing that no philosophic understanding that was not also grounded in philology would any longer be permissible. Despite the manifest differences in their styles and their interpretive arguments and results—and Szondi's essay is at crucial points, regarding the poem's beginning and end, explicitly directed against Heidegger—both readings depart from the same initial sense of Hölderlin's poetic imagery: the image mediates the visual realm into the verbal, poetic medium—the language—of the poem, and, with this, the image initiates the utterance that may be read and made to yield the understanding of the poem's statement.

It will profit our own, later close reading to look briefly and provisionally at the opening movements of Heidegger's and Szondi's readings of "Wie wenn am Feiertage." After several paragraphs about the text of Hölderlin's poem, and a paraphrase of its first strophe, Heidegger writes:

> The first strophe names this, almost as if it wanted to *describe an image*. Its last verse admittedly ends with a colon. The first strophe opens upon the second. To the "Wie wenn" at the beginning of the first strophe, there corresponds the "So" with which the second begins. The "Wie wenn . . . : So . . . " *indicates a comparison*, which, like a bracket, holds the opening strophe *in unity* with the second or even with all the following ones.[4]

Szondi begins his discussion of the poem with a general introductory overview:

> The hymn "Wie wenn am Feiertage . . . " is a poem about the poet and his work. But *the motif* that runs through it from beginning to end is something else, something belonging to the twofold sphere of nature and myth, a motif from which all of the hymn's assertions about poets and poetry issue *with the logic that is peculiar to metaphor.* It is the lightning bolt, the "himmlisches Feuer." . . . The lightning

motif gives rise to *the metaphorical joining of poetry and wine,* which at the highpoint of the hymn allows for the illustration of the genesis of poetry from the birth of Dionysus. [Turning then to the first strophe, Szondi continues:] Still veiled . . . *this metaphorics* is already at work in the great *landscape image* of the opening.[5]

Heidegger's commentary, as his entire paraphrase of the first strophe also confirms, begins with the poem's beginning as an *image* of a field after a storm ("Wie wenn am Feiertage, das Feld zu sehn / Ein Landmann geht, des Morgens, wenn / Aus heisser Nacht die kühlenden Blize fielen"),[6] and immediately correctly identifies this "image" as the first term of a simile. But the *doubled* character of the simile (As: So) is said to be in the service of *unity,* indeed, in the service of the unity of the whole poem. Szondi proceeds somewhat differently, but along the same armature of argumentation. A *motif* is drawn from the *double* region of nature and myth, and appears throughout the poem according to a "metaphoric logic"; the specific motif of the lightning bolt signals the metaphoric *joining of two* things, and this metaphorics is embedded in the opening strophe's *image.*

Via a motif and (as well as *in*) an image, both interpreters acknowledge a "doubled" structure of simile or metaphor, but would have this tropological structure yield a "unity" of the poem or a "joining" of two different sets or spheres. Both interpreters know that the first two strophes of the poem are a comparison, but whereas they disagree about the terms of the comparison,[7] they agree that the comparison begins with the imagery of the lightning in the landscape, and tends toward the unity of the poem's statement—which "unity" their own readings will then proceed to unfold, however differently.

What is a lightning bolt? And what is a comparison, or a metaphor—its "logic"—in Hölderlin? What is an image? What directions do they take, and give, and where do they end—if they do? Such questions will guide this chapter on the technique of poetic ending in several Hölderlin poems; and in their interrelations, the same questions have long been posed by Hölderlin's best readers. Whether a particular image in Hölderlin's poem

"Friedensfeier" is of a landscape and/or of a room—which question, if images are taken literally and visually, would seem easy enough to decide—was the question that led Szondi to ask "whether a passage is meant metaphorically or not," when he wanted an example with which to focus his inquiry into the "questions which are of decisive significance for the problem of knowledge in literary studies."[8] In a pathbreaking essay on the rhetoric of literature and literary interpretation, Paul de Man raised the problem of Hölderlin's places, rivers and landscapes:

> They are not synecdoches designating a totality of which they are a part, but are themselves already this totality. They are not the sensorial equivalence of a more general, ideal meaning; they are themselves this idea, just as much as the abstract expression that will appear in philosophical or historical form in the later parts of the poem. A metaphorical style such as Hölderlin's can at any rate not be described in terms of the antinomy between allegory and symbol.[9]

However Szondi might have decided the question of the singular image or the metaphoric comparison in a Hölderlin passage, and however de Man might have been able to assert the "total" and yet still metaphoric character of Hölderlin's images, their ways of posing the problem are but versions of the same problem of reading Hölderlin that we have already seen in Heidegger's and Szondi's interpretations of "Wie wenn am Feiertage." From the presence of a single term (an image, a motif, a landscape) to the acknowledgment of two terms, and hence a doubled structure (the two terms of the simile, the metaphor's vehicle for the metaphoric tenor, the images of landscapes paired with "abstract expression"), the impulse is to return to *one* term: the claim of unity, or of joining, or of a name for such a style.

The issue may be restated as one of *mediation,* namely the question of how a production or recognition of doubleness after the initial appearance of one term can be made a mediating step toward, or intermediate to, an achieved or reachieved oneness: how a third term or step, that of "mediability," can mediate between a first immediacy and a consequent stage of the mediate(d). At this level of abstract terminology, one is not far away from Hölderlin, nor from his interpreters. Whether it is in his philosophical and poetological fragments of the Homburg period,[10] or in Heidegger's use of these very terms (*das Unmittelbare, die Mittelbarkeit, das Vermittelte*) in his interpretation of "Wie wenn am Feiertage,"[11] or in de Man's trenchant critique of this very step in Heidegger's argument,[12] one confronts repeatedly the problem of mediation that in Hölderlin's texts is only apparently "abstract." Rather, "abstraction" (*abs-traho*) repeatedly appears as the means by which readers mediate Hölderlin's images: drawing away from them in order to arrive at, return to, *end at* some *one* meaning or statement.

But in Hölderlin's poems, his and his interpreters' rightly philosophic question—of a possible logic of mediation—is first and above all a philological one. How does one read images in his poems? And how could one read them not exclusively as images *of* mediation, but, reflexively, as *on* or *about* mediation as well? Let us return to Heidegger's commentary on "Wie wenn am Feiertage." The opening of the poem is, in his reading, an image, as if of something immediately visually given, as if: "As on a feast day, to see the field, / A peasant goes. . . . " And if the poem can apparently represent a man seeing a field, then this can become the key to Heidegger's reading of the entire poem, for the beginning of the third strophe seemingly presents the poet seeing something coming and turning it into words: "Jezt aber tagts! Ich harrt und sah es kommen, / Und was ich sah, das Heilige sei mein Wort." We may recall that Heidegger's commentary, in a carefully staged argument that need not be retraced in detail here, leads to the concluding interpretive assertions that the poem must lead to the "closing word[s]" that he (wrongly, unphilologically) constructs the text to have—"To the sacred the closing word of this poem must return"—and that "The word of this song is . . . the hymn 'of' the sacred. The sacred gives the word and itself comes in this word. The word is the happening, the proper actuality [*das Ereignis*] of the sacred."[13] The full arc of Heidegger's reading of this poem is from his understanding that what the poet *saw* in the poem's "now" became the poem's word of the sacred ("Und was ich sah, das Heilige sei mein Wort"), to his understanding that this poem of Hölderlin *is* the event, the coming of the sacred.

Now in criticizing this preposterous interpretation it is not only a matter of observing, as other readers have, that this early statement in the poem is in the subjunctive: that it is optative, and indicates prayer or desire, or wish and task,[14] and not achievement. One should also note that the lines restate the task or problem of mediation that is assumed by Heidegger to be already solved in the poem's opening. A *sight* of a field, a man, and the retreating storm is ostensibly rendered in words, while here, at the beginning of the third strophe, a sight *might* or ought to be, but is not yet, the poem's word. Furthermore, the specific structure of the visual scene seen and the word that may or may not be spoken or speakable is common not only to both of these parts of the poem, but also—as we will see—to the whole narrative and structure of the poem and its undoing.

Returning now to Szondi's essay on the poem, one sees that he departs from an understanding that shares significantly in Heidegger's view of Hölderlin's poetics: there exist in Hölderlin images of poetic mediation between gods and men, and the lightning bolt is one such image. "In thunder and lightning the god speaks to men," Szondi writes, naming such signs the "counterimage [*Gegenbild*] to the godless darkness" (with reference to Hölderlin's poem "Der Archipelagus") (43). The visual is here made to speak: mediation occurs poetically in the verbal images of the *Donner* and *Blitze*. This minimal structure of mediation, from the visual sight through its image to speech, is understood by Szondi in the context of a larger structure and problem of mediation: "As Bacchus was engendered by Zeus and Semele, by the highest god and a human being, or, as the legend originally had it, by heaven and earth, so the vine grows—according to a verse from the *Empedokles* tragedy—'drenched / By hot sun from out of the dark ground' and thereby testifies 'of earth and heaven.' No differently does the fifth strophe of the hymn have the song grow 'from the sun of the day and from warm earth' ('der Sonne des Tags und warmer Erd')" (43, 44). Bacchus stands between Zeus and Semele, heaven and earth, as the vine also does. And so does the "song," the poem, stand or come to stand between the gods and the poet. If the poet catches the lightning bolts, as Semele received Zeus or the earth receives the sun's rays, the poem arises and testifies to the mediation of the two regions:

> Doch uns gebührt es, unter Gottes Gewittern,
> Ihr Dichter! mit entblösstem Haupte zu stehen,
> Des Vaters Stral, ihn selbst, mit eigner Hand
> Zu fassen und dem Volk ins Lied
> Gehüllt die himmlische Gaabe zu reichen.

> (Yet us it behooves, beneath God's thunder and lightning / You poets! with bared head to stand, / The Father's bolt, it itself, with one's own hand / To grasp and to the people within song / Concealed the heavenly gift to offer.)

These lines themselves, in their verbs, sketch a tiered mediation of poetic stances and activities. The poets stand beneath the storm, like (recall the "Wie . . . So . . . ") the trees of the field stand beneath the weather in the first two strophes. This visually depicted stance would initiate a process whereby poetry is produced: the song could be given, itself verbally mediating or passing on the heavenly gift. In between—mediating—is the difficult stance or act of "grasping the lightning bolt." Not the least of its difficulty is that *this* "image" is at once visual, however extreme (grasping the bolt with one's own hand!), and verbally interpretive: to grasp the bolt as meaning to understand or comprehend it (*fassen*).[15]

Szondi's reading of "Wie wenn am Feiertage" by no means assumes that such mediations depicted in the poem are readily achieved, least of all in this particular poem. At this point in his analysis he asks: "Here, at the latest, with the invocation of the Semele myth that is supposed to illustrate [*veranschaulichen*] the origin of poetry, Hölderlin must have confronted the question whether the poet—whether he himself—is in a position to bear the heavenly fire, whether it is not also the poet who has to pay the price that Semele, turned to ashes, paid" (44). With reference to Hölderlin himself, as well as to an early version of a line in the poem, where Semele is spoken of not as "the divinely struck [*die göttlichgetroffne]*" but as "ashes, deadly [*Asche, tödtlich*]" (2/2, 675), Szondi directs his attention toward the larger mediations that the poem may also represent: not mediations of and by poetry explicitly depicted within the poem, but mediations within Hölderlin's poetic oeuvre that the poem may be taken to represent. As the subtitle of his essay already indicated—"On the History of the Genesis of Hölderlin's Late Hymnic Style"—Szondi turns from the fact of the poem's fragmentation and nonending to the evidence of another poem that appears on the same manuscript page, "to investigate, with respect to the history of its genesis, whether the poem that grew out of the uncompleted hymn and that, for its part, is complete, does not shed some light on the question of why the hymn itself could not be finished" (54).

With this different approach to Hölderlin's "Wie wenn am Feiertage"—not at all like Heidegger's, which asserted a completion both for the poem and for the mediation of the sacred within the poem's "word"—Szondi takes us at once in the direction indicated by the image of the lightning bolt, and in the direction of our question of how and what a poetic image mediates and how it might end. In the course of examining the genesis of the poem that emerged out of "Wie wenn am Feiertage"—it is called "Hälfte des Lebens"—Szondi also attends to the prose drafts of the hymn, and points there to the alternative versions of a line that dropped out altogether from the fragmentary nonending of the verse hymn. The version, "Aber wenn von selbgeschlagener Wunde das Herz mir blutet," first read "Aber wenn von anderem Pfeile das Herz mir blutet" (2/2, 669–71). Szondi asks:

> The poet's heart bleeds from another arrow—but from which other arrow? And by which arrow may, indeed, should the poet be struck? The hymn already gave the answer: by lightning, by heavenly fire. The word *arrow* appears four times in Hölderlin's poetry during the decisive years from 1800 to his mental collapse. Three times it designates the sun's rays or lightning. . . . The fourth passage, however, is that in which the "other arrow" is spoken of. It is corrected into "of a self-inflicted wound." The alteration sacrifices the connection with the thunder and lightning,

for the sake of clarifying what the "other" is. The *other arrow* comes not from the god, but from himself: man himself has inflicted this wound on himself. (50, 51)

The imagery of the lightning inverts, via the attention given to the image of the arrow, to yield not a mediation between man and god, but one between man and himself and his poetic efforts. This *other* mediation is of a "biographical wound" in Hölderlin's poetry: of the wound caused him by his mourning, elegiacally, for the loss of his love Diotima (biographically, she is Susette Gontard), which mourning, together with the corresponding poetic style of the elegy, must be overcome for the genesis (*Entstehung*) of the hymnic style to occur. The hymnic style would be, in Szondi's interpretation, the *Ent-stehung*, the arising out of, and the sublation or overcoming of the elegiac style and its "self-inflicted wound." In this reading, the very argument that acknowledges *unachieved* mediation as represented by the lightning bolts in "Wie wenn am Feiertage" converts them and their poem into a mediating step from lightning to arrow, and to an interpretive narrative of Hölderlin's biographical career and the full arc of his poetic oeuvre.

It is precisely such a reading of the *directionality* of Hölderlin's image—as the *Blitz* becomes the *Pfeil* under Szondi's interpretation, not unlike the way the lightning and thunder became the "event of the sacred" ("Ereignis des Heiligen") in Heidegger's interpretation—that is always in the service of the hermeneutic move, in analyses of Hölderlin and other poets, from poetic images to interpretive statements—readings—of their meaning. Here, in the case of these two understandings of "Wie wenn am Feiertage," the question is specifically of the *directionality of mediation*. What is mediated toward or with what? Does the poem mediate the sacred into language, or the poetic career in between the elegiac and the hymnic styles? More specifically, does Hölderlin's image mediate toward the ontological, or toward the biographical-genetic (*entstehungsgeschichtlich*) dimension of poetry— or in some other direction altogether?

The poem that arises on the same manuscript page as "Wie wenn am Feiertage" does not contain the words *Blitz* or *Pfeil*. It displays another image of directionality: the *Fahnen* or weather vanes; the last words of "Hälfte des Lebens" are "im Winde / Klirren die Fahnen." (2, 117). Weather vanes, as is well known, change directions—they are capable of indicating any direction on the compass. In order better to focus our attention on this image of direction-taking in the poem that arises out of "Wie wenn am Feiertage," we must first recall certain directions of imagery and mediation that appeared in that first poem. One that has already been touched upon was the pattern of descent: from the sun of heaven through the vine of earth to yield the wine, or from Zeus through Semele to yield Bacchus; the most complex version of this imagistic pattern is the descent of the *Strahl* into the poet's "grasp" to yield the song (*Lied*), itself a "concealed" (*gehüllt*) form of the "heavenly gift" of the lightning bolt. Another direction taken by imagery of mediation in the poem was from sight to speech, as in the lines that move from "Ich . . . sah es kommen, / Und was ich sah" to "das Heilige sei mein Wort." The avenue of sight—its site and sighting—is the one that leads most directly into the problem of Hölderlin's image and its possible mediation in, its possible aiming at and ending in, the understanding of poetic language.

In "Wie wenn am Feiertage," the peasant sees the field—a simple enough image of sight—and the poetic *Ich* saw *es* and *was:* still simple, perhaps, but less clear about what is seen. Of Semele, it is not said that she *saw* Zeus, but that she "desired to see the god visible" ("da sie sichtbar / Den Gott zu sehen begehrte"). The strange redundancy of "sichtbar . . . zu sehen" ought to attract more consideration than it has in previous commentaries upon this poem. To see something visible would be just that: to see it visibly, as visual, as if without further mediating effect or transformation. It is, of course, Semele who is nonetheless affected or transformed by this curious desire—burned to ashes. The poet, on the other hand, is said to see in order to transform into speech: to see so to speak, not "to see visibly." It is this metaphoric seeing—seeing that "carries over," that metaphorizes—that is the primary given of Hölderlin's images of sight in this poem, and not the visual donnée of what is ostensibly seen. But if this describes one aspect of the directionality of the image in "Wie wenn am Feiertage," from sight to metaphoric or poetic speech, another aspect concerns the *direction toward sight* with respect to the orientations of the poetic "I" toward the god and the god toward the poet.

The poem presents not only the vision of given sights (the peasant seeing the field, perhaps the poetic "I" seeing *was*), but the attempt at vision "on high," or even *of* the god—as Semele also had attempted. The second strong simile of the hymn, which occurs at the beginning of the fourth strophe and therefore corresponds to the opening simile in this strictly triadically constructed poem,[16] is of the poet in the face of incendiary sights:

> Und wie im Aug' ein Feuer dem Manne glänzt,
> Wenn hohes er entwarf; so ist
> Von neuem an den Zeichen, den Thaten der Welt jezt
> Ein Feuer angezündet in Seelen der Dichter.

> (And as in the eye of the man a fire shines / When he projects on high, so is / Once again with the signs, the events of the world now / A fire ignited in souls of the poets.)

"The signs, the events of the world" may certainly refer to the contemporary revolutionary wars between France and the Coalition.[17] But they just as certainly carry over or metaphorize the first strophe's signs of the earth marked by the weather ("In sein Gestade wieder tritt der Strom, / Und frisch der Boden grünt / Und von des Himmels erfreuendem Reegen / Der Weinstok trauft und glänzend / In stiller Sonne stehn die Bäume des Haines"). (The mediating step in this metaphorizing of the image in terms significant for the contemporary history is the line "Die Natur ist jezt mit Waffenklang erwacht.") As if "the fire ignites in souls of the poets" when visual signs—images—mark the world or come to earth, so does the opening of this simile suggest that as the man "projects on high," a fire appears in his eye. This visible sign—the fire in the eye—may be part of his projection out and on high, or it may be the reflection of a visible sign outside, shining in, but the whole simile appears to compose a correspondence or symmetry between the two directions of the visible signs: the poet looking up, the signs of the god—the weather become the "Thaten der Welt"—coming down.

The remainder of the poem draws out this symmetrical imagery of sight directed up and sights of the god or his signs coming down; and up to the point of its decomposition, the poem appears to be drawing it out as the structure of achieved mediation. The beginning of the seventh strophe—which corresponds formally (triadically) to the peasant seeing the field and the man glancing with fire in his eye as he projects upward—says conclusively, "Und daher trinken himmlisches Feuer jezt / Die Erdensöhne ohne Gefahr." ("And thus the sons of the earth now drink heavenly fire without danger."). And the eighth strophe began—before it decomposed—with "Des Vaters Stral, der reine versengt es nicht / Und tieferschüttert, die Leiden des Stärkeren / Mitleidend, bleibt in den hochherstürzenden Stürmen / Des Gottes, wenn er nahet, das Herz doch fest." ("The father's ray, the pure, it does not singe, / And deeply shaken, with the suffering of the stronger / Cosuffering, [there] remains amidst the storms tumbling down from high above / From the god, when he nears, the heart yet firm."). The god nears, in the storms. The poet would catch the lightning bolt. A project that looks on high would be met, correspondingly, by a god who comes down in his visible signs of the bolts.

But this corresponding symmetry of man's upward project and the god's descent has its exact counterpart in the fragmentary last part of the poem, in what would have been its ninth and final strophe. After the abrupt and shocking "Doch weh mir! . . . Weh mir! . . . ," these late lines turn precisely on the matter of the *direction* toward sight on the part of the poetic "I" toward the gods: "Ich sei genaht, die Himmlischen zu schauen, / Sie selbst, sie werfen mich tief unter die Lebenden . . . " ("I neared, to see the heavenly ones, / They themselves, they throw me far down among the living . . . "). It is not the god who nears, but the poet who nears the gods, and he draws near *to see* them. The image of sight here, with an explicitness that parallels and indeed matches the previous ones of the peasant seeing the field, the *Ich* seeing *was,* and Semele seeking to see Zeus, also recalls the man with fire in his eye, projecting upward. But here it is not the man who projects or throws out (*entwerfen*) on high, but, to complete the contra of the counterpart, the gods who throw him down. The "full" development of images of the directions of sight and mediation in "Wie wenn am Feiertage"—which is to say a development that is not full because the poem decomposes into a last image of misdirection and unachieved sight—is caught in this final crux or chiasmus: the poet would see and cast up ("hohes entwerfen") as the god nears, but if the poet nears to see—to sight—he is cast down.[18] The direction toward sight yields not images of the accomplished mediation of visual experience into poetry and its understanding, but rather the image of a broken directionality, a ruptured *visée*— the scene of the seen not achieving its mediation into speech, but nearing the spectacle of speechlessness, the poem breaking off *Dort* without further utterance or punctuation.

This tentative conclusion on the image in "Wie wenn am Feiertage" is not far from Szondi's understanding of the poem when, seeking to explain its decomposition, he turns to "Hälfte des Lebens." The final version of this poem is as follows:

Mit gelben Birnen hänget
Und voll mit wilden Rosen
Das Land in den See,
Ihr holden Schwäne,
Und trunken von Küssen
Tunkt ihr das Haupt
Ins heilignüchterne Wasser.

Weh mir, wo nehm' ich, wenn
Es Winter ist, die Blumen, und wo
Den Sonnenschein,
Und Schatten der Erde?
Die Mauern stehn
Sprachlos und kalt, im Winde
Klirren die Fahnen.

(With yellow pears hangs / And full with wild roses / The land into the lake, / You gracious swans, / And drunk from kisses / You dunk the head / Into sacred-sober water. // Woe me, where do I gather, when / It is winter, the flowers, and where / The sunshine, / And shadows of the earth? / The walls stand / Speechless and cold, in the wind / Clatter the weather vanes.)

Szondi's commentary begins with three precise and dense sentences that focus squarely on the question of the image and its possible mediating powers: "In image and counterimage the two strophes express the state of mind of the poet from which they arise. It is the feeling of darkness, of the remoteness of the gods, of the absence of love; the experience of isolation, whose expression is the missing and failing [*fehlen*] of language, whose image is the missing and failing of the shadow that mediated between sun and earth. The longed-for mediation is, in the first strophe, as an image, alien reality" (56). I shall return to these sentences several times, for in their precision they provide great if skewed insight into Hölderlin's two poems, their images and their ends, leading us in a rather different direction than the one that Szondi actually follows in his argument. He identifies the two strophes as contrasting images, and as arising (*entstammen*) from the poet's "state of mind": from his life's experiences, from his biography in effect. But as the echo between *entstammen* and *Entstehung/entstehen* readily reminds one, Szondi also examines their genesis from out of the manuscript page of "Wie wenn am Feiertage" and hence, from Hölderlin's *poetic* effort and project. There he finds "the verses that form or imagistically present [*bilden*] the transition between the hymn and the poem 'Hälfte des Lebens'" (57):

Wo nehm ich, wenn es Winter ist
Die Blumen, dass ich Kränze den Himmlischen winde?
Dann wird es seyn, als wüsst ich nimmer von Göttlichen,
Denn (1) wenn (2) von mir sei gewichen des Lebens Geist;
Wenn ich den Himmlischen die Liebeszeichen
Die Blumen im [nakten] kahlen Felde suche u. dich
    nicht finde.

(Where do I gather, when it is winter / The flowers, that I might wind wreathes for the heavenly ones? / Then it will be as if I never knew of the godly, / For (1) when (2) the life's spirit might have left me; / When I for the heavenly one the signs of love, / The flowers in the [naked] bare field seek and do not find you.) (2/2, 664)

Along with the imagistic allusion to the earlier poem's peasant (*Landmann*) in the field, the last two lines here also recall much of the unfolding of the unfinished hymn. Signs are *sought for* the gods, unlike the *receiving* of signs *from* the gods, but like the effort represented in "Wie wenn am Feiertage" of the poetic "I" to near the god ("Ich sei genaht, die Himmlischen zu schauen"). Here, too, the effort ends in failure: "[I] do not find you." Not finding the signs, becomes, in the completed poem "Hälfte des Lebens," *finding* the flowers and then losing them, in the "contrasting images" of a fullness of nature and its then missing or failing status.

With respect to these draft lines, Szondi writes that for "the lack . . . the impossibility of the hymnic [style] . . . , its image is the missing and failing of flowers" (58). And as he said of "Hälfte des Lebens" in the sentences quoted above, the first strophe presents "the longed-for mediation [between sun and earth] . . . , as an image, [as] alien reality." Szondi is correct that the hymnic style, as present in its genesis in "Wie wenn am Feiertage," aims at such mediation between heaven and earth. And he also seems correct to say that, from the perspective of "the missing and failing of the flowers" ("Die Blumen . . . suche u. dich nicht finde"), the *image* of such mediation would then appear as "alien." But is the "reality" of this "image," itself an image of natural reality, alien only to and from the perspective of the second strophe, with its *not*-finding of mediation? Does the poem, in other words, move indubitably from fullness to emptiness or lack? Is the image of the flowers and everything else in the first strophe *itself* a fully mediated, non(self-)alienated poetic text?

Szondi suggests as much, for he writes that "the land and the swans combine with the water, 'drunk with kisses' the one, 'sacred sober' the other: love and religion, the essence of both of which is union, are seen by the longing glance as nature in oneness. The state of mind of the poet [is one] for whom such a reconciliation is an alien matter in which he does not participate" (56). All of Szondi's highly controlled interpretive language preserves the "image" of the first strophe as a unified, combined image of a spectacle of mediation, from which the poet is nonetheless alienated. But are the different elements of this first strophe of "Hälfte des Lebens" mediated into unification? There is no doubt that the beginning lines appeal to a *full* image: "Mit gelben Birnen hänget / Und *voll* mit wilden Rosen / Das Land in den See." But the very dynamics of the image—dynamic in the accusative form of "hänget . . . in den See," and not the dative—suggest a contrast with another image of land meeting and joining with a lake. It is Goethe's in his famous poem "Auf dem See," which we may on good grounds assume that Hölderlin knew from the 1789 edition of Goethe's *Schriften*.[19] The image in the poem's last strophe is also of fruit and a lake:

Auf der Welle blinken
Tausend schwebende Sterne,
Weiche Nebel trinken
Rings die türmende Ferne;
Morgenwind umflügelt
Die beschattete Bucht,
Und im See bespiegelt
Sich die reifende Frucht.

(On the wave blink / A thousand hovering stars, / Soft mists drink in / The towering distance around; / Morning wind wings around / The shaded inlet, / And in the lake is mirrored / The ripening fruit.)[20]

The dative form in Goethe's title and last lines (Auf *dem* See; *im* See), which would represent a full union of the land (its fruit) and the water, signals that such "fullness" is an image: a mirrored or reflected image, a reflection. Szondi comes as close as is possible to indicating the importance of the image of reflection in Hölderlin's lines without actually doing so when he calls attention to an image from the fourth strophe of Hölderlin's "Menons Klage um Diotima" (initially simply titled "Elegie" and, in its composition, slightly earlier than "Hälfte des Lebens"), and affirms that "it is the image from 'Hälfte des Lebens'":

Aber wir, zufrieden gesellt, wie die liebenden Schwäne,
    Wenn sie ruhen am See, oder, auf Wellen gewiegt,
Niedersehen in die Wasser, wo silberne Wolken sich
    spiegeln.

(But we, joined contentedly, like the loving swans, /
When they rest on the lake, or, rocked on waves, / Look
down into the water, where silver clouds are mirrored.)
(2, 76)

These lines also recall Goethe's "Auf dem See," the first strophe of
which includes the line "Die Welle wieget unsern Kahn." ("The
wave rocks our boat.").[21]

From this collocation of Hölderlin's first strophe of "Hälfte
des Lebens," Goethe's "Auf dem See," and the lines from Hölderlin's "Menons Klage," we may draw the following analysis of
Hölderlin's image. At the beginning and end of Goethe's strophe,
the visual image is one of reflection, of the highest heights (the
stars) or the nearer nature (the fruit) reflected on the water's surface. There is not depth here but surface, a surface absorption of
the difference between height and surface, just as the middle
of the strophe absorbs or drinks in the difference between border
(the edge of the lake) and distance. In the lines from "Menons
Klage," the swans who are compared with the human "we" may be
joined with one another, but they do not join with the water except on its surface: they rest on its surface, and in looking *down
into* the water (*"Nieder*sehen *in die* Wasser"), they do not arrive at
depth but rather are met with an image of reflection ("wo silberne
Wolken sich spiegeln"). Here, too, heights are not received into
depths, but upon a surface.[22] In the first strophe of "Hälfte des
Lebens," then, the image indeed does begin with a full nature
hanging *into* the water. This image of land "joined" and "united"
with water—Szondi's terms and claims—is, however, only the
opening of that strophe. "The longed-for mediation is, in the first
strophe, as an image, alien reality," Szondi said, and the alien-
ation, the introduction of otherness with respect to nature as an
image, occurs already in and within the perspective of the first
strophe. "As an image," drawn as it is, in all likelihood, from the
Goethe poem, and, in near certainty, from the first version of
"Menons Klage," the first three lines of a fully mediated nature
are surface, not depth. The directionality of depth in the image's
"in die See" becomes reflected as an image—an image of an
image—"auf dem See."

Thus the swans do not become absorbed into the water (*pace* Szondi's claim, for which there is no evidence), nor merely hover or float upon it like an image of stars or clouds, but pierce it and break it. The quick, in-and-out meaning of *tunken*—as in our English "dunk"—indicates just this. As an image of reflection, the self-reflexivity is the otherness or determinate negation entering into and through the surface image of absorption. That this action should be represented by the swans not only repeats the lines from "Menons Klage," where the swans serve as a simile for the "we" who *see reflection*—and not just a reflected or represented visual scene—in the image, but also recalls the classical-mythological region from which "Wie wenn am Feiertage" drew some of its imagery: Zeus entering the world in the form or image of a swan, "a sudden blow," as Yeats put it in "Leda and the Swan"—sudden and powerful like thunder or lightning.

It is from this perspective, internal to the first strophe of "Hälfte des Lebens" and the verses surrounding it, that the "alien reality" may be understood "as an image": as an image of an image that no longer merely represents nor absorbs nor otherwise mediates the visual donnée, but reflects upon this and breaks the illusion or appearance of its representation in reflection. When we turn, then, to the poem's second strophe, the sagacity of Szondi's interpretation is now redirected toward the poem's directionality, and away from its ostensible origination or genesis from out of Hölderlin's "state of mind." The "experience of isolation" is between the initial "full" image and all that follows. Once their fullness is broken and broken with, and they reemerge as its negative reflection—negative in the sense of the negation of fullness appearing as surface—the surface images of "Sonnenschein" and "Schatten der Erde" in the second strophe take on a similarly *reflexive* significance.[23] The pathos-laden questions of "Woe me, where do I gather" sunshine and shadow repose as well the question of directionality. "The missing and failing of the shadow that mediated between sun and earth," in Szondi's words, is of course the symmetrical counterpart to the lack of sunshine—there is no shadow without sunshine—but neither sunshine nor shadow need be read as issuing from some interior or personal lack. They are missing and failing once the appearance, the *Schein*, of surface absorption has been pierced, ruptured, broken by the *tunken* of the first strophe: an image that "reflects" reality becomes, once reflected upon, the image of such reflection, the appearance of reflection rather than the mediation supposedly established thereby.

"Where do I gather" such images of mediation, once the mediation is broken, but also, quite literally, "where do I take them?": "wo nehm' ich?" What direction does the poem take now, having taken its steps of setting up a reflective image, reflecting upon and breaking its spell, and asking about what is then missing and failing? It takes the step of presenting an image, but of a special kind: "Die Mauern stehn / Sprachlos und kalt." This image is at once of the visual walls and of speechlessness; Szondi calls it "the expression" of a wounded poet, "the missing and failing of language." The "expression" *is* an image, but it is an image that refuses to express verbally, except as the metaphoric image of that speechlessness. We may say that this poetic expression *is* the image—the image of "Die Mauern stehn / Sprachlos und kalt"— but the image is one of what is *not* expressed, not spoken or speaking, of what is missing and failing. The image is, as Szondi said, of a *Fehlen*.

To say that the walls are speechless, and that this image both represents walls visually and presents a nonexpressive or speechless image in that poetic representation, is to have followed the directionality of "Hälfte des Lebens" through several steps: from visual reflection, to reflection upon and rupture with such representation, to the images of missing and failing appearance, mediation, and language. Poetic language says that the image does not speak. But I would emphasize that even this statement is still presented as visual and as visually significant; if it is speechless, it is not insignificant but rather signifies visually this speechlessness. And yet the image is on the very border of the visual, for while one can see walls, and therefore can understand the verbal representation or image of the visual walls, one cannot *see speechless* walls (in distinction from any other walls—the adjective is literally self-voiding). Speechless walls, then, are a visual *and* metaphoric image carrying over (*metaphérein*) and presenting the far side of a threshold of the image—of what can be represented as visual, and what cannot. Where walls can be said to be either speechless *or* speaking, we are speaking of unnatural walls, of walls that are no longer "images of nature."

It is here that the last lines of "Hälfte des Lebens" sustain to the end the problematic of images and mediation in this poem as well as in the unfinished hymn from which it emerged. Weather brings not only storms of thunder and lightning, not only sunshine and thus shadow, not only summer and its ripening fruit, winter and its cold. It also brings wind. Wind is invisible, nonvisual, or more correctly, its visibility and visuality are perceptible only as an effect redesignated as a cause. (Tropologically, the phrase "see the wind" is a metalepsis.) Hölderlin writes "im Winde / Klirren die Fahnen." We see the wind in the weather vanes, the quintessential signs or sign takers of direction. What we "see" when we read "in the wind the weather vanes clatter" is that the visual image indicates or tells no direction. If the weather vanes steadied, they would signal direction, or become a sign of direction—the direction of nature and its weather. The weather vanes would become mediating images, mediating between nature, the skies, and the powers above, and man and his understanding. Pointed like lightning bolts and arrows, they would point out unilinearly the direction and a meaning for the persona in the poem and the reader of the poem. But as it is, in Hölderlin's image they clatter.

Unlike the impossibility of *seeing* a speechless wall (in the sense of any meaningful opposition to a "speaking wall," similarly unvisualizable except as a cartoon of the Pyramus and Thisbe story, or its production in *A Midsummer Night's Dream*), one *can* see a clattering weather vane. In such a visual image, one sees the unstable, wavering sight of a sign that will not take sight—will not take aim—at any direction, and thus will not aim at mediation or the understanding of its significance. But *this* threshold of a visual image unstill and unmediating, is not just a determinate negation of "The walls stand / Speechless," as if it took the visible walls' invisible speechlessness and turned it into the visual image of signs that do not signify direction or meaning, but that are nonetheless of nature and its weather as what still produces such sorts of signs. The image of the "full image" of nature received into the lake was, upon its reflection—its mirroring—and its rupture by the dunking swans, the determinate negation of the self-sufficiently full visual image of nature. And the images of sunshine and shadow missing and failing in their mediation of heaven and earth were the determinate negation of the first strophe's breaking of and with the appearance (*Schein*) of mediation in natural signs such as weather and the seasons: they presented visually the missing and failing of representation. In their turn, the speechless walls negated determinately the missing representation by representing at once the visual image and its speechlessness or nonutterance, still "visible" in its conspicuously invisible metaphoric attachment to and border with—its limit of—the visual image. But here, "the weather vanes clatter" is both a visual image—what I have called the unstable, wavering sight of a sign that will not take sight—and an aural one. *Klirren*, clattering, is not the sound of signifying nature, nor that of speaking man.[24] If anything, in being nonhuman and altogether inanimate, it is the sound and utterance of the poetry of the sheerly *made*—ice pieces and glass fragments, for example, are capable of *klirren*—and at its threshold, it is the sound and utterance of the poetry of the *mechanical* (related, perhaps, to what Hölderlin considered the "law-governed calculus," the "gesetzliche Kalkul" of poetry).

It is also somewhere between—not midway, but somewhere indeterminately between—speechlessness and speech. As such, it is the indeterminate negation of this poem's determinate negations of visual images that might mediate into speech, and between heaven and earth, with the importance of this "indeterminacy" residing in its denial of the reader's capability to determine what the image means or what it does not mean—the impossibility, in other words, of bringing the image to its end. The image in its visual aspect refuses to stabilize and take sight at meaning; and in its aural aspect it is neither speech nor the previous image's speechlessness, but *not-speaking:* it withholds the distinction of, or will not mediate between, speaking and verbally representing speechlessness. In Hölderlin's terms from the Homburg fragment called "Urteil und Sein," such an image would be one of (not representing, but "of" in the strongly genitive sense) the *Ur-Teilung* or original cutting and partition, the decision and judgment performed by language and its power of *Setzen* (4, 216, 217). In Paul de Man's terms, when he criticized Heidegger's argument for the mediation of *parousia* into language in the commentary on "Wie wenn am Feiertage," this image of not speaking the difference between speech and speechlessness would be the other face of that performance when "in its moment of highest achievement, language manages to mediate between the two dimensions we distinguish in Being," but not by uniting them, because "their unity is ineffable and cannot be said, because it is language itself that introduces the distinction."[25] "Im Winde / Klirren die Fahnen" *marks* mechanically, in not speaking, the difference, and thus the condition for any possible or impossible mediation, between the visual image and its significance or understanding as either speech or speechlessness.

Such an interpretation of the directionality and itinerary of the image from the narrative and decomposition of mediating images in "Wie wenn am Feiertage" to the series of self-negating representational images in "Hälfte des Lebens" has led in and at the end to a nonending, an indeterminacy beyond speechlessness and yet still within the domain of poetic utterance's *klirren* or clattering. We can read into this domain, to its liminal conditioning, but not out of it to an end to our reading or an arrival at its meaning. This particular trajectory between two poems cohabiting in part—in fragments—on the same manuscript page is not, however, a last step, a cul-de-sac, or a dead end, as we will soon see in turning to a third Hölderlin poem, nor are the results of our analysis in themselves any obstacle to a possible argument about these poems' locations in the project of Hölderlin's late poetry. At first glance, the site of Hölderlin's image is still left—however suspended—in between the initial attempt at the "hymnic style" and the elegiac's mode of visual images of reflection.[26] But such a possible inquiry and argument could no longer pursue Szondi's direction of following the "healing" of the poetic "I"'s biographical wound toward the emergence of a nonegoistic mediating voice between gods and men; it could not, that is, operate any longer within the sphere of imagery of the full course or development of Hölderlin's poetry and the arc of his arrow.

Rather, the direction of the "other arrow" ("anderer Pfeil") may be, in Szondi's very terms, toward the other *error*, the missing and failing or *Fehlen* of language. The near homophony between *Pfeil* and *Fehl,* arrow and error, suggests in both contexts a lack: the lack of a healed, ascetic, even self-sacrificing voice in the first case, the lack of mediating language in the "Fehlen der Sprache" and "Fehlen des Schattens, . . . der zwischen Sonne und Erde vermittelte" in the second case. *Fehl* as lack or *Mangel*—in our interpretation, the lack of the image in not signifying the mediation of distinctions between heaven and earth, the visible and the spoken or expressed—immediately suggests as its other, in Hölderlin, his term and notion of *Mass:* the measure or ratio that balances deficiencies and excesses within poetic language. In the key line from the prose draft of "Wie wenn am Feiertage" that Szondi cited, Hölderlin wrote "Aber wenn von selbgeschlagener Wunde das Herz mir blutet, und tiefverloren der Frieden ist, u. freibescheidenes Genügen, Und die Unruh, und der Mangel mich treibt zum Überflusse des Göttertisches" ("But when from a self-struck wound my heart bleeds, and peace is deeply lost, & freely restrained pleasure, And unrest and lack drive me to the excess of the gods' table") (2/2, 669, 670). Here, there is not an image of *Mass* so much as a conspicuous lack of measure or an unbalanced ratio of lack to excess, *Mangel* to *Überfluss*—an imageless version of the "balancing" of which must await our third Hölderlin poem.

Indeed, in the still-customary understanding of Hölderlin—the familiar, developmental, totalizing one—this "Un-mass" is always supposed to lead, in his later hymns (or at least up to their rupture in madness), to its correction in the establishment of a *Mass* between images that are no longer missing or failing, and the poetic narratives that extend and meaningfully fulfill these opening images and thus make possible their full reading. Thus we would no longer find, as in "Wie wenn am Feiertage," *Mangel* and *Überfluss* yielding the poem's decomposition into images of nonmediation, but the *Fluss* or river yielding *Lied* or *Gesang:* the image of the river's flowing would flow into the narrative of the song issuing from that image. One thinks above all of "Der Rhein," but also of several other late "river" poems such as "Am Quell der Donau" and "Der Ister." Similarly, images of nature as the room of the gods, as in "Festlicher Saal! Der Boden ist Meer! und Tische die Berge" ("Festive hall! The floor is the sea! and tables the mountains") ("Brod und Wein," 2, 92), or "der altgebaute, / Seeliggewohnte Saal; und grüne Teppiche duftet / Die Freuden-wolk' . . . Zur Seite da und dort aufsteigend über dem / Geeb-neten Boden die Tische" ("the anciently built, / blessedly inhab-ited hall; and green carpets are wafted by / the cloud of happiness . . . On the side here and there rising up over the / leveled floor the tables") ("Friedensfeier," 3, 533), might fulfill themselves in the poems' narratives of the gods come to earth. But there is also in Hölderlin, in a persistently disequilibrious balance with such avowals as "immer bestehet ein Maas" ("a measure always ob-tains") ("Brod und Wein," 2, 91), the ongoing admission that "Gut machen will ich den Fehl / Wenn ich noch andere singe. / Nie treff ich, wie ich wünsche, / Das Maas." ("I want to make good the lack/failure/fault / When I sing yet other [songs]. / I never hit, as I wish to, / The measure.") ("Der Einzige," first version, 2, 155). Thus, in a counterdirectional inquiry into the directionality and itinerary of Hölderlin's image, one would be obliged to read one's way not only to images and poems of *Mass,* but also to *its* counter-part, which is *Gesetz* ("what is posited or laid down," thus, "law"). *Gesetz* in Hölderlin is less that which can be met, achieved, or lived up to—it is of course by no means clear that *Mass* can be, ei-ther—than what can only be violated and consequently submitted to.[27]

The law of images, including the imageless, almost invisible, scarcely readable law of their measure, continues to determine the limit of Hölderlin's poetry and its interpretation. At the limit of its excellence, where formal and structural laws are posited and observed so extensively and yet so effortlessly as to be almost in-visible, and where poetic and semantic statements are rendered so powerfully that reading seems to have no point, no aim, no end—no function or activity—but that of assent and repetition, at such heights of achievement, the determination of interpretation still remains: the question of determining what it is to be in the face of such poetry, the fact of its own determination to read on in the end anyway. We turn to such an exemplary instance of poetry in now coming to the third of our several Hölderlin poems. But a last remark on Hölderlin's explicit image-making will not be unhelp-ful in approaching our turn. All images are made; there is no such thing, in Hölderlin or other poetry, as a "natural image." The question, then, is not whether the direction of poetic images is from or to nature, but of the direction and ends of poetic image-making. The image of the image-maker in "Der Rhein," borrowed from Rousseau's *Pygmalion,* is "Der Bildner, Gutes mehr / Denn Böses findend, / Zur heutigen Erde der Tag sich neiget.—" ("The sculptor/image-maker, more good / than evil finding, / The day inclines to earth.") (2, 147), and this appears to represent a directionality, and thus a tendency toward mediation, of the sun's day toward earth. An interpretation of the poem, however, has never been able to convincingly sustain such an appearance, what with the final lines' statement of the return of a counterdirectional "uralte Verwirrung" ("primeval confusion"). An image of image-making in "Patmos" suggests, but still in the subjunctive or optative, that "So hätt' ich Reichtum, / Ein Bild zu bilden, und ähnlich / Zu schaun, wie er gewesen, den Christ" ("That I might thus have the riches / An image to image, and in the similar / To see, how/like he was, the Christ") (2, 170). But the very untranslatability of this image returns us to "Wie wenn am Feiertage" and its dissociative linking of images both with seeing and with similarity and metaphoricity (*wie*).

To reflect further upon the law of Hölderlin's images, which are oriented toward mediations of the visual into poetic speech, but which along the course of that directionality also swerve to reflect upon the appearances of images that are not visual except as signs or marks of a limit of language's direction and movement toward the goal or end of meaningfulness—of its direction toward and capacity for an end in reading—is, for now, the law governing interpretations of his poetry. Already over fifty years ago, Heidegger wrote of Hölderlin that "language must continually place itself within an appearance produced by itself, and thereby endanger its most proper achievement, authentic speech."[28] This dangerous law, which is the danger to the measure and mediation of images, governed both the appearance of images of mediation and the missing and failing of the mediating *Strahl, Sonnenschein,* and *Schatten* in "Wie wenn am Feiertage" and "Hälfte des Lebens." A further understanding of the language of Hölderlin's images, one that would be proper to their exact verbal construction and marking, is to be sought not only in their impropriety with respect to the law—their marking of the limit where danger to speech and statement becomes the law of the image and the image of the law. It is to be sought also in a poetic measure and beauty, the success of which displays both an endlessly instanced and returning reading and the invisibility—the nonimaged character—of its constitutive structure.

≥

"Andenken" is unlike any other Hölderlin poem—which would be an a fortiori proposition if it could be determined, as I suspect, that it is also unlike any other poem whatsoever. Being obliged, or at least tempered by caution, to restrict a survey to Hölderlin's poetry, we can readily recall some of the distinctive features of this uniqueness. It is a late poem, dating uncertainly from either shortly after his return from an exhausting trip on foot to and back from Bordeaux (thus, fall 1802 to spring 1803) or as much as two years later; and yet unlike most of his late poems (and as Hellingrath insisted on from the start), biographical details are inscribed in it with a remarkable precision and clarity. Although it is comparable in the grandeur of its themes to the most ambitious of Hölderlin's "hymns"—it praises heroic action, love, poetry, and of course remembrance—in contradistinction to those poems the gods are here absent as either themes or poetic vehicles, and classical motifs and images are almost equally absent, or at least highly muted and submerged. The language of "Andenken" is calm and controlled in an achieved poise unlike that of most of the other late poems ("Der Ister" and "Mnemosyne" appear to be comparable exceptions), even though it spares itself none of Hölderlin's famous syntactic and grammatical "muscularity"—what Hellingrath called his "harte Fügung" or "austere harmony," translating what Dionysius of Halicarnassus had designated as distinctive of the style of Pindar and other ancient Greeks. The poem is so unlike the other late poems called "hymns" (by their editors) and "vaterländische Gesänge" (by Hölderlin himself) that Hellingrath—to the embarrassment of his successors—called it "a lyric in the narrower sense,"[29] and whatever the shortcomings of this judgment (for the "hymns" are also lyrics), every subsequent editor has had to agree that the poem lacks the distinctively conspicuous triadic organization of form and structure that Hölderlin took over from Pindar for most of his late poetry.

"Andenken"'s reading has been different from that of other Hölderlin poems as well. It received the dubious benefit of Heidegger's longest commentary in his *Erläuterungen*, where he granted it such importance in his philosophy of the remembering and forgetting of Being and the foundational task of poetry that Friedrich Beissner scarcely exaggerates when he says that Heidegger took the poem "as the occasion to develop his philosophy."[30] It remained virtually immune from the politicized readings of Hölderlin in the late 1960s and 1970s, although it mentions France as much as any of his poems and is clearly a product of his only visit there, and so an ambitious and comprehensive reading published in 1970 by Jochen Schmidt, one of the deans of Hölderlin scholarship, has been able to remain authoritative.[31] More recently, the philosopher and scholar of German idealism Dieter Henrich has trumped Heidegger by publishing a 185-page reading of "Andenken" as both an important document in German idealism's philosophy of reflection and identity, and a landscape poem in its particular topographical and mnemotechnic traditions.[32] This reading in turn has received its critical reversal and extension in one of the few extant deconstructions of Hölderlin.[33] From biography to topography and its deconstruction, from Hellingrath to Henrich and Haverkamp, "Andenken" continues to force its readers to read it uniquely.

Except, that is, when it is not read very thoroughly at all, but taken—and retaken, and retaken—at its word at its end: "Was bleibet aber, stiften die Dichter." ("What remains however, the poets found.") (2, 189). It would be one thing to be able to explain to both German- and English-speaking audiences how "Andenken" is as beautiful and complex and yet poised a poem as Keats's "To Autumn," but the linguistic gulfs may be too wide for our mutual understandings to span. It is another and baleful thing altogether to recognize that a great poem can become a one-liner. More than "Patmos"'s famous and pathos-draped beginning—"Nah ist / Und schwer zu fassen der Gott. / Wo aber

Gefahr ist, wächst / Das Rettende auch." ("Near is / And hard to grasp, the god. / But where danger is, grows / What saves as well.") (2, 165)—and more than the enigmatic line that begins "Der Rhein"'s fourth strophe—"Ein Räthsel ist Reinentsprungenes." ("An enigma is what springs pure from the source.") (2, 143)—"Andenken"'s last line substitutes for the poem, and if parody is the homage that posterity pays to the banalization of greatness, then this last line, ever since its assault by Heidegger, has had its "gnomic" character first cracked by the weight of banal enchantment, then further pulverized by parodistic ridicule.[34] This must be faced up to from the beginning by a reading that wants to read to and at the poem's ending.

I am going to read "Andenken" selectively, that is, from privileged passages to its ending, then back to its title and its middle. We will be continuing the trajectory of our reading of the first two Hölderlin poems, in that we will be observing both the image of fullness claimed for—read into—Hölderlin's achievement, and the exploitation of a particular image for the emptying out of former interpretations. Through and then beyond these indications given by "Andenken"'s readers, we will also still be asking about Hölderlin's technique and "Andenken"'s device for directing reading to and from his ends and its end.

Schmidt's authoritative and totalizing interpretation of "Andenken" takes its point of departure from two widely recognized aspects of the poem and its contexts. The first is that the poem's most obvious references and coordinates are from Germany back toward Bordeaux (the perspective of the first strophe: "Der Nordost wehet" . . . "Geh aber nun und grüsse / Die schöne Garonne . . . ," ll. 1, 5, 6), thus a return in memory ("Noch denket das mir wohl . . . ," l. 13) after a return from abroad to the "fatherland." These features, together with the presumed contemporaneity of the poem's composition with that of Hölderlin's "Anmerkungen" to his Sophocles translations and his famous second letter to Böhlendorff in November 1802, authorize Schmidt to read "Andenken" as part and parcel of Hölderlin's poetics of the "vaterländische Umkehr" ("native reversal/conversion")—a trajectory out to the non-German, a countertrajectory back—that admittedly inform much of the late work with their "dialectic" of the native and the foreign, the source and the colony. This is a dense and weighty and much-contested issue in Hölderlin scholarship;[35] suffice it to say here that it gives Schmidt a context and a schema for organizing his entire interpretation: "The process of remembrance, the poem in its total structure is shaped by this dialectic of the near and the far" (24). Schmidt goes so far, in a practice not uncommon to Hölderlin interpreters, to see this one poem as consistent with all of Hölderlin's work, and not just the late texts; his commentary readily brings in passages from the youthful novel *Hyperion* (1792–95), for example, to round out the total image of Hölderlin's artistry and thought and the totalizing interpretation of the poem.

The second aspect of the poem that authorizes Schmidt's interpretation is the threefold division of what he calls the "realms" or "spheres" of its imagery and their thematics. Beginning with the famous three-and-a-half lines at the end,

> Es nehmet aber
> Und giebt Gedächtniss die See,
> Und die Lieb' auch heftet fleissig die Augen,
> Was bleibet aber, stiften die Dichter.

> (But the ocean / takes and gives memory, / And love
> also keeps the eyes intently fixed, / What remains
> however, the poets found.) (ll. 56–59)

Schmidt observes that the three regions of the sea, love, and poetry correspond to the imagery and thematics of the entire poem—heroic activity (*Thaten*, deeds, l. 36) and seafaring with the sea; gardens, women, and festivals with love; and of course remembrance with poetry—and that furthermore, the three "spheres" are distributed triadically across the poem (all three spheres in the first strophe, then love in the second, all three mixed in the third, then principally masculine activity—with love as its counterpoint—in the fourth strophe and the first half of the fifth, until the resolving summation at the end; 14, 15).

Thus Schmidt recovers a triadic arrangement otherwise conspicuously lacking in the poem's formal strophic structure, and one evidently directed precisely at and to a "dialectical" interpretation in which a whole poem and its full understanding over-come and elevate all partial passages and stages. The first strophe, he claims, already "contains, but not yet unfolded, the three realms of existence in one complex structure of imagery" and so it "relates to the later strophes like a hint to its interpretation [wie die Andeutung zur Deutung]" (17). The third strophe is the ef-fective point of dialectical transition in this understanding:

> The middle strophe has the function of transition and mediation toward reflection, in that it represents the sit-uation of the reflecting persona in such a manner that, from out of the strophe, the concluding gnomic utter-ance of the poem develops as the result of the thinking-over [*Nachdenken*]. . . . The third strophe constitutes the axis in the five-strophe poem, it displays the poet in the "middle" of his remembrance, insofar as in the reflection he achieves the transition from the remembering re-pres-encing of the past and the transient to the consciousness of what remains. The entire structure thus testifies to the same decisive self-consciousness of artistic shaping that is to be observed in the structure of the strophes, in the se-quence of the images, and in the value of the location of the gnomic utterance. (24)

I shall return both to Schmidt's privileging of the third stro-phe—which is not at all incorrect—and to his specific and insight-ful terminology of "reflection" throughout this privileging. For the moment, however, I conclude this presentation of Schmidt's influential and holistic interpretation by bringing it to the end that he brings it to: the claims for the achievement of the last lines, in which the received Hegelianism of Schmidt's "dialectical" read-ing together with its unilinearity are especially visible:

> The poetic "Andenken" is a process of consciousness, the decisive agents of which are "Liebe" and "Taten"; but the consciousness that has finally developed out of its process spans the stages of its becoming in that it sublates [*aufhebt*] them in a higher coherence—in the notion of the total unity of life. This notion is an a priori form of

sentiment for the poet who finds himself in proximity to the origin, to the "Quelle" (source), albeit at first a form of sentiment that is still unconscious and that then in remembrance develops itself to full consciousness. (40)[36]

Combining a thoroughgoing thematization of the poem's movements with a self-satisfaction in such paraphrase that approximates smugness as it covers and replaces—"sublates"—the poem's poetics with a hermeneutics of "coming to consciousness," Schmidt's reading could risk being dismissed as facile overstatement were it not still so influential for and representative of the celebratory understandings of Hölderlin's own "full" achievement.

If Schmidt risks self-parody in his unfolding of a unilinear "dialectics" of the poem's poetics from its beginning to its end, Anselm Haverkamp's commentary on "Andenken" risks self-parody in its deconstruction first of Dieter Henrich's own reading, then of the poem itself. Henrich reconstructs at once "Andenken"'s German idealist-philosophic intertext and the poem's topographic and historical context in Hölderlin's Bordeaux experience, but for Haverkamp, while this is admittedly a reconstruction of what the poem presupposes of philosophy, it is only a one-sided interpretation of what actually takes place in the poem (74). Quoting Henrich's admission that he reads what "can only *complete* [*vollenden*] itself in the thinking [*Denken*] of the poem," Haverkamp counters that "he [Henrich] cannot read the completion of this thinking *in* the poem—a completion that in the present case approximates a failure of the same thinking in the poem" (75). Counterposing failure to completion, Haverkamp returns at the end of his interpretation to the claim of "the failure that is held fast in the course of this poem, in 'Andenken'" (88)— without having made very clear just what this failure is, apart from an inability of remembrance to overcome mourning. "'Andenken' thinks its 'remembrance' as the impossibility of its and every remembrance and leaves behind in the trace, in the excluded figure, the sign of this and every remembrance" (92). If this runs the risk of deconstructive self-parody—every accomplishment a failure, every possibility an impossibility—it is nonetheless, as we will see, Haverkamp's considerable achievement to have noticed a figure in the poem that indeed reverses Henrich's and others' claims for "Andenken"'s particular powers of reflection.

Henrich's argument about "Andenken"—to summarize greatly—is that its "course" (*Gang*), its "act," its activity (which is, then, also its value as a reading-experience) is to re-presence (*vergegenwärtigen*) a remembered experience in poetry in such a way that the reflected, inwardly directed remembrance qua poetry yields greater understanding and worth than the re-presenced experience itself. To be able to make this subtle and rigorously dialectical argument convincingly, Henrich has to give all due credit to Hölderlin's precise poetic "re-presencing" (not representation) of Bordeaux in the poem, in order then to credit more highly its sublation in remembrance. The turn from the one to the other is located most powerfully by Henrich in the turn from the last five lines of the first strophe to the first four of the second:

Dort, wo am scharfen Ufer
Hingehet der Steg und in den Strom
Tief fällt der Bach, darüber aber
Hinschauet ein edel Paar
Von Eichen und Silberpappeln;

Noch denket das mir wohl and wie
Die breiten Gipfel neiget
Der Ulmwald, über die Mühl',
Im Hofe aber wächset ein Feigenbaum. (ll. 8–16)

(There, where along the sharp bank / The landing goes and in the river / Deeply falls the stream, over which however / Gazes a noble pair / Of oaks and silver poplars; // All this still comes to mind and how/ The broad peaks are bent by / The elmwood, over the mill, / In the courtyard however grows a figtree.)

From the exact precision of the image—the imaging, the "re-presencing"—of the steep bank of the Garonne at Bordeaux, with its sharply cutting "port de la lune" (known since Roman times as *portus lunae*), its wooden landing (*Steg*) that gave way sharply to the waterline at low tide, its picturesque streams emptying into the river, its oaks and poplars held already at that time to be characteristic of the region[37]—from all this precision captured in the poem's first strophe, Henrich signals the poem's turn inward, *in* to the perspective of memory ("Noch denket das mir wohl . . . "), *in* toward the inside of the courtyard, *in* to what he calls the "still more corporeal present" of a self-reflexivity upon one's own standpoint that is embodied in the remembering, in contrast to the objective re-presencing of the landscape that one had just been poetically performing and presenting. In the middle of this inwardness turned to in the act of remembrance, Henrich underscores the figtree as the very symbol of remembrance: the tree before the walls of Troy invoked in "Mnemosyne," the tree at Semele's grave included in Hölderlin's translation from Euripides' *Bacchae* (and recalling her death in "Wie wenn am Feiertage"), the tree of paradise "at the entrance into the history of human consciousness" (Henrich, 92, 93).

From this powerful interpretation, Haverkamp turns precisely upon its centerpoint—the figtree—by bringing out the crucial detail that the perspective that gave both upon Bordeaux and, in turning, upon the courtyard—the perspective, in other words, of the Hölderlinian persona in his remembrance—is from *Lormont,* the (in however spurious an etymology) "laurel mount" above Bordeaux. Drawing upon John Freccero's well-known article "The Figtree and the Laurel,"[38] Haverkamp calls into question any original fullness of perception, let alone its sublation in its poetic remembering, and elaborates instead the Augustinian-Petrarchan duality of the topoi before deconstructing the difference between them. The figtree in the garden in Milan under which Augustine claimed that he experienced his conversion (*Confessions,* 8, ch. 12), was already for him a topos for the divine promise of a fullness of the Logos in the fullness of time, linking past and present with a future disclosure and fulfillment—a closure—of their meaning;[39] artfully employed in the fiction of a "true" experience, Augustine's figtree is a rhetorical one. Petrarch's laurel, which he himself (in his *Secretum*) skillfully and disingenuously plays off against Augustine's figtree as an empty sign of poetic vanity and idolatry in contrast to the full sign of divine promise, is thus both the *other* to the figtree, and—here enters Haverkamp's deconstruction, counter to Freccero's argument—the explicit rhetoricity of the topos that was already implicit and readable in Augustine. "For Petrarch leaves no doubt that he sees through the rhetoric that, in Augustine's autobiographical fiction, gives priority to the figtree over the laurel" (86). When Hölderlin, then, turns on the "laurel mount" (Lormont) to the figtree in the courtyard (also *hortulus,* thus a carrying-over of Augustine's "garden"),

> the view is retracted from an implicit laurel to an explicit figtree—a silencing of poetic ambition that, in this silencing, is not so much retracted as heightened. . . . Both [Petrarch and Hölderlin] in the end do away with the play of empty words, which the laurel crowns, as the foregrounded pretext of poets, in writing the play to this end. . . . "What remains," so the figtree displays, is the signifier that it is and that it has remained throughout the changes of context—regardless whether Augustine invented the figtree of his conversion or owed it to the arbitrariness of circumstances that allowed Hölderlin to re-find or imagine it in the courtyard of a mill. (84–87)

Thus the dualisms of fullness and emptiness, sincere conversion and poetic vanity, are erased in Haverkamp's reading. "The success of the figtree—far from 're-presencing' an original experience, but rather employed in order to call up a powerful tradition that has as its object the illusionary effect of such fictive immediacy—is the success of the laurel, which, even in the denial of all empty ambition, remains active as the silenced desire in the text" (88). In a "Postscriptum," Haverkamp goes further and is more explicit still:

> The historicity of the motif [of the figtree] in Hölderlin reflects within itself the rhetoricity of the medium [of the topos] and establishes the constancy of the figure within the changes of context—including its own. . . . In Augustine's *conversio* the figtree signified a turning point that in Petrarch's reading becomes visible as the turn signal for poetic convertibility (*tropus*) and that in Hölderlin, in the completion [*Vollzug*] of the turn, disappears, having be-

come transparent to itself. The figtree *is* a laurel . . . but a displaced one. As denied ambition and silenced desire it remains—"however"—still active in the text that it discredits, it still testifies—"however"—to the efficaciousness of the discourse that it—having fallen into discredit—continues to write, a *crossed-out* discourse [*durchkreuzter Diskurs*, with reference to Derrida's *sous rature*]. (90, 91)

Haverkamp's argument is a brilliant counter-reading to Henrich's interpretation, let alone to Schmidt's. I have cited it *in extensio* not to allow it the last word on "Andenken," however. Rather, the direction of inquiry Haverkamp sketches, from Henrich's topography via Freccero's topos-ology to his own tropology, needs to be pursued more rigorously and poetically, that is, with greater attention to the guiding precision of the poetic workings of Hölderlin's text and with more consequential reasoning about what it means to try to read "Andenken" to the end. For, no less than Schmidt with his "full development of consciousness" and "notion of total unity," or Henrich with his "completion in the thinking of the poem," Haverkamp also has "Andenken" writing through a topos's tradition *and being read, in his very reading,* to an absolute end: "in writing the play of empty words to the end," "in the completion of the turn," a turn—a full conversion in its own right—to an absolute transparency of the poem's rhetoric to itself and its reader.

All three of these highly skilled and informed readers of Hölderlin adopt a strikingly similar terminology and rhetoric in making their ways to these similar ends: it is the language of reflective effects and reversals or conversions. Haverkamp spoke of the "illusionary effect of fictive immediacy" and the "trace or 'momentary evidence' left behind as the motif of reversal [*Umkehr*], of *conversio*" (88), following his critique of Henrich's preoccupation with both the reflection of reflection (which in German idealism makes the subject what it is and provides Hölderlin's philosophic context) and the particular self-reflexive turn of the perspective upon one's own point of view in "Andenken"'s passage about the figtree. And we recall Schmidt's sentences about the poem's middle strophe: "The middle strophe has the function of transition and mediation toward reflection, in that it represents the situation of the reflecting persona in such a manner that, from out of the strophe, the concluding gnomic utterance of the poem develops as the result of the thinking-over [*Nachdenken*]. . . . In the reflection he achieves the transition from the remembering re-presencing of the past and the transient to the consciousness of what remains" (24). He added: "The middle strophe displays the poet as the one whose horizon surmounts the other two realms [of action and love] in that he reflects them" (37). The interpreters' language of reflection and reversal can serve as our guide back to the poem and its poetics of ending in remembrance, with a final signal from one of them.

In poetry and its poetic figures—its tropes—reflection and reversal combine, as we saw already in Shakespeare's sonnet 43, in chiasmus, the crisscrossed pairing of similars or parallels (grammatical constructions or semantic units) that displays the reflection of the similarity or parallel as a reversal or mirror inversion. It is Schmidt's considerable merit to have been the first to observe that in the second strophe, precisely in the lines that have so preoccupied Henrich and Haverkamp, there is a chiasmus, and he describes it exactly with the language of reversal or conversion and with attention to what is perhaps the poem's most powerful word, the adversative *aber:*

> The adversative conjunction "aber" in the phrase "im Hofe aber . . . " explains itself through the reversal [*Umkehrung*] of the imagistic movement with respect to the preceding verses: while the elmwood bends its broad peaks over the mill—nature thus surrounding the place of human activity—the figtree is brought into the space of human activity. This meaning of the image—harmonious reciprocal interpenetration—is also made clear, in these verses that are constructed with the greatest artistry, by the impressive chiasmus. (18, 19)

The chiasmus, represented schematically, is:

neiget / . . . über die Mühl',

       ×

Im Hofe aber wächset . . .

as not only the prepositional phrases of location ("über die Mühl'" and "Im Hofe") are inverted in their surrounding/enclosed representations and in their syntactic locations with respect to their verbs, but the verbs are themselves inverted in the directionality they indicate (*neiget* [down], *wächset* [up]). The adversative *aber* represents the exact point of the turning, the twisting, the inverting and reversing—the point of the *chi*, the turning of the parallel construction into a ×—that its grammatical description also suggests: *ad-versus,* turned against. This is one of eight uses of the word *aber* in the poem, and although we know from his Pindar and Sophocles translations that Hölderlin sometimes used the word rather indifferently, together with *nehmlich* (namely), *doch* (yet), *denn* (then), and *und* (and) to render the different Greek particles *gar, men,* and *de,* we have reason here with "Andenken" to ask if *aber,* its adversative, inverting power, and its place in a beautiful and conspicuous chiasmus do not direct us more deeply into the poem's poetics. Heidegger, in perhaps the most lasting insight of his outlandish interpretation, concluded by calling the whole poem "a single structure, joined in itself, of the *aber*" ["eine einzige in sich gefügte Fuge des *aber*"].[40]

There are other constants in the poem that may perform an organizing function with respect to the whole. One could argue, for example, that given the connections of fire, festivals, and wine with one another that were established already in "Wie wenn am Feiertage" and "Brod und Wein"—in "Wie wenn am Feiertage," a *Feiertag* is a *Feuertag,* with fire coming from above—in "Andenken" each strophe similarly displays the homophonic and/or semantic feature of the same triad: "feurigen Geist" (str. 1), "Feiertagen" (2), "dunkeln Lichtes," which is Hölderlin's brilliant oxymoron for red Bordeaux wine (3), "Feiertage" again (4), and finally "Traubenbergen" (5). But this red thread that runs through "Andenken" may lead only to a thematic blunting of the poem as one jumbles it together with the Dionysian thematics of other Hölderlin poems (and we have seen how subtle and complex they can be in "Wie wenn am Feiertage"), and it may only be a red herring. The chiasmus in the second strophe is different.

For, together with the repeated appearances of *aber,* it leads us to ask after other chiasmi, other reflections-as-inversions. There is no other such elegant, classically poised a chiasmus in the poem, but there is arguably a form or version of a chiasmus in each strophe. In the fourth,

. . . nicht . . . / Die Feiertage . . .

×

Und Saitenspiel und eingeborener Tanz nicht

is a chiasmus, where the inverted positions of the *nicht* invert the otherwise parallel construction. (Schmidt, 30, calls this *kyklisch,* cyclical, as the second *nicht* "circles back" to the first.) There is momentarily a near-chiasmus in the fifth strophe's "Ausgehet der Strom. Es nehmet aber," where the verb/subject word-order of the first half of the line is inverted after the caesura to the impersonal subject/verb word-order, as semantically the "going out" is inverted by the "taking." (I say this is only momentarily a near-chiasmus since the next line brings in "die See" as the actual subject of the clause.) The third strophe, over several lines, sketches a minimal chiasmus in "Nicht ist es gut, / . . . / . . . Doch gut / Ist . . . ," with the inversion of "ist . . . gut" to "gut / Ist." And in the first strophe there is, quite remarkably, a phonetic chiasmus:

ed*el Pa*ar

×

Silber*pappel*n

A chiasmus in every strophe, indeed. "So what?" the skeptical or merely curious coreader may be expected to ask. I want to argue now, in pursuing these markers, these *reflections,* of reversal as inversion, that in "Andenken" we have to do not with an artful poem that decoratively scatters versions of the trope of chiasmus upon its formal surface, but with a chiastic tropology and structure of deeper significance, particularly with respect to how the poem arrives at and departs from its ending, and how the reader gets wrapped up in it as well.

Henrich, on the grounds of his argument's own coherence as well as on the intuition and taste of a fine Hölderlin reader, had focused on the line "Im Hofe aber wächset ein Feigenbaum" and the gnomic closing "Was bleibet aber, stiften die Dichter"—what Haverkamp, following Henrich, had called "the two focal points of the poem" (78), between which both an interpretation and its deconstruction could be strung and unstrung. Between these two "focal points," we now realize, is not an ellipse, but a chiasmus:

aber wächset

$\times$

bleibet aber

What grows in Bordeaux—with all the temporality, transience, and mortality implied in growth—becomes, via its reflection and inversion, what in "Andenken" remains. The poem's "whole" chiasmus is in effect the protostructure for Henrich's interpretation: the imagery *in* the poem becomes and remains the image *of* the poet and his poem in the course of "Andenken."

With this we are talking once again, with all our interlocutors, the language of the image of Hölderlin the poet ("the poet of poets") and of the poetic images of his poem in all their fullness, but we are not yet talking about or reading at the poem's end and beginning. The last strophe, as the exception to the other four, contains only eleven instead of twelve verses. Beissner unconvincingly suggests this is an "oversight" on Hölderlin's part (2/2, 802)—unconvincingly, that is, because anyone who, like Hölderlin, could write very long poems of highly complex triadic construction, where the slightest variations are motivated by the poems' arguments, has to be credited with knowing how to count and knowing the difference between eleven and twelve.[41] There is no surviving final clean copy of the poem's manuscript but a draft version of the last strophe exists, and there we see how Hölderlin shortened two lines (which would have given the strophe its full complement of twelve lines) into one: "Ausgehet der Strom. / Wohl nehmet und giebt" became the single line, "Ausgehet der Strom. Es nehmet aber und giebt," then the final version, "Ausgehet der Strom. Es nehmet aber" (2/2, 801). Hölderlin's conspicuous *aber* marks the turning of two into one—the *re*turn of a once "extra" (or numerically sufficient) line as a now "missing" one. From this remarkable poetic gesture he gains not one but two caesuras: turning two into one gets back, as its return, not one but two. The first caesura is the obvious one in the extraordinary line itself: "Ausgehet der Strom. [pause] Es nehmet aber." But the second, extended caesura is the caesura at the end, the caesura of the ending: "Was bleibet aber, stiften die Dichter." The poem cuts and breaks with this line—it is a caesura in an extended, prosodic, formal, and line-numerical sense, not in the strictly metrical sense[42]—and the reader sees and hears the missing, lacking, failing (*fehlend*) line, the empty spot that remains, that is found founded. The end, with its lack, is the "failure" (*Fehler*) of the poem to end, the fault (*Fehl*) and fault line at its nonend.

But not only does virtually every reader know that the poem ends with its last line; she or he knows that what is missing (whether one noticed the missing twelfth line or not) isn't really missing because it had been provided from the beginning. The "gnomic" end-line "Was bliebet aber, stiften die Dichter" is no impenetrable wisdom since the answer has been given from the start: What remains? "Andenken." What remains, and what the poets found, is remembrance and is the poem titled "Andenken." The extended caesura at the end, then, in its missing twelfth line, points back to the beginning, to the first line—if not the first verse—of the poem: its title, "Andenken." The poem does not end at its end, but returns to its beginning to make up its lack of and at the end. Only at the end can the poem begin as its "full" remembrance, as the remembrance of the remembrance, the remembrance (*Andenken*) of "Andenken," the beginning of its and any remaining (*Bleiben*).

This is a doubling in self-reflection that produces the doubled, reflected remembrance and "Andenken"—the doubled mental activity or consciousness of Hölderlin's (or his persona's) depicted imagery of remembered experience preserved and elevated in poetic remembrance, in the poem and in its reader's understanding; and the poem "Andenken" doubled into its self-reflexive, self-conscious rereading—and that occurs, I am arguing, as ending and beginning are inverted and (re)turned into one another: the end makes up its lacking line at the beginning, the beginning only makes sense and has the authority to be the title and first "line" of the poem when it remains and is found and founded at the end. But how this doubling, self-reflection, and inversion between ending and beginning occur has not yet been understood. We are not, I had said, in an ellipse between two foci, nor simply circling back and around from end to beginning, beginning to end. Rather, as the schematic chiasmus "aber wächset / bleibet aber" suggested, a twisting—as if in a figure eight—occurs in the looping back and around from the terminal point and the point of departure, and a cutting—as in a caesura (from *caedere*, to cut)—also occurs as first a line is cut, then a surviving line is cut in two, then a cut remains in the missing last line, wherefrom one cuts back to the beginning and finds the end in the beginning, the beginning in the end.[43] If one combines a twisting with a cut, one gets the "figure" we have already encountered in the previous chapter: the Möbius strip, where a cut is necessary for the twisting and rejoining to yield a shape whereon one side *is* its other, as here where an end is at the beginning and a beginning already at the end.

If we look in the middle of the poem, we can find this point of twisting and inverting, corresponding to the cut at the end to the beginning and the reflection of the beginning in the end. I have already pointed out a minimal, even uninteresting chiasmus in the third strophe: "Nicht ist es gut, / ... / ... Doch gut / Ist." But within this chiastic frame, which is to say at the exact formal middle of the poem, are the lines:

> Nicht ist es gut,
> Seellos von sterblichen
> Gedanken zu seyn. Doch gut
> Ist ein Gespräch.

> (It is not good / Soulless from mortal / Thoughts to be.
> Yet good / Is a conversation.)

The end of the poem had too little—a missing or empty line—that was inverted into the structurally compatible "too much" of the "first" line (the title) plus the first strophe's twelve lines: 12 − 1, or 11, was thus converted into 12 + 1, or 13, and 13 back into 11. Between *Mangel* and *Übermass*, a Hölderlinian *Mass* thus obtains. The needy end takes away (*nimmt weg*) and measures the excess or surplus that the beginning anticipates (*vorwegnimmt*). The axis, the turning-point, the crossing (the *chi* or ×) of this inversion and conversion of end and beginning, too little and too much, is to be read in the middle strophe's middle lines, and precisely in the crossing-over or enjambment "Seellos von sterblichen / Gedanken." I say it is to be read there, because it cannot be imagined as seen, like "Im Hofe aber wächset ein Feigenbaum," nor can it be found remaining fixed and founded, like "Was bleibet aber, stiften die Dichter."[44] It cannot be imagined as imaged in the perhaps deceptively convenient shape of a Möbius strip. We are here in an imageless line, beyond the limit of the image in "Im Winde / Klirren die Fahnen," and we have arrived at a point of reading that can be neither phenomenalized as perception or intuition, nor hypostatized as a fixed meaning.[45] *Seellos* means "too little," from its suffix *-los:* "soulless" or "without soul," "to be" too little, to have too little. And too little because of, from "too much": "von sterblichen / Gedanken," "from mortal thoughts." If one is too full of mortal thoughts, then one is too little, "soulless." But this very inversion of too much into too little—too many mortal thoughts, too little soul—is itself the turning-point of its own inversion, where the lack is overcome: "Doch gut / Ist ein Gespräch und zu sagen / Des Herzens Meinung, zu hören viel / . . . " The lines indeed turn, invert from a line-beginning *Seel*los to an end-line *viel*, from less to much.

What are "sterblichen Gedanken" and what does it mean to be "von" them? "Mortal thoughts" cannot just be tautologically understood as those that are not about immortality, or not yet about the remaining and founding provided by poets and poetry, thus not yet immortal thoughts immortally expressed. This would amount to the further tautologies that "mortal thoughts" are those that render us soulless instead of soulfull, and that the midpoint of the poem is not (yet) its end.[46] For what other thoughts are there but the thoughts of, that is, by and belonging to, mortals? Once one notices—reads—that there is an incipient inversion within the phrase "sterblichen Gedanken," from "mortal thoughts" to "thoughts of/by mortals" ("Gedanken der Sterblichen"), then one can begin to read the lack inverting into its compensation and reversal. Beissner had already intuited this in his nontautological gloss of the line, allowing that it itself somehow got the poem and its reader to the next step: "Nonetheless it is occasionally allowed to man—'in festive hours' ('Die Titanen,'

l. 5)—to rest in 'sterblichen Gedanken' from the tension [of anticipation of the future and the appearance of the new god]. The following sentence ('Doch gut ist . . .') provides the positive equivalent" (2/2, 803). With the self-inverting, chiastic power within the phrase "sterblichen Gedanken" thus noted and read, its preceding preposition *von* likewise elastically turns and inverts: from "from" in the sense of "because of" (*von* in the sense of *wegen*), to "from" or "of" in the sense of "with." For to be "soulless with mortal thoughts" already allows one to read it turning—adversatively, *Doch*—to the consequence that one can be "soulfull with mortal thoughts," having a conversation about the heart's conviction, and hearing much of days of love and deeds that have occurred. From thoughts about mortality to thoughts of or by mortals, from consequences because of them to being *consequent with* them, is the reflection and reversal within the writing and reading of "Seellos von sterblichen / Gedanken zu seyn." Even an alternate scansion of the lines in question provides the turn: not intoning "von sterblichen / Gedanken" as if they were an indifferent causal appositive to *Seellos*—soulless because full of or with mortal thoughts—but rather "Nicht ist es gut, / Séellós von sterblichen / Gedanken zu seyn. Doch gút / Ist ein Gespräch. . . . " *From* soulless thoughts—from *out of* soulless thoughts—one thus gets the soulfull, from out of a con-versing and speaking of the *von* and the ad-versing *Doch*.

The middle of the poem as the axis, the turning-point, the crossing and inverting of less and much, negative and positive, loss and gain, and indeed, end and beginning, is in a writing and reading of an imageless line. Every word of the crucial sentence—"Nicht ist es gut, / Seellos von sterblichen / Gedanken zu seyn"—is without or on the far side of an image, is invisible as perception, is unthinkable except as inscription and legend. It cannot be filled up, completed, and ended (Schmidt) because it keeps inverting, inverting an end of too little back into a beginning of too much, a beginning of premature excess back into the ending of measured founding—except for its lack of measurable, fixed measure. It cannot be found—then to be sublated—in any original experience to which the text would mark a difference (Henrich), because its original experience is its textual difference from itself: each word's difference "from" and "with" itself, "less" and "more" than itself. It cannot be read in any positive, negative, or indifferent relation to topoi of semiosis (Haverkamp, with his parodistic "*Was bleibet,* is the signifier"), because the line is its uncommon place—its utopia, I would call it—where the poetic power of the writing keeps the poem from being read to any one end or from any one beginning. "Andenken" so twisted in its middle, so cut, reflected, and inverted at its ends, is for all its exquisite imagery a poem of the inscription and remembering of the imageless. The crux of soullessness, which is the chiasmus of each and every strophe and of the poem's larger structure, inscribed then with its caesuras, is that it cannot be filled with consciousness, cannot be seen turning inward, and cannot be read in a tradition from a Christian cross to an idolatrous crossing-out. The crux is that the crux can only be read as the ending of the poetic image in the nonending of its trope, its turning, its reflection, and the thought it returns to itself.

6

Passage to Reading in Baudelaire's "A une passante"

❧

Someone who sees without hearing is much more
unsettled than one who hears without seeing.
—Georg Simmel, quoted by Walter Benjamin

Baudelaire's poetry in *Les Fleurs du mal* has for so long been so
well known and so easily placed in literary history that it has become hard to read. Baudelaire, the last French romantic, the first
symboliste, the French heir of German romanticism, the anticipation of French surrealism, the first universally modern poet, the
most infamous in a line of decadents and *poètes maudits:* these and
many other such characterizations—part scholarly truth, part
popular wisdom, partly contradictory and partly complementary,
and all clichéd—cover Baudelaire's book of poems so thoroughly
that one has half the sense that there is nothing further to be
gained from actually reading them, half the sense that no light
can penetrate them through all the surrounding foreknowledge.

The poet as albatross, the mood of spleen, the hair and eyes of cat-women, the mystical correspondences, the invitation to the voyage: a pastiche of titles and themes like this may make one, in a Baudelairean image, swallow it all in a yawn rather than sit down, open the book, and start reading.

Walter Benjamin, who has been widely credited with stimulating new interest in Baudelaire's poetry, participated in the massive epochal situating of the poet. On the first page of his essay "On Some Motifs in Baudelaire," drawing attention to the first poem of *Les Fleurs du mal*—its programmatic "Au Lecteur"—Benjamin insists on the epochal shift effected by the historical conjuncture of the book, its audience, and its future. Nothing less is at stake than the lyric. "The conditions for the acceptance of lyric poetry have become less favorable," and in three respects: "First, the lyric poet has ceased to stand for the poet per se. He is no longer 'the singer,' as Lamartine still was; he has become a representative of a genre." Second, "a mass success has not reoccurred in lyric poetry since Baudelaire." And a correlative third circumstance: "The public became more reserved even toward lyric poetry that was handed down from earlier times. The span of time we are talking about may be dated roughly from the mid-1800s. In the same period the fame of the 'Fleurs du mal' has spread without interruption. The book that counted on the least inclined readers, and that at first found few that were inclined, became a classic over the course of decades; it also became one of the most widely printed ones."[1] Benjamin's paradoxical image is of a bad time (a declining literary history) for lyric poetry, a good time (a success story) for Baudelaire, and an implicit and ironic prediction that becoming a classic as Baudelaire did can lead to a non-reading a short time later, as he comes down to later generations as the poetry from the olden days.

Unless, that is, Baudelaire is no longer counted as a lyric poet, but as anything and everything else: modern poet, poet of the urban, *poète maudit*, prose poet, and the like. Benjamin participates in this recharacterization of the generic alignment of the poet. Memory as defense, the experience of "shock," modern life in the big city, all this according to Benjamin makes Baudelaire a nonlyric poet and, a fortiori, a survivor in the struggle for literary-historical reception, readership, and afterlife. Unless, that is, his popularity acts as a shield against reading. So widely printed, possessed, taught, and invoked, the poems of *Les Fleurs du mal* are more likely to receive their close readings from abroad than from France's lycée "explications de texte" and university "histoire littéraire," while other French writers shed light not through intense interpretation but through the brief and general observation or the enweaving of a reading in their own writing of another poem.[2]

My study has not much worried about the distinction between "lyric" and "poem," and I do not intend to take Benjamin's bait here. I introduce it nonetheless because Benjamin's attention to Baudelaire, while admittedly long on psychoanalytic speculation and sociohistorical location, focuses its sights several times on a lyric poem par excellence, the sonnet "A une passante." Not only is it in one of the canonical forms of modern Western lyric poetry; the poem is also of that subgenre that dominates so much lyric: it is, after its fashion, a love poem. Benjamin remains one of Baudelaire's best readers, albeit in elliptical and often surprising fashion. "A une passante," a sonnet of desire, attraction, and near-love, attracts Benjamin's insight in interesting *reprises*. This conjunction of the rare reader and the exquisite poem can become our occasion to study how one Baudelaire sonnet (and some of his most famous poems are sonnets) leads its narrative, its form, and its reader to an ending in singular and spectacular exchange.

> La rue assourdissante autour de moi hurlait.
> Longue, mince, en grand deuil, douleur majestueuse,
> Une femme passa, d'une main fastueuse
> Soulevant, balançant le feston et l'ourlet;
>
> Agile et noble, avec sa jambe de statue.
> Moi, je buvais, crispé comme un extravagant,
> Dans son oeil, ciel livide où germe l'ouragan,
> La douceur qui fascine et le plaisir qui tue.
>
> Un eclair . . . puis la nuit—Fugitive beauté
> Dont le regard m'a fait soudainement renaître,
> Ne te verrai-je plus que dans l'éternité?

Ailleurs, bien loin d'içi! trop tard! *jamais* peut-être!
Car j'ignore où tu fuis, tu ne sais où je vais,
O toi que j'eusse aimée, ô toi qui le savais![3]

(The deafening street howled around me. / Tall,
slender, in full mourning, majestic grief, / A woman
passed, with a fastidious hand / Raising, balancing the
festoon and the hem; // Agile and noble, with her leg of
a statue. / I, I drank, contorted like an eccentric, / In
her eye, livid sky where the hurricane grows, / The
sweetness that fascinates and the pleasure that kills. //
A flash . . . then night!—Fugitive beauty / Of which the
look made me suddenly reborn, / Shall I see you no
more but in eternity? // Elsewhere, quite far from here!
too late! *never* perhaps! / For I don't know where you
flee, you don't know where I go, / O you that I might
have loved, o you that knew it!)

Benjamin presents two versions of his reading of "A une passante," one in the book manuscript, unpublished in his lifetime,
"The Paris of the *Second Empire* in Baudelaire," the other in his
essay "On Some Motifs in Baudelaire."[4] Each version itself has two
aspects or sides to it. On the one hand (to begin with the book
manuscript's version, 547, 548), love in the sonnet is, according to
Benjamin, represented as fleeting and fugitive: "The sonnet 'A
une passante' represents the crowd . . . as the asylum . . . for the
love fleeing the poet." On the other hand, love is nonetheless experienced: "The enrapture of the city dweller is a love not at first
but at last sight." The reversal of a negative experience into a positive one, of a flight into a contact, goes to the essence of this first
reading by Benjamin. "The 'jamais' is the culmination of the encounter, where the passion—apparently frustrated—in truth first
flashes out of the poet like a flame." But this achievement of passion becomes, as Benjamin's reading continues, problematic for
him insofar as the poem presents a properly poetic problem, that
of the relation of the two tercets to the two quatrains. Seizing on
the word and the image of the figure *crispé* (contorted), Benjamin
adds that this is not an image of self-possession; it is rather the case
of a figure in shock, "of the shock with which an imperious desire

surprises the solitary man without any mediation [*unvermittelt*]."
(Benjamin also alludes to the word "extravagant" in the phrase
"crispé comme un extravagant," where the "outside" [from *extra*]
and the "errance" [from *vagari*] together express the excessive
and the centrifugal rather than the mediated and well-com-
bined.) Benjamin insists on what he calls the formal "rupture"
(*Bruch*) in the poem: "There is in truth a deep rupture between
the quatrains that display the incident and the tercets that transfigure it."

This last word, "transfigure" (*verklären*), is a signal for the entire interpretation of the poem in this first reading by Benjamin,
for it is an interpretation of a failed transfiguration, where the
"rebirth" in the tenth line ("Dont le regard m'a fait soudainement
renaître") promises a continuity neither with the "body" of the
sonnet nor with its continuation and end. The poem is as if a cru-
cifixion and transfiguration without resurrection, where—in the
last sentence of this reading of Benjamin—the theme remains
"stigmatized": "Love itself is recognized as stigmatized by the me-
tropolis."

In its second version (622–24), Benjamin's reading of the
poem—although it repeats several phrases from his first word for
word—gives it a slightly different inflection. A language of crossing, of reversal and inversion, displays itself in a visible and legible
manner. "An unknown woman crosses [*kreuzt*] the poet's gaze." "It
is a leave-taking forever which in the poem coincides with the instant of rapture." (Here I have tried to preserve the crossing, the
chiasmus that we find in Benjamin's own German: "Es ist ein *Ab-
schied für ewig,* der im Gedicht mit dem *Augenblick der Berückung*
zusammenfällt.") Then there is this phrase that doubly develops
the one from the first reading: no longer a "shock without any mediation," but "the figure of the shock, indeed, the figure of a catastrophe," and this is something that the sonnet does not *re*present
but presents or puts in place ("So stellt das Sonett die Figur des
Chocks, ja die Figur einer Katastrophe"). This doubly develops the
first reading, because now there is mediation in a figure—the
mediation of or by a figure—and a specifically tropological name
for this shock: the *cata-strophe,* or reversal (the *kata-strephein* of
Greek tragedy being the overturning or reversal of the hero's fate).

And instead of a "deep rupture" in the poem, of a formal kind and formalistically readable, the rupture now appears in Benjamin's second reading itself. Its last sentence this time (after an interesting but obscure comparison with Proust) is that in this poem, love's fulfillment remains unachieved, without realization—less "refused" than "spared" (or "saved," as for a later time), still escaping the poem ("die Erfüllung sei ihr [der Liebe] minder versagt als erspart geblieben").

We know that in the "whole" (and totalizing) argumentation of Benjamin's posthumously published book on Baudelaire, this "fulfillment" that is still lacking, "spared," "saved" from, and "escaping" ("fugitive") in Baudelaire's text, aims at a possible act, indeed at a possible historical act that would reverse mourning (Baudelaire's *deuil*, Benjamin's *Trauer* and *Traurigkeit*) in a heroic action: this would be the *revolution*, the overturning or *Umsturz* that is the formal and structural counterpart and complement to the poem's catastrophe. The revolution was still lacking, still repressed, according to Benjamin's argumentation, during the *second empire* of Baudelaire's time; and according to the same argumentation—as its allegorical underside—still lacking up to Benjamin's days, during the 1930s, on the eve of a mourning still more inconsolable: that of World War II and *its* catastrophes. I believe it is for the sake of this rationale for a thinking of the heroic, of a hidden and latent revolutionary heroism, that Benjamin drew a faint but readable connection between the figures in "A une passante" and those of heroes. He translates two different words from Baudelaire with the same German phrase when he says that the body of the "I" in the poem, *crispé*, "im Krampf zusammenzieht" (contracts in a convulsion) (548, 623), and then—recalling "the fascination exerted upon the poet by the passing lady of his sonnet, dressed in mourning" while translating from the last paragraphs of Baudelaire's "Salon de 1846"—writes that Balzac's characters, named "heroes" by Baudelaire (more heroic even than those of the *Iliad*) while wearing their black suits as "the symbol of a perpetual mourning," endure sadnesses "unter dem makabren, wie im Krampfe zusammengezogenen Frack" (under the macabre frock-coat, contracted as in a convulsion; Baudelaire: "sous le frac funèbre et convulsionné que nous endossons tous") (580). To wear the black bourgeois frock-coat—I draw out and summarize the suggestions in Benjamin's argument—is to await a heroic "convulsion": to be *crispé*, convulsed, is to await a reversal, a revolutionary overturning.

We should not read Baudelaire any longer toward this end, in this direction, which is a direction and ending beyond his text and history and into its possible and revolutionary future.[5] It is not just bad—outdated and condemned—politics; it is bad reading. Furthermore, when reading for poetic ending, one must realize that poems end in *their* present, not ours, or rather in the present (ending) to which they give (us) directions. Poems are never historical, which means that while they are always historical artifacts, they are never historical activities. Where Benjamin might have had (we must remember these are only suggestions in his text) an overturning to complement and overcome, set aright, the figure of the "catastrophe" in the poem, he also leaves this prophetic heroism in a subtle but noteworthy tension with what Baudelaire called, in the "Salon de 1846," the "deuil perpétuel" of those figures clothed in their "uniforme de desolation." The desolation recalls Benjamin's "catastrophe," the perpetual mourning recalls the sonnet's *deuil* and *éternité*. Rather than try to read Baudelaire's poem by aiming beyond it, we should read further into its weave of mournfulness and postnarrative eternity, literal crossing and figurative catastrophe, already most effectively brought out for us by his reader Walter Benjamin.

≥&

"A une passante" is a network, an interlaced knot, an assemblage of movements and countermovements, mounting and suspending their efficacy to the very end. We read the poem best when we read this texture in several turns and returns, remarking the patterns and structures of force at work in it so as to bring out the poem's remarkable guidance of its reader to its and his or her end. A first pair of turns and returns, I want to suggest, is "A une passante"'s staging of *passages,* linear and temporal experiences of passing, that then lead to, encounter, or turn into their blockage.

The first quatrain's second line is a sequence, a listing of features that build and add up to their subject and her activity, which is itself passage: "Longue, mince, en grand deuil, douleur majestueuse," then followed by "Une femme passa." This second line is one of the most "linear" in the poem in its forward-directed motion and momentum, although the entire first quatrain continues this tendency: "d'une main fastueuse / Soulevant, balançant le feston et l'ourlet"; and just when this image of poised balance would arrest and suspend the forward motion at the semicolon, the enjambment carries the sentence on over the spatial gap between quatrains: "Agile et noble, avec sa jambe de statue." The poised balance gives way to renewed activity or passage in the "agility," and the formal (syntactic) *enjambement* also enacts its corporeal (semantic) embodiment in leading the mind's eye down the woman's body from her hand to her hem to "sa jambe."

At this point of forward progression, which is one of considerable erotic advance, linear passage encounters and becomes its blockage. The very line we have just glanced at itself comes to a stiffening, ossifying end—from agility to the statuesque—and in its end-rhyme, it anticipates a dead end as well. For in rhyming *tue* with *statue,* the eighth line not only brings out the incipient Medusa-izing of the woman's statuesque leg (a glance at her offers "the pleasure that kills"). It also arrests the line's elegant formal parallelism—progressive in the very noticing that one element leads to a second, its parallel ("La douceur qui fascine" paralleled in its exact grammatical double "le plaisir qui tue")—in an abrupt instant and end-line of death.

There is a similar, if lighter, pattern of passage meeting its blockage in the tercets. "Un éclair . . . puis la nuit!—Fugitive beauté": between the semantic motion of the lightning bolt and the fugitive, fleeting quality of the beauty, the temporal marking of the *puis* and the rapid alternation from light to dark, and the punctuational rapidity of the ellipses, the exclamation mark, the dash—it doesn't get any quicker than this. But the formally symmetrical and parallel repetition of a pattern of passage in the first line of the second tercet—moving us elsewhere ("Ailleurs"), far away in space ("bien loin d'içi!"), excessively far away in time ("trop tard!")—comes upon an abrupt and italicized *jamais:* as negating or dead an end ("peut-être!" but *peu importe)* as that *tue* was at the end of the second quatrain.

Passage to blockage, a passing away of motion into stasis, possibility into possible impossibility: this may describe the poem's action through line 12. Passage *and* blockage are combined, and in the most extreme reach of its resonances—already noted in Benjamin's first reading of the poem—it attempts to recombine the passage to blockage (to the death at the end of l. 8) with the overcoming of that blockage in a renewed passage (to the possibility of a rebirth in l. 10), which however leads only to its own impossibility (the end of l. 12). This pattern in the poem may itself be redescribed as an *inversion,* the inversion of passage into its other that is the blockage of passage, of possibility into impossibility.

At first, perhaps most subtly and in a way that is only subconscious to the reader before a formal analysis brings it out, "A une passante" communicates inversion in its sound patterns. The very first line inverts the initial sequence of vowel sounds in its first half ("r*ue* ass*our*dissante") into its mirror opposite in the second half ("aut*our* . . . h*ur*lait"), and this pattern of inverting *u* and *ou* sounds continues throughout the two quatrains.[6] The quatrains also display the inversion of masculine and feminine end-rhymes: masculine, feminine, feminine, masculine, the pattern itself then inverted to feminine, masculine, masculine, feminine. From sound to sight, one can spot the graphic inversions of the pairs of vowels in "*oe*il, c*ie*l." Since so much is made, across the tercets, of the rhyme *renaître-peut-être,* with its semantics of posing rebirth and then negating (possibly) a possible reencounter, the reader's eye is drawn to the intervening *éternité.* A pattern of graphic inversions of consonants and the *e* vowel begins to emerge:

renaî*tre*
é*te*rni*té*
-ê*tre*

And while this aural and graphic evidence of a pattern of inversions into mirror reversals is irrefutable, perhaps the most readily evident and persuasive instance of the design will be the elegant chiasmus that is the eleventh line, "Car j'ignore où tu fuis, tu ne sais où je vais": elegant because the obvious and powerful parallelism of mutual ignorance about motion (I don't know where you flee, you don't know where I go) has upon it the inversion of the pronoun-shifters:

$$je \ldots tu \ldots$$
$$\times$$
$$\ldots tu \ldots je.$$

Our reading has come upon knowledge of the chiasmus of mutual ignorance in the penultimate line—which ignorance will itself be inverted into the last line's last word's claim of knowledge (*savais*). From passage's inversion into its other of blockage, from patterns of inversions of sound to sights of inversions of letters, and now to the trope of inversion—chiasmus—our reading is observing and listening to the poem's dynamic and its governing structure without yet having read much (apart from some motifs of eroticism, death, and resurrection). From the trope of chiasmus and the figure of inversion, we must now read the motion and structuring of observation in the poem, all the way to its passage to reading.

The basic events of the poem in a representational sense are two, accompanied and followed by their figurative elaborations and epistemological consequences. A woman passed before the perspective of the poem's male (Baudelairean) persona or "I": "Une femme passa." And the "I" drank in from her eye sweetness and pleasure (however Medusa-izing): "Moi, je buvais . . . / Dans son oeil." This minimal representation of two events is all that is really known. We do not know—the poem does not tell us— whether, for example, the woman even saw the man. Claude Pichois, in his Pléiade edition of Baudelaire, reproduces a passage from Pétrus Borel's tale "Dina, la belle Juive" (in his volume *Champavert*) that may have served as a source for "A une passante," and in which looks *are* exchanged: "elle égara sur moi ses beaux yeux pers; ses deux prunelles . . . me frappèrent droit au coeur . . . on lui a jeté un regard, on a reçu une oeillade . . . c'est déjà de l'amour."[7] But nothing is so transparent, so grammatically or semantically clear, in Baudelaire's poem.

The last three lines of the second quatrain, where the look is made, are the most densely metaphoric and figurative in the poem. We have already seen Benjamin observe and elaborate the

"I" in its simile, "crispé comme un extravagant." Our interest can be directed to the multiple metaphoricity of the "I" drinking in an eye that is a sky where a storm grows (*germe*)—followed by the hyperbole of a pleasure that kills. This unmistakable and impacted metaphoricity nonetheless represents, as I have already said, one of the poem's two basic represented events: he looked in her eye(s). The literalism (he looked) within the metaphor (he drank in her eye-sky) leads to an extension of its storm-metaphor in another metaphor, tired as it is—the *éclair*, like a proverbial *coup de foudre*, which jumps across the eyes or out of the eye-storm. The poetic ambiguity and interpretive uncertainty in the representation here is that perhaps the *éclair* is his glance at the woman's eye (his *coup de foudre*), perhaps it is her glance back at him. A unilinear passage, or its reversal and return? The ambiguity and accompanying uncertainty are sustained in the next line-and-a-half: "Fugitive beauté / Dont le regard m'a fait soudainement renaître." Did the "I"'s glance ("regard") at the passing beauty cause him to be suddenly reborn, or did her glance ("regard," although tellingly not "*son* regard") at him provide the renaissance?

We may read this ambiguity and uncertainty more precisely by noticing that the ambiguity regarding the literal version of the "regard"—is it he literally looking at her, or she literally looking (back) at him?—need not be resolved by its double literalization in the completion of the literal, interpersonal exchange (one looked at the other *and* saw that the other looked back) but may be complemented, doubled, giving and getting something back in return, by the "regard"'s literal reflection and the observation of this self-reflection. That is, the "I" looking in the woman's eye would not have to see her looking (back) at him in order to get a glance back in return: he could see his glance reflected back to him in her eye. A unilinear aiming and sight at the image of a lover—a literal "regard" at a *passante*—is enough to get back, by self-reflection, the look that was, literally, one's own but looks, has become, "like," like it comes from the other: the doubling of the look in its literal reflection, its observation in and as self-reflection.

Perhaps all looking at love-images is Narcissistic. Perhaps all "drinking in eyes" is likewise Narcissistic, with the three-dimensionality of eyes becoming liquid, watery mirrors. (Although we remind ourselves that the glass of non-Ovidian mirrors is also a liquid, and also has three-dimensional depth to the point where the glance reaches the tain and reflects back.) But certainly this moment—this passage—in the poem, where a literal glance, however ambiguously literal, doubles into a literal reflection, is the moment—the passage—where the literal reflection itself becomes metaphoric, a reflection of reflection or a self-reflexivity where the reader no longer needs to represent any persona seeing himself looking into (and back from) another's eyes. For, just as certainly, this is the point and passage in the poem where, as Wordsworth put it, "the light of sense / Goes out," where phenomenal sight is extinguished: "Ne te verrai-je plus que dans l'éternité?", where the negative question leaves less hope for its affirmative refutation ("Si!") than it points to the consequent invisibility. For nothing is seen in the remainder of the poem.

What I have called the metaphorizing of the reflection of the "regard" into a self-reflexivity at the very moment of the disappearance of sight occurs at the poem's passage into an intense reinteriorization. The mutual ignorance that is averred, as well as the possible love and the asserted knowledge thereof, all are spoken in a tone or voice that is far from its interlocutor, far from a beauty that is fled, no longer seen, elsewhere, far away from here, perhaps *never* to be seen again. This interiorized "speech" is part of a *re*interiorization because the poem began with the "I" in a similar, bookended position of interiorization, surrounded ("autour de moi") by a deafening noise that allowed him neither to hear anything else nor to be heard, surrounded by an inhuman, inarticulate howling. The "I" was—following Benjamin following Simmel—condemned to see without hearing. At the end, at the *re*interiorization, the "I" sees no longer, either, and if it hears at all, it hears, like a deaf person, inwardly.

Do we hear the last lines? We certainly read them. Perhaps all reading is Narcissistic, as we look for our project of comprehension to be reflected back as another's meaning that we are intended to understand. As we read the poem's last lines, after the "regard"'s literal reflection and self-reflection (self-observation of the literal reflection) as metaphoric doubling and self-reflexivity, we no more hear anything than the persona could—than anyone in this poem could—from the first line onward. The only sound represented as outside the interiority of the poem's perspective of sight and "speech" is a deafening that oblides all other sound: to hear one thing in this poem is to be represented as deafened. In the last lines, the reader sees the loss, the fleeing of the spectacle of sight, she or he hears the deafened, interiorized "speech"—perhaps better, after our reading of Hölderlin, to speak here not of "speech" but of articulation, of joining (*Fügung*)—she or he reads the passage to reading of "A une passante."

Reading the passage to reading at the end of "A une passante" means reading the closing lines not as any possible (audible, vocalizable, communicative, interlocutory) address to "une passante," but as the send-off, the envoi, the closing of a poem that opens it to its reading. The lines are addressed not to "une passante," but "A une passante"—their address is the end of the poem and the beginning of its entitlement.[8] The *tu* who can "hear" these lines within the deafening, who can "see" them within the absence of the passing woman to whom they are nominally (phenomenally) "addressed," is the reader who finally, in the last appearance of the second-person pronoun, is the seat of an end in knowledge that would reverse the mutual ignorance between "I" and "you," Baudelairean man and passing woman.

The seat of knowledge in a site of reading at the last words of the last line—"ô toi qui le savais"—is of course in the imperfect tense: its declaration comes too late with respect to the declared cognition. Even reading's knowledge at the end of the poem is outdated, past, in a passage backward and away. To understand better the significance of the verb's tense in relation to the other tenses of the poem, we ought first to reconstruct the structure of exchange and inversion that has led to its reading and address to its reader at the end. I recall that there are two basic representational events in the quatrains of the poem, and their relation may be represented schematically as a chiastic exchange:

Une femme passa [before the "I"'s perspective]

×

Moi, je buvais / Dans son oeil . . .

(The schema of the chiasmus is feminine subject-verb-preposition-male object inverted into, and yielding the exchange—the passage from passage to drinking in—of, male subject-verb-preposition-female object.) The second part of this chiasmus constitutes the first part of a subsequent one:

> Moi, je buvais / Dans son oeil . . .
>
> ×
>
> Dont le regard m'a fait . . . renaître,

where the "I"'s activity (*buvais*) upon the "eye" is inverted into the activity of the eye (*regard*) upon the "I" ("m'a fait renaître"). The second part of this chiasmus in turn becomes the first part of a subsequent—if virtual—one, virtual in the sense that it is there only to be read, not to be seen:

> Dont le regard m'a fait . . . renaître,
>
> ×
>
> [Moi, le poète envoie "A une passante"]

This chiasmus, readable as the reconstructable infrastructure of how the "regard" yields self-reflexivity and the departure of all other sight and spectacle—what I have called the passage to reading—has all looking and seeing (*le regard*) inverted into the reception and reading of "A une passante," and the claim of the persona's rebirth inverted into the birth of the poet of the poem "A une passante" (which is what allows critics to refer so casually to the "I" of this poem as "Baudelaire"). Finally, the second part of this virtual but reconstructable chiasmus builds the first part of a last chiasmus:

> [Moi, le poète envoie "A une passante"]
>
> ×
>
> . . . ô toi [lecteur/passant(e)] qui le savais!

In the passage to reading, and the address of the last lines to the send-off, the envoi of the poem, the passing woman has passed out of the picture and the poem, while the reader has become the "you" addressed in passing over the lines of "A une passante," the consequence of which is that the poet attributes knowledge *of this*—the passage to reading—to the reader. "O toi qui le savais" means you knew what has happened in this poem—glance, *coup de foudre*, love at first and last sight, loss—because you have read it to the self-reflexive self-address of the last half of its last line.

From passage to blockage to the structure of a series of self-inverting chiastic exchanges and inversions: this is the passage to reading that would yield an ultimate knowledge that undoes a penultimate mutual ignorance ("Car j'ignore où tu fuis, tu ne sais où je vais"). But we are now in a position to return to the question of the poem's verb tenses. The knowledge that is attributed at the end came too late, I had said: to read it is to have read it. The end of the poem is too late for itself; it is over and already "A une passante," speaking to no one but being read as having been "spoken." The poem, in fact, is a past-tense narration (the imperfects *hurlait* and *buvais,* the historical past *passa,* the *passé composé* of "m'a fait") that jumps to the future tense of its own denial of a continuity of sight and spectacle: "Ne te verrai-je plus que dans l'éternité?"

The love declared is only possible in the "unreal condition" of the past subjunctive ("O toi que j'eusse aimée"), and the knowledge is presented as already having been. The exceptions to this recounting of the poem's verb tenses are of course the two-and-a-half lines of the present indicative, first in the highly figurative description of the passing woman's eye and what can be "drunk" in it ("ciel livide où germe l'ouragan, / La douceur qui fascine et le plaisir qui tue"), then in the penultimate line of mutual ignorance and departure ("Car j'ignore où tu fuis, tu ne sais où je vais").

These present indicative verbs and verses are, I suggest, the non-narrative present—the present-tense time that the poem presents (posits, performs) and gives—that enlivens or, better, empowers and renders dynamic the surface of the text for and in its reading. The penultimate line, in its elegant chiasmus, presents and preserves forever the personae's mutual ignorance as it also is sending them out of the picture and out of the poem forever—forever sending them out—in the *fuis* and *vais* of flight and evasion. The surface and depth of the eye, made the surface and volume of a sky where there "grows," in an uncannily permanent present, the storm that shoots lightning and *coups de foudre,* and the liquid where a sweetness always fascinates and a pleasure always kills: this surface is, we have read, the surface of reflection that becomes, in the poem's narrative, the surface, site, and sight of self-reflection and, beyond the poem's narrative (at the ending, the evacuating of its narrative of spectacle), the surface of self-reflexivity. The eye is what we read in "A une passante"'s passage to reading.

We may recall that, in *Les Fleurs du mal*, the eye's "ciel livide" is self-reflexive in the additional sense of being intertextual. The poem "Horreur sympathique," which is situated only a few poems before "A une passante" and is addressed to a *libertin* in an exercise of self-address, has as its first line "De ce ciel bizarre et livide." Asked what thoughts descend from such a sky, the *libertin* answers by entering into a spectacle of self-reflection with the sky: "Cieux déchirés comme des grèves, / En vous se mire mon orgueil." And from this positing of self-reflection ("se mire"), the poem goes on—it is also a sonnet—to reflect a word and an activity of "A une passante":

> Vos vastes nuages en deuil
>
> Sont les corbillards de mes rêves,
> Et vos lueurs sont le reflet
> De l'Enfer où mon coeur se plaît.

We will return in a moment to the reappearance of the *deuil*. The explicit naming of the sky as a surface of reflection ("vos lueurs sont le reflet") draws us back to the self-reflexivity of the two uses of "ciel livide." "Horreur sympathique" rhymes its *livide* with *vide*, bringing out already the vanity and aridity of this *libertin*'s prideful self-reflection ("De ce ciel bizarre et livide / . . . / Quels pensers dans ton âme vide / Descendent?"), and then—via the third rhyme of *avide*—concludes the rhyme scheme with the laughable but telling lines (in reference to the complaining *Tristia* and *Epistulae ex Ponto*), "Je ne geindrai pas comme Ovide / Chassé du paradis latin."

Perhaps reading *ciel* in Baudelaire is always Narcissistic—not only that that liquid eye like a "ciel livide" in "A une passante" becomes the surface of self-reflection and self-reflexivity, recalling Ovid's Narcissus, but that reading *ciel* will lead to *Ovide*. We recall, in this widening weave of intertextuality which is *Les Fleurs du mal*, that "Le Cygne," even nearer to "A une passante" in the volume, has *ciel* and *Ovide* in a single line that is then rhymed with *avide:* the poem presents the swan "Vers le ciel quelquefois, comme l'homme d'Ovide, / Vers le ciel ironique et cruellement bleu, / Sur son cou convulsif tendant sa tête avide." Perhaps even the *convulsif* here recalls—anticipates and echoes—*crispé.*

What this weave of repeated rhymes brings out is the *vide* in *livide* and *Ovide* (and *avide*), a sky-surface and Narcissistic mirror with fictional volume and actual—here, textual—emptiness. If the depth, in becoming a surface, can fascinate, pleasurably seduce, and then kill—so "A une passante," retelling Ovid—it leaves a void, and thus an occasion for mourning, *deuil.* But it also leaves, as an actual, textual sur-face or "over-face," the readable mark of the void as the sign of the poem's self-reflexivity: its address to the reader, to the passing reader in passage to reading the epitaphic, mournful, self-voiding narrative. "Halt, traveler" (the epitaph's conventional *sta viator*) has here become "pass, passing one, to reading." The liquid eye, having—via the "ciel livide" and the Ovidian Narcissistic subtext that is everywhere readable here—become the reflective surface of a *regard* seeing itself, self-reflectively and self-reflexively, becomes the reader's eyes seeing and reading the voided eyes of the evacuated personae of the poem, the woman gone to and for eternity, the man become the extratextual poet, both monumentalized and so mortified (the woman raised on a pedestal as a statue, having a poem dedicated to her in her absence; the man inscribed and immortalized as its author).

The eyes to be read here appear and look back out of the text in a passing, fleeting, fleeing motion that is the very passage to reading. As the penultimate line declares mutual ignorance about where (*où*) the "you" flees and the "I" goes—all we know is that they are already out of sight and spectacle, and out of the poem's narrative—the balanced repetition of "où . . . où . . ." becomes transformed and reflected in the last lines' "O . . . ô . . ." The directional *ù* attached to *o* to give direction ("where"), but that here directed representational and narrative direction right out of the poem—declaring ignorance of direction—collapses and tips into the "O/ô," as if the grave accents have combined into the circumflex, or the *u* has tipped upside down—inverted—to become a circumflex. If we weren't deafened, we could hear in these apostrophaic *o*'s (via "Le Cygne"'s phonetic and semantic chiasmus of "sans eau"/"Ovide") the watery, drinkable eye homophonically recalled.[9] Deafened or not, we can recall Paul de Man's adventurous association of the apostrophaic *O* of address and invocation, of anthropomorphism and prosopopeia, with the tropological giving-of-face to the human subject—here, to the absent lover and the present reader as well—and its extratropological, deconstructive defacement of sight, voice, and subjectivity in epitaphic inscriptions.[10] Indeed, after de Man, we are here at the threshold between the phenomenal sight of voided eyes and hollow sightlessness and the reading of inscription—the passage from one to the other. Passing to reading and reading to the end of a poem, we see ourselves reading the sight of the disappearance of our eyes and of the knowledge—too late, now past ("toi que le savais")—they had been given, and had taken from them, in passing to the site of reading. We read in the end the doubled "oeil . . . vide" of the text's reflexive surface reflection of two eyes—"O . . . ô," as if "ô . . . ô"—looking, with raised eyebrows or winking eyelashes, back in specular recognition at our sightless eyes and in Narcissistic recognition of their reading.

7

End and Ending

On the Lyric Technique of
Three Wallace Stevens Poems

In several of this book's chapters—on Coleridge, say, and on
Hölderlin—we have seen how individual poems and poets' entire
oeuvres invite the preunderstanding (the *Vorverständnis*, the horizon of expectation) that the texts and the poetic careers, in their
imagery and themes, their origins and goals, lend themselves to
explication. That is, major themes or images, their sources and
aims, unfold themselves along and across the lines of individual
and successive poems, and understanding—the hermeneutic response to such poetic activity—would be, in this view, the venue
and the very goal of such unfolding from origin to end. But in between the origins and goals of a poetic career or, for that matter,
of an individual poem, are of course its words and their ends, and
their very letters, and I have tried to attend to those words and letters—Leopardi's *questa* and *quella*, Keats's *still*, Hölderlin's *seellos*,
Baudelaire's *ô*—in my series of close readings of great lyric poems.
The shaping of words and letters toward their poetic ends has

been seen to be a formal achievement of the poems' techniques that may be responded to—with precision, with unexpected turns, sometimes with considerable difficulty—by each reading's attempt at a corresponding achievement of its goal and end that, we have also seen, may not be a thematic understanding at all and, indeed, may be a kind of understanding of poetics that is obliged to abandon thematics or to pass to their far side. The lyric relations of words and letters to ends, then, may be where the possible articulations and disarticulations of poetics and hermeneutics are most concretely accessible. Our series of case studies into how poems end has challenged received understandings and opened new dimensions regarding the thematic interpretations of what poems mean and what they mean to do. This consequence leads quite obviously to the methodological question of how poems are to be read: of how hermeneutics is supposed to respond to and supplement poetics, or of how poetics are supposed to direct and redetermine hermeneutic responses.

Wallace Stevens, with an outwardly placid, ample, and celebrated poetic career, would seem to present material very different from Coleridge's self-advertised "fragmentary" "Kubla Khan," from Keats's abandoned Hyperion poems and interrupted (if spectacular) trajectory, from Hölderlin's often fragmented texts and their mode of poetic composition that, in its intensity and complication, sometimes seems to reproduce or pass on a tortured state of mind. But for all that Stevens' work seems to exude a sense of completion and achievement unlike some of the poems and poets already studied here, his poetic technique of endings is as daring and astonishing as any of those we have encountered in their perhaps more immediately compelling instances. So, too, attention to his technique of ending may help resituate him in a context and tradition different from those that inform some of his most expert and influential recent interpreters.

Harold Bloom, for example, has helped us understand Stevens in his alignment with and "swerving" from Emerson, Whitman, and "High American Romanticism,"[1] but I find that once we attend to Stevens' language in provisional suspension from his themes, it more interestingly recalls the high *English* romanticism of Wordsworth, Shelley, and Keats. Here Helen Vendler has been our most helpful reader in tracing out Keatsian echoes and their implications in Stevens.[2] With respect to his poetic technique in general it may be that his real ancestor and neighbor is no English or American poet at all, but Stéphane Mallarmé.[3] A more specific tradition for Stevens' technique of ending suggested by our context is that of Shakespeare's sonnets.[4] Stevens still writes from out of his readings of that astonishing sequence of poems, just as we saw Keats's use of the word "still" to be in the wake of Shakespeare's sonnets and the way they virtually invented the poetic use of that word in English, otherwise a mere case of an "invisible word," as Rilke would call it.[5]

Although one could also trace Stevens' use of "still" from its Shakespearian-cum-Keatsian intertext, his relationship to the sonnets is yet more complicated.[6] The bundle of themes that dominates the sonnets—erotic desire, idealized love, metaphoric metamorphoses of romance, time's passage, poetic self-reflection and its possible resistances to time—provides many of the motifs for Stevens' lifetime of poetry. The form, on the other hand, is foreign to Stevens: although there are fourteen-line poems in his work, especially from the last decade of his career—"The Dwarf" (1937), "Man Carrying Thing" (1946), "The Good Man Has No Shape" (1946), "The Poem That Took the Place of a Mountain" (1952), "On the Way to the Bus" (1954), "Reality Is an Activity of the Most August Imagination" (1954)—there is not, to my knowledge, a single sonnet in *The Palm at the End of the Mind*. But it is with regard to poetic techniques of moving poems and their words and readers across their formal and structural space—of moving between beginnings and endings—that Stevens' poetry is in its most interesting relation to Shakespeare's sonnets. For the sonnets represent a formal road not taken as well as a semantic and rhetorical thesaurus repeatedly visited. The richness of Shakespeare's example, precisely in the ambivalence of such richness, is what compels Stevens to write, at once, so differently and in so similar a vein.

To move to an analysis of Stevens' technique of ending, then, I first make a claim that I cannot detail or defend here: that Stevens rarely if ever in his poetry comes to the point of a poem's goal and end as we saw Shakespeare do in two of his sonnets (nos.

145 and 30). I follow this with a hypothesis that will guide the readings that follow: that Stevens does (here the similarity with, after the difference from, the sonnets) write his poetry squarely in the tradition of reflection and self-reflection that we have observed from Shakespeare's sonnet 43 through Coleridge's "Kubla Khan" and Keats's "The Fall of Hyperion" and "This living hand." Stevens' poems do not end with the attainment or achievement of a goal—an arrival at a target—so much as with their lingering ending upon words. The first two Shakespeare sonnets that we examined, and that stood for a kind of unilinearly narrative and thematically communicative poetry in general, have as their goal their end. Stevens' poems, moreso perhaps than any of those in the lyric tradition I have been studying, have as their endings their last words.

"The Snow Man" moves from "The" to "the nothing that is."[7] The impersonal "one"—a common gesture by Stevens—gives force to a claim of mock universality, and thus the appearance of the imperative is less forced and manipulative than it might otherwise be felt to be; "One must" here (in "One must have a mind of winter") is like "One feels," or "One sees," and not at all like "Du musst dein Leben ändern." The phrase "a mind of winter" suggests a slight abstraction amidst the concretions of the definite particles and their objects: the frost, the boughs, the pine trees. And the suggestion of abstraction, once noted, hints at an ambiguity in the genitive construction: "a mind of winter" may be a winterlike mind or a mind belonging to winter. (The verb "regard," with its faint Gallicism, its non-native sound among Anglo-Saxon neighbors, also perhaps hints at an abstraction.) As the sentence continues—the whole poem is a single sentence—the parallel construction of "And have been cold a long time / To behold" complicates the earlier abstraction: "cold" is, momentarily, concrete—a part of the weather, the winter, even if it is also, almost immediately, metaphoric, in the sense of dispassionate. And the verb "behold" reinforces the lingering gaze invoked by "regard." Perhaps without having paid any notice to it, the reader has also been given even more repeated uses of the word "the," lodged among concrete particulars, from "the frost and the boughs, / Of the pine-trees" to "The spruces rough in the distant glitter / Of the January sun."

The poem's tension breaks out in its middle tercet, in mid-line, with the strong negation and the strong act of intellect signaled in "and not to think / Of any misery in the sound of the wind." At this point, to have had a mind of winter, to have been cold a long time, to be regarding and beholding the winter scene, all this becomes in its consequences a statement of mind, and specifically of antipathos: a statement of abstraction, of drawing away (*abs-traho*), to be precise, from the feelings and valences associated with things to the extent that "the mind" draws away from itself. (Can the mind draw away from itself? In Stevens it can.) The logic of this turn in the middle, in other words, is to call the scene to the mind and, in the immediate negation, to call the mind away from it. It is an abstraction that renders concrete.

The scene has come to mind, and the mind would be gone. It is as if there would now be a beholding and listening of and to the winter itself. One may say a listening of the winter because it is as if the sound is not even heard, so much as produced and absorbed by the scene: the repetitions of "of" draw the sound—"the sound of the wind, / In the sound of a few leaves, / Which is the sound of the land / Full of the same wind"—back into the sources that produce it. This relation of sound coming out of something even as it remains in or of it, also emerges in the tension in the penultimate tercet between "full" and "bare": "Full of the same wind / That is blowing in the same bare place," a place that is "full" of the same repeated sound without any thought of pathos, is a "bare," mere place. ("Mere" is also, of course, a favorite word of Stevens', and one is justified in hearing an intertextual rhyme here with "bare.") How does the poem's tension resolve itself? Or does it? What could be the goal of such a poem, and how could it end?

At the level of a conceit, the poem would resolve its tensions of fullness and bareness, of a mind not thinking, by exposing or rather confirming the "one" spoken of in the poem as "the snow man" of its title: an inanimate object, made of the winter scene itself; a "man" of the winter like the sound of the wind, the leaves, the land. This would be "the listener, who listens in the snow, / And, nothing himself, beholds." The force of such a resolution would hinge on the first word of the last tercet, "For." The wind is said to be blowing "for the listener." If the listener is the snow man, then to have the wind blowing for him is to have a natural closure, as it were: a teleology, a goal and its achievement, among winter, snow, and sound—"the same bare place / For the listener." But to the extent that the conceit—one might also say, the joke—is suggested already from the title and the first line onward, it is also obviated or struggled against by the very metaphorics of "mind" and "cold" and "not to think." These can only be "literally" of a cold, mindless, nonthinking snow man (in another conceit, that of the pun: "this no man") to the degree that they are "first," or immediately, metaphoric of one thinking man: one with a bleak, cold, wintry, pathosless mind ("this know man"), thinking indeed but not thinking (or not to think) of any misery. The "conceit," in other words, is composed but also undone in the poem's first move between its title and its first line. The snow man may be figured as a man, but a man—"one"—must already have been figured as like a snow man.

Who is this "one"? By the end of the poem, there is what one could call the natural teleology of the scene "for" the listener–snow man, undone by a poetic teleology of the poem's scene of sound and wind blowing "for the listener" who can and does listen. This one listener—the listener—has curiously become every bit as concrete as the poem itself has. One might note that, after the second semicolon and the injunction "not to think / Of any misery," the poem has repeated the definite article "the" nine times up through "this listener, who listens in the snow." An indefinite, impersonal "one" becomes a "the" along with every other "the" (the sound, the wind, the land, the same bare place, the snow). Any "one" imagining, writing, or reading this poem becomes, at this point in its directed enactment, the listener.

Which is to say, "nothing itself." Far from resolving any tension in a final unveiling and closing of a conceit, the last tercet returns upon each of the poem's twists. For while "naturalistically" the poem's representation has been of a winter scene with its winter things—including a snow man—its poetic production has been of a mind emptied of pathos, emptied out to the regarding and beholding and listening of and to the things. Sufficiently oriented toward the things in their spare bareness, beholding and listening only to them without addition or supplementation, the reader/listener is minimally there and in a minimal differential relation to anything else. He is himself, but also nothing, and the minimal difference is between all the things (including the listener) and the nothing that, in this reading, the mind still is.

Things without thoughts of pathos are the things, and the mind that beholds them is at once the listener and no thing. This installed difference, which is the poem's tension reinstalled or established anew at its end, is the perspective from which the listener/reader beholds the last line: "Nothing that is not there and the nothing that is." A difference between "the listener" and "nothing itself" is transferred in between the two halves of this line, and within each half itself. To behold nothing that is not there is—like the phrase "nothing himself"—to encounter first nothing as if it were something (the litotes or double negative suggesting that nothing that is not there is indeed the something, the bare thing that is there), and then, as the litotes turns into a metalepsis, to note that the word "nothing" is there precisely because it is "that [which] is not there." Nothing posits itself and takes itself away for the beholder/reader. If this double gesture of giving and removing occurs in the first half-line, it expands across the whole line, as "Nothing that is not there" becomes, qua double negation, something, while the half-line "and the nothing that is" becomes the negation of this first "something."

What is "the nothing" here? It is the phrase, the word, the point at which the poem will not end. The tenth "the" in the second part of the poem, "the nothing" at once makes it something— a noun with a definite article, and with the predication of existence—and defines and determines it as the nothing that is there, in the winter scene and in the poem, beyond "Nothing that is not there." To behold everything, and only everything, only the "bare place," is to behold nothing that is not there (no misery, for example), and this is to behold the nothing that is. At this point one realizes that the word on which the poem is ending—but not to end—is not "nothing," nor "is," but "the." The most awkwardly but also the most unavoidably stressed syllable in the line is this "the." Nothing has become a thing and a place like the frost and the boughs, the land and the snow, and it is not abstract, for it is the concrete thing and place of language.

This remark should serve to underscore and develop a point made earlier when commenting upon the middle turn of this poem. To call "the nothing that is" into the poem, and to the reader's mind, is—consistent with the poetic logic of the entire poem—to call the mind away from it. It is to read "the" not as any abstraction or representation except as the verbal presentation of the point where "a mind" abstracts or draws away from the very reading. For if a mind—say, the reader's mind—reads as the poem's listener listens, and comes to see not only nothing that is not there, but also the nothing that is, this means that one sees the nothing as just what "the" in this poem is: nothing that is, and the _____ [the word "the" as a blank or placeholder] that is: bare language. The poem will not end at this point, but counters its point by recalling or echoing all the "the"'s of the poem back to its first word "*The* Snow Man." One might even note that because one does not know how to pronounce the word in question—"thé nothing" or "the nóthing"—the "the" echoes a premorphemic or diphthongic level of the letter across this line and back across the entire poem: "No*th*ing *th*at is not *th*ere and *th*e no*th*ing *th*at is," back to "not to *th*ink." Drawn to the letters, reading can abstract only from itself, from its own customary abstraction.

In two later Stevens poems we can pursue some of the implications for reading that his poetics of last words presents. A Stevensian ending, we have seen on the evidence of "The Snow Man," is not a philosophic aphorism but a poetic word. In turn, a reader does not so much read abstraction as abstract from reading—abstract, that is, from the semantic and interpretive sublation of language into thematic meaning that is otherwise the goal and end of reading to and at the end of another norm (a more narrative norm) of lyric. Such other reading is then, seen from this new perspective, an abstraction, a drawing away from the material of language to its sense. Here, on the contrary, reading abstracts from such abstraction, drawing away from itself as it is drawn to linger upon the words themselves. Their concrete indication and determination was the "the."

"The Man on the Dump" is, like "The Snow Man," another famous Stevens poem, but unlike the earlier one, it is rich to the point of being cluttered; this clutter is in fact a part of its poetics.

A good deal of it may be summarized rapidly. The down and up of the day's and moon's passages, quickly metaphorized as flowers, are sarcastically characterized as so many "poetic" images on the dump. The times, the signs of their passage, poetic garlands, all are like yesterday's newspapers, wrapping garbage. The sarcasm gives way to weariness ("The freshness of night has been fresh a long time") and to indifference of allusion, of comparison, of simile ("it puffs as Cornelius Nepos reads, it puffs / More than, less or it puffs like this or that"). With a return to sarcasm in the scornful repetition of poeticisms around the word "dew," the poem then reaches its first recognizably Stevensian line: "One grows to hate these things except of the dump."

There is here the authoritatively impersonal "one," and the exact denomination of excessive poeticisms as "these things," but what makes this line powerful, and indeed the turning point in the poem, is the word "except." For "to hate these things" is said to be the result of a process ("one grows"), but precisely their being "on the dump"—which is, after all, the process and result of the poem—is what is said to exempt them from hate. And so the end of the line undoes or grants exception from the first part: "one grows to hate these things except on the dump." One is perhaps justified in hearing here a poetic echo of Shakespeare's turn in sonnet 145: "I hate she altered with an end."

Thus, in the middle of the poem, in its "now," the movement is momentarily suspended between "that" and "this," between everything that is on the dump and everything (the same everything) that will be, and this *point de suspension* is already the change marked by the "except" in the previous line. In this point of poetic "now," it is said that "One feels the purifying change. One rejects / The trash." But if this is a decisive, reiterated change, how does the poem continue on the far side of a rejection of its trash dump? It returns to images immediately to undo or to "shed" them: the phrase "the moon comes up as the moon" sheds the preceding image of "the moon creeps up / To the bubbling of bassoons," which itself echoed the poem's beginning on the dump ("The moon is creeping up"). (The moon coming up as the moon also completes the undoing of the poeticisms of the moon begun in "Lunar Paraphrase"'s "The moon is the mother of pathos and pity.") To see an image here is to see its other, image-less, an "as" that would match "the moon" to "the moon," "a man" to "a man." This would be (in what has also been a deft introduction of direct address to the reader, to "you") to "see the moon rise in the empty sky," which would also be, it seems, to see as the snow man does, "in the same bare place." (Compare here as well several lines from "Anatomy of Monotony": "earth grows / The same . . . And over the bare spaces of our skies / She sees a barer sky that does not bend.")

If this is nonetheless still to have an image, it is an image that is neither a poeticism, nor—evidently—a visible one. It is significant that the final stanza turns so dominantly to sound. Its first two lines, perfect pentameters, move from a visual image to the sonorous, alliterative one of rhythmic beating, and also to the apparent abstraction of belief. This is an apparent abstraction because "that which one believes" is immediately qualified as something concrete, spatial, something that one can "get near." A line of insinuated argument is readable in the series of questions that lead to the stanza's ending. This line issues from the internal rhyme of "what one wants to get near" with the threefold "ear," and from the overwhelming aurality of the whole last stanza. "That which one believes" and "what one wants to get near" might be, the question and its internal rhymes suggest, "merely oneself, as superior as the *ear* / To a crow's voice." The sense of "merely oneself" may also be related to "the same bare place" that the snow man's mind attended to, listening to its wind. That is, "oneself" and "the place" are counterparts, the place listened to and beheld in its bareness, oneself seeing the moon in the empty sky, or a man as a man, and approached or neared as such. The intertextual echo of "mere" and "bare," and the semantic resonance between empty and bare, underscore this nexus. "That which one believes," "what one wants to get near," "merely oneself"—these are not, or do not yield, an existential or substantial presence. They are rather, as the three line endings indicate, the ear: what a much later poem ("The Course of a Particular," 1950) calls "the final finding of the ear." The ear opposes itself to the crow, to the Keats-ian romantic nightingale, to the "peevish birds" from which it will not allow itself solace. But to or toward what does it listen?

The ear rejects "the blatter of grackles," just as the poem, with its final dose of sarcasm, implicitly dismisses the murmuring, saying, or crying of poeticisms. In this extremely literary series of questions, alternately cacophonous ("Pack . . . and scratch") and mellifluous ("stanza my stone"), the more one hears, the more one should see. That is, one should see what one hears—one should read—and try to hear in what one reads. One hears and reads the final question: "Where was it one first heard the truth?" Within "where" one may read "here"; within "heard" one may read "hear," visually rhyming with "near" and "ear." The meeting point between seeing the moon as the moon, rising in the empty sky, and nearing the ear to hear the truth, is, as the poem says and ends, "The the." This is the only answer the poem gives, and it is strikingly visual and aural at once: "the" as "the," face to face, and "the" echoing and rhyming "the." But what is this?

Here, at line's end, where one finally reads what the whole stanza has been listening for, one sees "the" as "the": the definite article as itself the subject of itself, reflective and self-reflective of "the truth" to the extent that it irreducibly reflects itself as "sheer language." A claim for "sheer language" here is not Mallarmé's "donner un sens plus pur aux mots de la tribu," nor Benjamin's "reine Sprache."[8] It is, in Stevens' words, empty, bare, mere language that is also full: "Nothing that is not there," in a poem, "and the nothing that is." Rereading the last line of this poem, the "first" hearing of "the truth" does, indeed, occur at the first word one comes upon in the phrase: the "the." The answer reflects the temporality of reading within the question. That it is also the "the"—every "the"—of Stevens' concreteness of language and hearing and vision, may also rush in at this point, "here." Thus "the ear," "the empty sky," "the moon," "The Man on the Dump," "The Snow Man."[9] The concreteness of the point is indisputable; that this is also linguistic—a writing of the linguistic character of "the truth" for Stevens—is also concretely reflected.

Precisely the doubleness of the ending phrase is what will not end. One scarcely knows how to read it, to scan it, and thus one does not—or even cannot—hear it in any one strict sense. It cannot be accented "thé thè," but it could be "thè thé," or "thé thé," or "thè thè." To read this line asking one to hear a "first" something, and to hear that one cannot hear one thing, just as one cannot hear one "the" but always only two and more—the "the" of "the the," of "the truth," and of all the "the"'s before Stevens' things—this is to see hearing, or to read, and above all to read the loss of the sight and site of reading, to read reading reading itself away. "The truth" is no abstraction, but concrete language; it is reading that, in the face of it, withdraws from any other sense.

"A Clear Day and No Memories," one of Stevens' very last poems, echoes and intensifies much of what we have already read in "The Snow Man" and "The Man on the Dump." "A clear day" sounds like an *ear* day, a day just for listening and hearing, without misery, being merely oneself. The poem begins in as strongly negative or privative a way as "The Snow Man" concluded: here, "No Memories," "No soldiers," "No thoughts." The day is being cleared of the past, is focused upon "now," is just "today." The marvelous pairing of the last line of the first stanza and the first line of the second establishes a scene of reflection that, visually and conceptually, is a condensation of the relations between the mind and the bare place in "The Snow Man," between oneself and the empty sky in "The Man on the Dump." In these lines,

Today the mind is not part of the weather.

Today the air is clear of everything.

"Today" reflects itself, above and below, while "the mind," having been parted from the weather, is echoed by "the air" that is cleared of everything in this immaculately clear day.[10] Weather without a mind is a clear day indeed—cleared of everything. The word "everything" subtly recalls the "something" two lines above—a something that might, in the past, have been touched—while a line later, there is not even "nothing" but the abstract "nothingness," given that everything—even a nothing—has been cleared away.

The phrases "except of nothingness" and "without meanings" risk a banality of pseudophilosophic statement, exactly the sort of thing that would give abstraction a bad name. Stevens is actually doing something more nuanced in these two lines. As the mind is not part of the weather, so the weather is not in mind or on the mind: the mind is clear, as when one says one has a clear head or mind. The line "Today the air is clear of everything" thus paradoxically invokes the mind as well as—in contradiction—the air clear of the mind. So, too, in the next line: "It has no knowledge" refers to the air, but does so by continuing or drawing out the incipient personification of the air as if it were a clear mind; at the same time—in contradiction—the phrase may mean that the air, clear of everything, contains or brings no knowledge to the mind before it, except of nothingness; "has" may have this meaning of bearing or bringing. And so, as well, the line "And it flows over us without meanings" allows itself to be understood, because of the presence of the "over us," as speaking both of an air without meanings and a flow over us that is without meanings. In each of these lines, then, a paradoxical shuttle or exchange occurs between air and mind free of one another, and the mind like the air, receiving or feeling its pressure.

There is here not only the explicit phrase "over us" that keeps a human presence in the air; there is also the more subtle but poetically more powerful coimplication of mind in air and air in mind: the mind and the air reflect one another, as they do above and below the divide in the poem. The proto-personification of a phrase like "the air is clear of everything" suggests that a mind cleared of the weather can flow over itself without meanings from the scenery, just as the air cleared of mind—say, memories—can flow "over us" without human meanings. This incessant and unstable exchange—unstable because contradictory—confuses "us" and "it" across two different versions of keeping them apart, and it is this situation that the poem would focus on in its final lines and words. The lines "As if none of us had ever been here before / And are not now" do not so much advance the poem's dilemma as restate it. The "as if" about our past nonexistence repeats the "no memories" of the first three lines; the "as if" of our present nonexistence continues the claim of an air "clear of everything." But the poem's series of strong negations—"No memories," "No soldiers," "No thoughts," "not part," "no knowledge"—appears here under the sign of "as if," and the specific negation of "And are not now" is not only a fiction, an "as if," but the impossible fiction of "not now" now, just as impossible as a "none of us" following directly below the phrase "flows over us."

The fiction is an impossible one because a fiction can tell any story except of its nonreading. (The graffiti Jacques Derrida has told of—"Do not read this!"—is the exemplary teaching of this lesson.) This poem can, as a capstone to Stevens' career, tell the story of thoughts about nothing, of a mind without memories, of an air clear of everything, of knowledge only of nothingness. But the representation of a meaningless flow over us who "now" would not be here (or there) is a limit both for fiction and for reading.[11] For fiction, it attempts to represent absence by representing not first its representation, but rather its meaningless reading: a flow of lines over a reader. For reading, the "we" who are here "now," reading, appear as the meaning of, and on the far side of, the attempt to represent "our" absence. The fiction of the "as if"—absence, meaninglessness—means the presence of reading. As a representation, the closing lines of the poem similarly do not close. They represent, within the thematics of the poem and those of much of Stevens' career, the abstraction of pathos from a landscape or place, of memories from a mind, of a world of things from a mind full of ideas: all this is represented in an adjective like "shallow," which but for its pathos would line up with the series "bare," "empty," "merely," and "clear." It is when one stumbles over this slight contradiction of a pathetic sense to "shallow spectacle" that would run counter to the current of the entire poem that one realizes one is still not yet reading Stevens à la lettre. For on the far side of the attempted representation of a world of scenery and weather and air without "us" is the actual presentation—present, "now"—of reading.

The phrase "in this shallow spectacle" is neither pejorative nor pathos-laden, but very precise. Like the lines in "The Fall of Hyperion" that we glanced at in the Keats chapter—"a square-edg'd polish'd stone, / That in its lucid depth reflected pure" (canto II, ll. 51, 52)—this phrase of Stevens' has a lucid depth and pure reflection in its "shallow spectacle." The "spectacle" reflects, specularly, the "we" who are reading their presentation in the (impossible) representation of the "us" who "are not now [here]." The "shallow" is the precise measurement of a language that is read, and confused with nothing else—"no memories," "no soldiers," "no thoughts of people now dead"—confused, in other words, with no dimensions or volume of a world. For what is the volume of language on the page of a volume of poetry? As "this shallow spectacle" gives way to "This invisible activity," the spectacle of reading reading becomes even more precise, for while one can see readers—in the "flows over us," for example, or in the hands on the edges of the book before our eyes—one cannot, strictly speaking, see reading: it is "this invisible activity," itself nonvisible, and an activity that renders invisible.

The repetitions of the locative pronoun "this" keep the meaning and the reading focused on the very lines and words. Ultimately, the reader of Stevens has come from "the nothing" to "the the" to this "this . . . this . . . this . . ." What is "this"? "This" at the end of a thirteen-line nonsonnet reads, and in so reading recalls for its reader, the famous "this" in two Shakespeare sonnets that themselves, like Stevens' poem here, turn deictics into the self-reflection of language: "But thy eternal summer shall not fade, / . . . When in eternal lines to time thou grow'st. / So long as men can breathe or eyes can see, / So long lives this, and this gives life to thee." (no. 18); and "The worth of that is that which it contains, / And that is this and this with thee remains." (no. 74). "This" in its last word in this poem is "this sense." In a late poem such as "An Old Man Asleep," Stevens could conflate "[t]he two worlds [that] are asleep, are sleeping, now" ("The self and the earth," in the poem) into a single occasion for a single "sense"—"A dumb sense possesses them in a kind of solemnity"—and then give the reader explicit directions for parsing out the self's sense as meaning ("your thoughts, your feelings, / Your beliefs and disbeliefs, your whole peculiar plot"), the earth's sense as mere being. In the much greater "The Ultimate Poem Is Abstract," Stevens splays these two meanings apart in order to have them come together again, in the penultimate and then ultimate lines: "enough to be / Complete because at the middle, if only in sense, / And in that enormous sense, merely enjoy." In the way in which this second use of "sense" allows what it resists to overtake and retake the sheer sensuousness of the first use—"Knowledge enormous makes a God of me." (*Hyperion*, III, 113)—Stevens not only recalls Keats's great intellect beyond his great sensuality, but also edges over to Hegel's lesson. Sense is meaning, sense is the material level and letter of the meaning; it is, in Hegel's famous formulation, the essential (*das Wesentliche*) and the outward, the exterior (*das Äusserliche*).[12] Reading "this," reading both this shallow spectacle (of reading) and this invisible activity (of reading) is reading "this sense" of reading suspended between letter and meaning—sense and sense—like a Stevens poem suspended between mind and air, one's ear and the empty sky, man and snow. It is to read this poem, this poet's poetic technique, as examples of how lyric poems can end without ending reading and of how reading can read everything except its making an end of its sense.

8

Scrolls, Projectiles, and Plunges;
Endings, Rejections, and Collections

Three Celan Poems

Paul Celan's poetry stands not only at the end of this book on poetic ending, but at the end of Western poetry. By this I do not mean something so fatuous and stupid as the claim that there can be no poetry after Celan. Celan's own example caused Adorno to revise his famous (and fatuous) claim that to write poetry after Auschwitz is barbaric, and of course poetry goes on in the quarter-century since Celan's death. I mean rather that Celan's poetry exists as the heir to the entire Western lyric tradition, and it is difficult to imagine a poet more resourceful, more full of resources, in this inheritance. Perhaps only Derek Walcott will one day appear as rich: Walcott and Celan share a command of the classical and Judeo-Christian traditions, although Celan's grasp of continental European poetry and Western philosophy makes his oeuvre a deeper and wider vein than that of any other poet of our half of this century.

I recall Celan's poetically rich importance here because it

Vincent van Gogh, *Wheatfield with Crows*. (Van Gogh Museum, Amsterdam [Vincent van Gogh Foundation])

presents his reader with a double challenge. As much as with Hölderlin, Baudelaire, or Stevens, to choose one, two, or three poems for extended examination is to confront a surplus of possibilities and a conflict of interests, tastes, and pleasures. Celan is varied in his excellence, and no small selection may "stand" for his achievements, including his achievements of poetic ending. The second side of the challenge to reading in the face of such multiple variety is one of economy. Celan's poetry is so dense and intricate in allusion and poetic technique, and so original in its uses of the German language's semantic, syntactic, and grammatical resources—in these respects only Hölderlin is his peer—that the analysis, understanding, and appreciation of individual poems becomes a struggle of measure, of *Mass*, as well as of pace. There are furthermore no easy indices to guide one's choices: the work does not get demonstrably better or worse, easier or more difficult, across the decades or the volumes of verse, and Celan's very short poems—and many of them are very short indeed—can be as long in interest and reward as his several long ones.

Any choice of three Celan poems for an examination of their directions for reading toward and for their poetic ends must be, then, an arbitrary selection. Celan is meticulous in his attention to and respect for his reader; the guidance his poems give can sometimes appear overwhelming, but it is never missing, and nothing could be further from the mark than to accuse the texts of being hermetic. His longest poem, "Engführung," speaks of guidance (*Führung*) already in the title, and the entire poem is an exercise in the reader's being led literally by the hands and fingers. In their incessantly discursive character—addressing, conversing, questioning, directing—with the corresponding engagement of an "I" with a "you" and a "we," even the briefest, densest, and apparently most private lyrics open out to their audiences (think of "Du warst," for example). The present reading of three poems from Celan tries to respect the dilemma of his rich oeuvre and our need for economy by avoiding the longest texts. And in the face of his particular strengths as a poet who directs his readers to his ends, it treats two poems (mid- and late-career, more or less) in which the I-you exchange is especially intense and productive, and one in which it is entirely mute without its for that reason being absent, and where instead all the directions for reading are with respect to a painting, Van Gogh's "Wheatfield with Crows," that the poem imagines before its reader's eyes as she or he reads. The thematics and the formal and structural determinants of these three poems will recall classical ekphrasis and baroque emblematics, Judeo-Christian apocalypse and non-Christian drowning, flights and descents of such variety, that we will, by and with the endings of these last poems, have looped back across much of the Western poetic tradition and returned to both its sources and its theoretical consequences.

ə♠

when the light of sense / Goes out
—Wordsworth, *The Prelude*

Celan's poem "Unter ein Bild" (I, 155),[1] an ekphrasis—the verbal representation of a visual work of art—of Van Gogh's "Wheatfield with Crows" appeals, as such an ekphrasis, at once to last works—the painting is thought to be one of Van Gogh's last, if not *the* last—and to first: in the founding work of our Western literary tradition, Homer's *Iliad*, the famous ekphrasis of the shield of Achilles (Book 18) introduces not only the subtradition of ekphrastic writing, but in the same gesture the cosmic reach of Western art—for the literary representation of the imagined shield's visual representation portrays a concentrically and cosmically ordered series of worlds—and the representational device of the *mise-en-abîme* (for the representations on the shield re-present in miniature the whole of the story of the text, the *Iliad*, which contains them). I recall these founding features of Western ekphrasis here because Celan's ekphrasis is, for all its brevity, no less grand in its reach and scope. All of four verses long, "Unter ein Bild"'s title should be treated as a fifth, or first, line, for it both sets up and as quickly upsets the specific convention of ekphrastic writing that the poem employs. This is the convention of the *emblem*, especially popular during the baroque period, in which a visual image is combined with its (literally and visually subordinate) verbal naming, elaboration, commentary—its verbal re-presentation—according to several regular steps.[2] The image comes first (known as the *pictura*), followed by the title or sometimes a motto (the *inscriptio*), followed in turn by a caption—or sometimes the motto in this position (the *subscriptio*); the visual part of the emblem was also known as its *cor*, the verbal part as its *anima*.

Celan's title invokes two aspects of this emblem structure: the image (*Bild*) above, the text "under" (*Unter*). (We are to imagine a reproduction of Van Gogh's painting before the reader as she or he reads the poem, or Celan before the painting itself, now in Amsterdam's Van Gogh Museum.) But just as quickly, he alters this convention. For if the poem is literally *under* the painting with respect to conventional location as well as subordinated status, it is not literally, that is, grammatically *located under* or beneath the image because "Unter ein Bild" is in the accusative case, not the dative. The title, in other words, is not referential or re-presentational with regard to the visual object "before" (or above) it, but introductory and self-referential to and self-presentational of the text that is indeed still discursively and conspicuously *under* the image (for if it was just discursively "about" the object, it would be "über ein Bild," also in the accusative). In terms of the emblem structure, the first line of text—the *inscriptio*—indicates or introduces the *subscriptio*, the actual four-line poem that follows underneath (*sub*). The title above, called "Unter ein Bild," is actively (accusatively) *going* under; we might even imagine it rolling or curling under.

The poem's first line, a single phrase, a single pair of two compound words, represents the Van Gogh painting's image with utmost economy, precision, and evocativeness: "Rabenüberschwärmte Weizenwoge." ("Raven-overswarmed wheat-wave."). Like the title in an emblem, this line names the image's name—borrowing the key words of the birds and the wheat from *its* title—and so helps entitle the following text and its representations. (Let us not quibble over the ravens and the crows, remembering that the title does not come from Van Gogh.) The words are specifically literal and referential with respect to the middle of the painting. The shape of the wheatfield is a wave, in the picture as in our colloquial phrases ("amber waves of grain"), and the birds swarm over or above it. The prepositional prefix *über* does further and specific work, however—unsurprisingly, given the contrasting signal already given by the title's "Unter." As the first line directs our gaze at the painting (or recalls it to the mind's eye by name), its *über* re-presents two dimensions—the two-dimensionality of the painting itself, its horizontal and vertical Cartesian coordinates—that in turn yield or represent three dimensions, the three dimensions of perspectival and spatial reality. That is, above and below (*über* and *unter*) indicate as well the third dimension of depth, as in any employment of perspective, and in the Van Gogh painting specifically, the *über* names the visual, highly palpable sense in which the paint that represents the birds is on top of that representing the wheat (which is underneath, below), so that the word doubles and splits, to indicate both a two-dimensional version of the painting as a visual art object (a rectangle of verticals and horizontals) representing a three-dimensional scene, *and* a three-dimensional version of the same painting (its above and below with respect to higher and lower in the rectangle, *and* its on-top-of and beneath with respect to the depth and texture of the paint on the canvas). There are thus two three-dimensional "overs" in the line's version of the painting: the above that represents perspectivally representational depth—the birds above and also, painted variously large and small, in the foreground and background, the spatial depth, with respect to the wave of wheat—and the above that names the materiality of the painting's own (nonrepresentational) three-dimensionality of canvas, paint, and paint on top of paint. The implying or enfolding of the image's materiality in the *über* points, then, directly to its other, that is, *textual* materiality.

For by seeing—by means of reading—that *über* refers, splits and doubles, and re-presents as such, the entire line (all of its two words) becomes multiply and materially dimensional as well. It is, considered graphically, a two-dimensional line, more long than high, which furthermore tends, in the very term and image "line" (as in the German *Zeile*), toward unidimensionality. So, too, in its semantic representation, for if it performs an initial and highly effective reduction of the image to two dimensions (ravens and wheat, above and below), then the determinant is one dimension—the line or horizontal, roughly in the middle—that "divides" the painting into its two main halves, above and below. But the *über* in the line contravenes any unidimensionality, the *schwärmte* indicates a disorganized dynamism that similarly moves above and below, and back and forth, from any one determinant,[3] and once such up-and-down and back-and-forth motion is introduced by *schwärmte,* then *woge* doubles and redoubles it, for waves move circularly, not going down without another part going up, not going forward without another part going backward. The thin line becomes thick, wide, and deep indeed. It is even the case that this thickening of the thin can be traced in the line's sonority and its representations. After the variety in the vowels and consonants in *Rabenüberschwärmte,* the alliteration of *Weizenwoge* indicates a thinning out of the line, but semantically the same sound-pattern suggests the two dimensions of undulation, and the three dimensions of solid upon liquid sounds.

This far, the title and first line of the poem have each been doubly referential and representational: referential and representational of the Van Gogh image they are "under," subordinate to, and about; self-referential and self-presentational in their going under the image to their own self-sighting and self-siting, directing the reader to their own readability and locating or positing themselves as verbal and graphic images in their own right. Literally about the painting, they are also figuratively (in the tropological, and not the painterly sense of this term) about their inscription in and submission to the emblem's structure of figurative or allegorical meanings derived from a visual image—here, the figuration of self-referentiality in the process of the literal ekphrasis. This doubleness then continues and in fact raises itself to self-conscious address and interrogation in the following line: "Welchen Himmels Blau? Des untern? Obern?" ("Which sky's blue? The lower? The upper?").

Wholly interrogative, the line also posits; undeniably and indelibly positing and representing the painting, the same line questions its very priority. Undeniably the line is literal with reference to the presence of darker and lighter blues in the Van Gogh painting, and it invokes both the thematics of mood and tone in this as in many of his paintings—darks that may be troubled in one manner, lights that may be dazzling and disturbing in their brightness in another manner—as well as a painterly convention according to which a darker sky may be situated lower and thus as if farther away, representing either an already rapidly departing storm or an already rapidly arriving one. Let us further acknowledge—with, if only momentarily, Stevens' "To be blue, / There must be no questions"—that for a line to name "blue" is indelibly to name the world of color, be this the world of a painting's colors or its representations of the colors of the real world with its real sky. But positing and interrogating the doubleness of blues and, in Celan's version, the doubleness of skies, of heavens (the same word, *Himmel,* in German) in Van Gogh's painting, also continues and even reinjects the under/over structure of the title and the first verse: in fact, it reinjects it in its concentrated form, this being the one line that names the full pair of "under" and "over" that had previously been divided—by inversion—between the first two "lines," "under" (*Unter*) in the upper position, "over" (*über*) in the under position. If one can be directed to look up into the upper half of Van Gogh's image and see *two* skies or heavens, one of which is *under* the other, then quite literally the sky is falling: to look up toward the source of light can be to descend into darkness; to rise into darkness is to fall. The structural inversion of the title and first verse—upper line naming "under," lower line naming "over"—is as such sustained in this verse: the lower (the sky and its sky-blue) might be the upper (question mark), or in turn (inversion), might it be the lower after all (after the return or reinversion)? The distinctions and inversions of the title and first line are rolling into one another in this one.

When it is seen—and this is as it, the line, is read—that the verse repeats and unfolds the bobbing up and down, the double motion of the previous lines' under and over and the immediately preceding one's undulation, such a focus on the line allows it to reclaim the very name and claim of "blue." "Which sky's blue?", indeed. The "lower" one is quite literally the "under" line's "sky," underlying an "upper" one that, from the title onward, the poem was going *under*. Underlying the blue "above," in the Van Gogh painting or its reproduction or its locus in the emblem structure, is this line that says "blue," and thus allows blue or blueness to be two places at once, doubled and split, painted and said, over and under—seen and read. To read "blue" is not to see it (we see black on white in reading *Blau* or "blue"), to read *Himmel* is not to see a sky or a heaven; they are as decisively separated as the bipolar opposition of "under" and "over," even as the line and the poem also render the dimensions invertible, revolvable, enfolded, and as such inseparable. The "blue" of the under-line's "sky" refers to the "blue" of the upper-image's "sky," after all, even as it self-referentially names itself in its difference. "Under" refers to and revolves toward "over," even as the line posits and interrogates their difference.

The poem's next line, its penultimate one, appears to multiply its doubled references to a painting literally before one and to another level of meaning "below" or "above." "Später Pfeil, der von der Seele schnellte." ("Later arrow, that sped from the soul."). With reference to the Van Gogh painting, the single line is doubled, doubly representational. On the one hand, it delineates something visible in the image, the path that cuts diagonally (in a slight zigzag, more vertically than horizontally) through the wheatfields and terminates, or rather disappears, at the horizon: this may be designated as a vector, and thus, imagistically, as an arrow. On the other hand, it abstracts from the specifics of the image and speaks about it as allegorizable but still with its literal determinants: as a late (very late) work, issuing from Van Gogh's troubled and avowedly spiritual interiority, the painting is in this line *visualized as*—allegorized as the literal image of—a "later arrow"

"speeding" (we know of his speed of execution) from his "soul."
Two levels of representation, we may say, emerge in this one line
about the one image—what it might look like (or be seen as), and
what it might mean (or be "seen" as).

But if this reading of the line has it pointing unilinearly from
itself to the image and the image's maker's life—and we observe
that this is the first line that does not double matters with "below"
and "above"—the line nonetheless comes back (turns around,
curves or reverses direction, boomerang-like) when we inquire
after the "arrow." There is, in other words, an implicit doubling of
matters with respect to "later" and "earlier." For in the first sense
of the arrow—referring to and representing the painting's path
as a vector, an "arrow"—it flies away from the viewer, with its
"point" being the perspectivally narrowed path as it nears the horizon. But in its other sense—referring to the entire painting issuing from Van Gogh's "soul"—the painting must be there before
the viewer, having been "sent" (having "sped") there *from* the
painter: the vector points and the arrow flies in the opposite direction, *toward* the viewer. The one "literal," representational
sense (a vector points away from the viewer) can only be seen by
way of the other "allegorical," but still-representational sense that
would found and be the source (the "soul"-source whence the
"arrow"-painting "sped") of the literal view of the image and its
path-vector, but the second sense inverts the former into the latter—for to be its source, the "later" version must come earlier.

And seeing this representational doubleness turn and revolve
upon and invert itself is predicated upon *reading* the line as the
doubled, that is, allegorical re-presentation of the literal (the
image, the visual or visualizable, the shapes on the painting) that
has an underlying or overarching, more fundamental or higher
meaning (the painting in an artist's creative life and struggle). If
the painting as an arrow must have sped and come to the viewer
from the painter's soul, the line similarly points and directs and
comes to the reader—we are its direction, its directionality—who
is then, and yet from the first, the point of departure for its entire
meaning: the reader is the source of the "later arrow" that issues
from his (or her) perspective, his viewing, his "reading" or inter-
preting of the image and painting, "Wheatfield with Crows," by

Vincent van Gogh. He or she—Celan the viewer, and any of his readers—projects back out and up from the interiority of a viewing mind or "soul." This is also the projection back up, to the literal picture or image or *cor* of the emblem, from its allegorical *anima* or "soul."

The most imagistic line so far, also the one most imaginatively and allegorically abstracting from the literal determinants of representations in the painting and paint on its canvas, has shown itself to be—has directed its reading toward—a revolution into its self-referentiality as the very condition of possibility and point of departure for its ekphrastic representations. We must read ourselves seeing the painting—and this means we must also read ourselves reading—in order to see it as the reversal of the directionality of that reading: we must read the arrow having come to us before we can see it having sped from Van Gogh's soul. This is the tropological structure of hysteron proteron, "the last before the first."[4] The next and last line continues and even heightens the imagistic and allegorical imaginativeness of the preceding one, while it returns to the poem's explicit structure of doubleness and further unfolds as well as enfolds the emerging structure of the hysteron proteron, the last before the first.

"Stärkres Schwirren. Näh'res Glühen. Beide Welten." ("Stronger whizzing. Nearer glowing. Both worlds."). The line recalls, symmetrically, the second verse's division into three utterances, but here each is assertive, not interrogative. I continue as I have with each line, inquiring first into its literal, representational-ekphrastic sense with regard to the Van Gogh image. Here less is certain than ever. The "stronger whizzing" may represent the comparatively stronger—with reference to the "arrow from the soul"—whirling and swarming of the birds. The "nearer glowing" may represent the blaze of glowing gold color, "nearer" in the foreground of the picture, which is apparently a splay of wheat or such that looks as if it might like to be a Van Gogh sunflower. The "both worlds," most banally in their repetition of reference to doubleness, would represent the plays and, more significantly, the *combinations* of foreground *and* background, sky *and* earth, which the painting achieves.

As faithful a closing commentary, a well-rounded ekphrasis,

as such a version of the last line would be vis-à-vis its brilliant art-object, it is too banal and scarcely begins to read the line itself. For the first important word to read is *schwirren*. We will marshal much of the textual evidence regarding this word in Celan's oeuvre when I turn to the analysis of his poem "Aber." Here I simply note first that *schwirren* is always aural, and one can't paint sound. Furthermore, *schwirren* means a limit of visibility, as velocity overcomes stable sight and is supplemented by the whirring, buzzing sound of flying objects. Finally—and here one must accept the generalization drawn from Celan's oeuvre, some examples of which will be presented below for the poem "Aber"—*schwirren* in Celan brings with it the sound and velocity, the mark, the *inscription* (the blasting or boring in) of language and its letters. The last claim is in the case of "Unter ein Bild" motivated or justified by the first two: if *schwirren* as sound cannot be painted, and if it also marks the limit of visibility, and as such another limit to painting, then the *schwirren* here must be the whizzing and buzzing of language—Celan's language, his words on the page of "Unter ein Bild." This also explains the comparative "stronger," for the swarming ravens, however much they might caw and swirl, are still highly paintable, fixed on the canvas in their minimalist, "checkmark" fashion, while the "stronger whizzing" is to be looked for not in the literal reference to visual representation "above," in the image, but in the self-referential presentation "under" the image, in its *inscriptio* and *subscriptio*. There, in writing, we understand the re-presentation of sound that cannot be painted, and the limit of visibility that can be seen but only as the sight and site of the overcoming of vision and visual representation into reading and its other, nonreferential, nonrepresentational modes of meaning.

Once the comparative of "stronger" is associated with Celan's writing, "under the image" or on its near side, then the companion comparative "nearer" makes self-referential sense as well. It also, as part of the second phrase, advances upon and goes beyond the first phrase, for "Stärkres Schwirren" still marked a linkage of sound and sight and a *limit* or threshold of visibility—still visible as a blur—while "Näh'res Glühen" makes its way beyond both. In *Näh'res*, the contraction, marked with the apostrophe, is its distinctive feature, and the written and readable punctuation mark cannot be sounded—voiced or heard—as making any of the difference it does as written or read. *Näh'res* sounds exactly like *Näheres*, but *Näheres* is not written or read as *Näh'res*. In other words, the mark marks the limit, the divide, and the leave-taking between writing as sensuous re-presentation—of the visible, of sound, of their possible linkage in birds flying or arrows whizzing—and writing as a means of presentation that is only readable at and beyond the limit of its visibility: the same threshold on which we saw and then read Hölderlin's "Hälfte des Lebens" and "Andenken," Baudelaire's "A une passante," Stevens' "A Clear Day and No Memories." To see the apostrophe is not to see or hear the missing *e*—one can't hear the difference anyway—but to see the mark as the *cut*, the *contraction* as *omission*, between the audible and visible world on one side, and the readable one on the other. This mark without sound, this sight and site without anything represented there except a cut, an omission, a lack—this is the sign of the writing of the limit of the readable.

We are, at this point or mark, reading what *isn't* there, or is there no longer: the image, an image. Just as it was tempting to try to read, to "see" and to hear, *Näh'res* as showing or displaying its missing *e*—when, of course, the middle *e* is nowhere to be seen and impossible to hear missing—it is perhaps still tempting to try to read Celan's writing "under the image" as still referring up to and re-presenting the image above. Specifically, this would mean the temptation of "seeing" the centered cut in *Näh'res*—which is also roughly in the metrical middle of the line—in, and therefore taking a representational value from the priority of the visual in, Van Gogh's painting. Is there not a centered cut on the line of the horizon, roughly in the middle, where the path—the "arrow"—has disappeared, but a cut in the wheatfields still marks its disappearance? Or are we then "seeing things," and in the realm of the invisible and the unreasonable—or the ghostily returning, the revenant—altogether? Instead of "seeing" what is not there, and may not even be marked as such, we do better to *read* what is there, in a quintessential Celanian bilingual pun: *Näh'res, näh res, ne res,* no thing, nothing.

Which explains the *Glühen*. It is a glowing that takes away things, that renders invisible, that destroys. In a word, it is apocalyptic. On the near side of "Under an Image," the image that "came first" is gone, and in the writing that survives, first as the mark of the cutting-off and -away, then as the sight and site of a burning, "both worlds" both stand written and stand consumed. Written as the end of the poem and the end of the world, the end of words referring and deferring to the visible world of things and their images, and the end (the goal, the terminus) of words readable—to their limit of unreadability—as meaning the *in*visibility of their presentations and their meanings.

This is how "both worlds" would stand written: one world is the world of the painting, of images of the visual world, once "above" and now glowing in its disappearance, its consumption by apocalyptic fire; the other world is the world of the poem, its writing, glowing with its apocalyptic message and meaning. But to read the second world this way is to not yet fully read its unfolding and enfolding, is not to read its own autoconsumption, its glowing and burning away. Whence my remark about the limit of unreadability in the preceding paragraph. For if the "other," "lower" world of script, "under" the now proscribed and banished image, really means apocalypse and the invisibility of its meaning, its own end and goal cannot be its own visibility and hence readability, but rather its ending in its own inscrutability. The text that ends the world ends itself as a text: they all fold up their tents and go away together, "both worlds." Text and picture, the poem "Under an Image" and the image of any and all worlds, folded and rolled up upon one another.

This is the image—but a specifically textual and scriptural image—of apocalypse: how it ends, according to the Book. "Tout, au monde, existe pour aboutir à un livre."[5] In the Old Testament, Isaiah 34:4, *Et complicabuntur sicut liber caeli:* "And the heavens shall be folded together as a scroll" (as *liber* has been understood). In the New Testament, Revelation 6:14, *Et caelum recessit sicut liber involutus:* "And the heaven departed as a scroll when it is rolled together." The poem's ending, as a writing of apocalypse under the sign of the heavens' and the heaven's rolling-up—whence my conviction that Celan's plural "Welchen Himmels Blau?" justifies the allusion to both Old and New Testament versions of the apocalypse—leaves itself, rolled back *up,* under a different image: that of the world of images enfolded into a script and a scroll readable only on the far side of man and world. The ending of the poem returns to and is enfolded in, looped and tongued into, its beginning, its title, as it "begins" with its end—hysteron proteron—"under the image" not of Van Gogh's painting but of Scripture's scroll.

The reversibility of end and beginning, one kind of imagery (painting, the visual, the world) burned away and another kind of imagery (the scroll of divine writing as the limit of human readability and unreadability) appearing at the beginning and end—the apocalypse—of its significance, enfolds within it and has been unfolded across the poem's structure of the emblem, with its literal image and its allegorical inscription and meaning. So, too, it has been uncovered across the steps and reversals of literal reference or representation and allegorical self-reference, themselves two models of poetic language vis-à-vis the world. Language might seek to "cover" the world referentially: to "map" it, as eyesight scans what's there and painting can try to represent it. But in allegory, such "covering" is *not* seeing, but is rather a blocking that must itself be covered, blocked, rolled up, or burned away. It is the persistent and teleological seeing of the literal image that is both covered or blocked and burned away and overcome in the uncovering, discovering, or revealing of the allegorical: in this case, the canvas of the image rolled up by the lines of the poem to become the scroll and sign of apocalypse.

The structure of the poem "Unter ein Bild," to summarize schematically then, is that "under" means first that the image is above and the text is under, then that the text below or under rolls up, covers the previously covering or upper part, and thus discovers or reveals the allegory of the apocalyptic loss of the visible world and the discovering of the scroll "under the image." The loop of reversibility of under and over, end and beginning, "both worlds," sky/heaven and scroll—which is the structure of the hysteron proteron, the last (the apocalypse) before the first (the title of the poem)—is ultimately the reversibility of letter and spirit, the emblem's *cor* and *anima*, to the limit of their unreadability. The writing that directs its reader under an image means that the poem's letters assert their meaning over the image, which means

that the poem's spirit takes precedence over, but only after, its letter, because the letters, as the poem now rolled up as a scroll, are
readable only as and by spirit, by no reader in this world at all. The
poem "Unter ein Bild" is eminently, immaculately readable—to
the limit that its ending and its beginning, all rolled up and enfolded together, spell out the message of an ending we cannot
read, and a beginning we therefore cannot be present at.

ᔓ

The image and structure of the scroll of heavens rolling up
and inverting the relations of heaven (once encompassing, now
contained) and earth (once the guarantor of representation and
reference, now unreal) is rarely—with exceptions[6]—associated
with the lyric genre, let alone with a lyric as short as "Unter ein
Bild," although an inversion of skyward and earthbound, which
also inverts ground into groundlessness, is famously associated
with Celan.[7] The inversion of earth toward heaven is rather—albeit usually in a highly diluted, conventionalized, anti-apocalyptic
mode—an image of an infrastructure of narrative par excellence
with its recuperative closure and transforming retrospection—
turning character into authorial-narratorial possession, story into
meaning and understanding—and as such it is particularly suited
to the long and ambitious narrative forms of epic, conversion autobiography, philosophic Bildungsroman, and novel. Dante's *Commedia* mixes and combines several of these narrative forms and, we
may note in passing—and in anticipation of an afterword—its
Paradiso is perhaps the principal instance for the nonlyric backdrop against which Celan's startling allegorical ekphrasis plays
out its lyric counterpoint to the allegorical-eschatological tradition.[8]

The example of Dante must also be recalled, as he was for
Leopardi, as part of the backdrop and context for the other two
Celan poems we now turn to. In these poems, however, the images
and figures at work are as familiar to the lyric tradition as they are,
broadly and commonly, to Western literature per se. In our Western tradition a sea voyage and an aerial flight have always been
privileged occasions for and images of the poetic act. Ulysses' return to Ithaca closes the circle of the cycle of the Homeric epics

that began with the Greeks' voyage to Troy, and Aeneas's voyage to Latium carries the epic tradition from one shore to another, from one city and culture—now fallen—to another, newly founded. The successful flight of a javelin, the victorious speed of a charioteer likened to wings' flight, the boy's winning dash to wings of glory, the success of one wrestler throwing another, and the corresponding flights of the Muses' arrows, are all celebrated in Pindar's victory odes (Olympian 1, 9, 13, and 14, Pythian 8, Nemean 7); and a story of harm and death is often transformed in Ovid's *Metamorphoses* into an afterlife of survival in the form of a bird's flight: Alycone's kingfisher, Philomela's nightingale, Procne's swallow. Just as the completed sea voyage as an object of representation is also already, in the ancient epic, an image of the poem's successful closure or continuation, so the trajectory of a flight—or the sheer capacity for one—may, in its poetic representation or celebration, attract and reflect the image of the poetry's effort to hit its mark in one case, to rise above its terrestrial material in another. Pindar's odes repeatedly bring the arcs of their praise to explicit approximation of and mimicry with the flights they celebrate, and Ovid's tale of the flight of Daedalus and Icarus may, in telling of Icarus's fall, also reflect in its own narrative afterlife the *ars ignota* that Daedalus's equipping of man with feathers represents. Arrows flying through the air are feathered objects, and men with feathers may try to fly, but men with the feathered objects that are (or were) pens turn the former into poems and thereby themselves into poets. If this is already implicit in Ovid's several tales of the feathered survivor who figures for the poetic rendering and preservation of its own transformation, then it is explicit in Dante's repeated association of the feathers of his poetic flight with the feather of his writing pen (*penna, penne*). So, too, Dante's repeated linking of a sailing vessel with the progress of his poem recalls and reaffirms the ancient epic's traditional doubling of the object of representation with the image of the means or vehicle of that representation.

But with Dante (again, if not already with Ovid)—and as we noted in our discussion of Leopardi's "L'Infinito"—the poetic sea voyage begins after a shipwreck that Dante-pilgrim survives in *Inferno* I. Sea voyages risk shipwreck short of their successful sailing into port; in the case of the *Commedia,* the successful voyage of Dante-pilgrim and of the poem is predicated upon that initial shipwreck and failure, and its overcoming or survival. Similarly, aerial flights may fail (like Icarus's), but these, too, may—as with Ovid's tale—be converted into their successful poetic afterlife and achievement. A flight that does not attain its goal may be memorialized in a poem, and become the occasion for celebrating the poetry that does attain *its* goal, its flight of narration and commemoration; and a shipwreck survived may, with its pathos of risk and overcoming, empower a poetics of survival and even, as with Dante, one of baptism and resurrection.

What I have just briefly sketched here in elementary literary-historical and thematic terms may be recharacterized in equally basic structural terms, and with this we will be coming closer to Celan's poems. In the Western tradition certain kinds of poems have told of the trajectories of objects (ships, javelins) toward their goals, and the poems' narrative paths and formal structures have embodied the voyages and flights from departure, through uncertain suspension or sure speed, to arrival, such that the representation of the object in motion is at once the image of the poetry of that representation. Within these kinds of poetry there are subsets that entail a shipwreck of the attempted voyage or the fall or missed target of the object flying through the air. In the latter cases, the apparently negative features of wreckage, drowning, fall, or failure can in fact be recuperated within the dimension of the poetry's representation—its achievement and, indeed, its very existence. A shipwreck risks a drowning, and hopes or aims at its survival, even as the sinking ship aims downward; but a *poetry* of shipwreck and drowning, given its "Archimedean" position beside or after the event, is conditioned from the very beginning on a poetics of survival. For there to be a poetry of shipwreck and drowning, the event(s) must both occur (be represented as occurring or having occurred) and be negated, undone, overcome —sublated—in the survival and afterlife that is the poem on the far side of the wreckage and the watery death. So, too, an object in flight may or may not attain its goal (a target or a safe landing), but a poem of flight may in either case end with a poetic achievement. In fact, the poem of a flight's failure will be able to redeem—or preserve, cancel, and elevate, that is, *sublate*—the failure in a successful trajectory from intention to goal, from beginning to end, from represented events to their continuity within a poetic afterlife, even if this be one of mourning or lamentation. The missing or failed is in such cases still written, measured, and read by the standard of the flight and goal achieved. At least since Dante (to return to literary history), shipwreck and drowning have been the conditions—not so much the risks, as the conditions of possibility—of a higher, that is, revived and redeemed poetry; to recall the words of one of his closest successors, "E il naufragar m'è dolce in questo mare" (Leopardi, "L'Infinito"). And at least since Ovid, a poetry of failed flight can be and indeed has been read as the celebratory achievement of the poem's arc and mark.

As summary and naïvely unproblematic as these introductory remarks have, for heuristic purposes, been made to appear here, they have been necessary to set the background for the analysis of two Celan poems which, in their semantics, their poetics, and their hermeneutics, emerge and depart from the Western literary tradition's poetry of shipwreck and failed flight. Celan's poetry is everywhere, it is well known, a poetry of survival and afterlife, but scarcely anywhere—"Einmal" would be among the small number of ambivalent exceptions, perhaps (so its title) the only exception—one of redemption or salvation. Shipwreck and drowning—within the poetry, not to speak of the life—are not something undergone in order to be undone and overcome, but something beneath and within which the poem comes to construct itself and the terms of its understanding: paradoxically, Celan's poetry of shipwreck survives not a drowning (that is, survives not after or on the far side of a drowning) but by and in and beneath the wreckage and the watery immersion. His poetry of the flying object neither celebrates successful flights nor mourns their misses, but is conditioned upon a missed mark and missing moment such that the poem does not move along a trajectory from beginning to goal and end, but loops elliptically between approach and return, flight outward and deviation back toward but not to the departure; it is what I shall call a poetics of the "double miss." The poetry and poetics of Celan's texts of shipwreck and flight, as much as they turn from and break with the dominant Western (postclassical, post-Dantesque, Christian) models and traditions, in turn confront their readers with the poetological and hermeneutic events of shipwreck and deviation. How to read these poems becomes the question of knowing where and how a text and a reading may end when they will not stop sinking or missing.

There exist in Celan's oeuvre clusters of poems, the imagery, motifs, and narratives of which concern shipwrecks and flights that miss their mark, or find it only strangely and by deviation. Although, as a practical matter of economy, my analysis will treat extensively only one poem from each "group," the existence of such clusters nonetheless offers an exegetical service beyond that of merely allowing the reader to recognize the repeated practice of certain themes such as shipwreck and missed flight. Rather, the hypothesis here—however provisionally held, and always to be put to the test of actual reading—is that Celan's oeuvre may be read, not, certainly, as a single text, but as a set of thematic and imagistic nodes that cast light and shadow upon one another, that throw lines and tie knots between them. In this manner, which reads a poem within the network of the other poems that reflect and connect with it, that write and rewrite across it—not as "parallel passages," but as palimpsests and as skin sutured and rescarred[9]—the poetic material and its operations become the more remarkable both in the depths of their repeated practice and in their unique manifestations. To invoke "Engführung" again, the kind of reading I am proposing responds to the directions given to the reader there—"Lies nicht mehr - schau! / Schau nicht mehr - geh!" (I, 197)—by reversing them: go, see, read, in a going back to what has already gone on in Celan's texts, to see both what's maintained and what's different.

Celan's work is not a single text like Dante's *Commedia*, in which a progressive and hierarchical movement is built into the very thematics and poetics of the text; nor can there be any easy assumptions about progress, "improvement," or increased value across the chronology of Celan's writings. While some changes across his career can be recognized more or less unilinearly—the shortening of verse lines, for example, or the increased division of prefixes from their verb stems—changes in poetic density or precision or statement cannot be similarly charted. An earlier poem or image or word may anticipate a later one, a later text may echo or rewrite an earlier one (including its direct citation: see "Zwölf Jahre," citing and rewriting "Auf Reisen," I, 220 and I, 45), and their relations are not those of a narrative as it unfolds and progresses, nor of some aesthetic "timelessness," but of a poetic temporality—more instantaneous, iterative, and aleatory than sequential—of writing and reading within and across one another. A shipwreck in one poem is not saved in a later one, nor is an object astray in its flight going to find its aim in a later correction of its path. Clusters of wreckage and submersion, skewed flight and missed marks, remain suspended in Celan's work and its understanding, "beim Wabeneis . . . ein Atemkristall" ("in honeycombed ice . . . a crystal of breath") ("Weggebeizt," II, 31).

&

das Auge, . . . das mich verformt

(the eye, . . . that transforms me)

Celan's poems of objects in flight are highly varied and almost never intuitive, never as expected by our experiences, in the images they sketch and the trajectories they articulate. In one of the last of such poems, the object that is thrown appears as that which might somehow be thrown not outward, but out of itself—out of its conventional fling and flight: "Wurfscheibe . . . // wirf dich / aus dir hinaus" ("Discus . . . // throw yourself / out of yourself") ("Wurfscheibe," II, 267). But one thing at least is both common and entirely intuitive in Celan's employment of images of projectiles: the persistent reappearance of the verb of the sound of the objects buzzing, whirring through the air that we saw already in "Unter ein Bild": *schwirren.* Celan's uses of this verb that indicates the coproduction of objects' rapid motion and distinctive sound can be conventional almost to the point of banality—"Pfeilige, wenn du mir zuschwirrst" ("like an arrow, when you whir toward me") ("Ein Ring, zum Bogenspannen," III, 99) could come from an illustrative example in Wahrig's *Deutsches Wörterbuch*—or they can be ambiguous, as in "Schwirrhölzer fahren ins Licht" ("buzzing pieces of wood fly in the light") ("Schwirrhölzer," II, 67), where it is unclear whether the *Schwirrhölzer* incidentally make their noise, or are the cultic noisemakers, the whirligigs, designed to be whirled overhead. Or the associations can be stunningly unexpected, as when it appears that an *eye* is whizzing through the atmosphere: "kometenhaft schwirrte ein Aug / auf Erloschenes zu" ("cometlike an eye whizzed / toward what's extinguished") ("Soviel Gestirne," I, 217).

But to this unsurprising, lexically conventional linkage of a conspicuous sound with flying objects—which renders sensuous as sound the increasing invisibility of the objects' ever greater velocity, their overcoming of ever more space within ever less time—comes the addition of Celan's distinctive touch: the objects and their sound are associated with language and—perhaps more unexpectedly still—less with speech than with writing or inscription. Two examples (others may exist—or may be interpretively unpacked, as in "Unter ein Bild") are from "Beim Hagelkorn" and "Les Globes." In the first instance, "deine Pfeilschrift schwirrt" ("your arrow-script whizzes") (II, 22) was, in an earlier version reported from the manuscript variants by Hans-Georg Gadamer, "Dein [dann, gestrichen: 'lesbares'] Pfeilglück schwirrt" ("Your [then, deleted: 'readable'] arrow-fortune whizzes").[10] The notion of one's fortune or destiny approaching with an arrow's speed and force (a classical Greek image), and thus becoming readable, is yoked into the single compound noun *Pfeilschrift*, so that the script might still buzz with the arrow's velocity. (The traditional association of feathered objects with writing is also preserved here.) In the other instance, from "Les Globes," the sequence of writing and flight—in the text's linearity this time, and not, as with the manuscript variants of "Beim Hagelkorn," in its origination (*Entstehungsgeschichte*)—is rather the opposite. First there is an image of faces inscribed by or as writing, "Aller / Gesichter Schrift" ("Script / Of all the faces"), then the account of the inscription that also introduces the word *schwirren:* "in die sich / schwirrender Wortsand gebohrt" ("into which / whirring word-sand bored itself"). But as if by the introduction of the "schwirrender Wortsand," flight is then prompted: "Alles, / das Schwerste noch, war / flügge, nichts / hielt zurück." ("Everything, / even the heaviest, was / fledged, nothing / held back.") (I, 274). Writing, like a flying object, whizzes; or, having been inscribed, script takes flight. Like the flying object, writing is inscribed by velocity, and inscribes its recognizable sound.

Perhaps this association of writing and the flying object stems, as Werner Hamacher hazards, from an ancient Greek pun between the word (*lógos*) and the javelin (*lógxé*).[11] Perhaps it is no more than a twist on the classical association of feathered, winged soaring and poetic flight.[12] Be this as it may, the project of a Celan poem may be constructed repeatedly—like Pindar—around the image of not just any flying object, but around that of a thrown object, a projectile. But as the reappearances of the accompanying word *schwirren* suggest that there is uncertainty—or, more correctly, reversibility—as to whether projectiles whir and then there is writing, or whether writing whirs and then there is flight, so in the poetry of projectiles it can be not only uncertain but at the same time decisively determining whether the imaged objects are coming or going. If all the thrown objects were arrows or javelins, pointed at one end and pointed or aimed *at* their end or goal, then the flights would be unilinear arcs, and all one would need to know is who is the archer or thrower, and who or what is the target. But as with the circular discus that spins on its flight and might even, in Celan's version, fly out of or over itself, a poetry of projectiles might turn on itself, revolving from a flight either outward or toward—the bipolar perspectives of unilinear flight—to a kind that is both and neither. This is to say that an object's flight could be both outward and back—directed toward *two* goals, but unilinearly toward each in its turn, as if rebounding—but, more curiously, it could have as its goal or aim the attainment of neither end, neither the outward target ahead nor the point of departure toward which the projectile returns. The achievement of such a poetry of projectiles would be, paradoxically, a *double miss*. But precisely in the writing of such poetry of a doubled trajectory, and in the traces and whizzings that guide its reading, the wider arc of Celan's poetology inscribes its mark.[13]

This is the threshold of Celan's poetry of the *boomerang*. There are two explicit instances in his work, only one of which I shall read here, as the other, directly named "Ein Wurfholz" (I, 258), has already received its most incisive and demanding reading in Hamacher's "Die Sekunde der Inversion."[14] The instance at hand is the poem "Aber" (I, 182). It introduces in its last and most difficult strophe the turn of the *Wurfholz*, but this is itself a consequence of the exchanges, engagements, and desires articulated across its first three parts. The axis of these encounters is itself ambiguous, duplicitous, polymorphous—that is, it is alternately unilinear and bipolar, and then elliptical and bifocal. Take the first, parenthetical strophe,[15] as if a stage direction for the remainder of the poem:

> (Du
> fragst ja, ich
> sags dir:)

> (You / ask indeed/yes, I / tell you:)

On the one hand, a question goes from a "you" to a "me," followed by the "I"'s response directly back to the "you." Language is apparently directed outward to its goal (this is the question) and received back in the response (this is the statement or answer) that is symmetrically aimed or targeted. The symmetry is brought out by the alliteration and internal rhymes: "*D*u fr*ag*st . . . *s*ags *d*ir," which has the effect of underscoring the two-way, reflecting character of the bipolar exchange.

But we must acknowledge that neither the "you" nor the questioning (nor the "I," for that matter) has any semantic clarity: more is missing, left out, than said. And we cannot not notice that the strophe, parenthetical as it is, appears as an incomplete—elliptical—circularity, with the two parentheses indicating two small arcs, the rest of the "circle" (or ellipse) remaining to be adumbrated or sketched in. And in this now-circular or circumlocutory exchange, the single affirmation in the "middle"—*ja*—splits into two foci and is the very sign of its missing other, its double: it is the sign of the ellipsis. That is, the parenthesis reads as if it were a double-parenthesis, each interlocking and embracing part of the other; schematically: [. . . (. . .] . . .).[16] Semantically, the strophe reads: first parenthesis, "You ask indeed";

second parenthesis—with the *ja* splitting and doubling—"yes, I tell you." In other words, the elliptical circularity of the strophe is, recalling "Der Meridian," a "detour from you to you" ("Umweg von dir zu dir"), as the affirmation does not get the last word—if truly unilinear, the statement could read: "Du fragst, ich sags dir ja" ("You ask, I tell you yes")—but is rather the point, *and the missing doubled point,* the switch-point or point of exchange in the "middle" of the "circularity." The present, *nonmissing* doubled point in the strophe is, of course, the *Doppelpunkt,* the colon that denies the strophe any last word and any closure: paradoxically opening within closure, speaking out but against the barrier of the second parenthesis, the colon keeps the quasi-circularity of the parenthetic strophe elliptical, maintaining it as the poem's opening.

Such a remarkable combination of linearity and reflexivity, symmetry and circularity, enclosure and ellipticality, informs and directs the second strophe as well. Here there are most immediately straight lines and reflections back, and in this mirror-scene, in which Bernhard Böschenstein is surely correct to understand as well the outward, natural mirroring of the night's stars on the Lac Léman's surface,[17] each line in the strophe appears to reflect, double, and keep in line or straight with its preceding (linear) image:

> Strahlengang, immer, die
> Spiegel, nachtweit, stehn
> gegeneinander, ich bin,
> hingestossen zu dir, eines
> Sinnes mit diesem
> Vorbei.

> (Corridor of rays, always, the / mirrors, night-far, stand /
> across one another, I am, / come to you, of one / mind
> with this / over-and-done.)

The "corridor of rays," already (and "always," *immer*) straight as beams of light, unfolds from the end of the first line to the beginning of the second into its specular double, the plural "mirrors," which is what the *Strahlengang* already was—the reflection of a "corridor of rays" between two "surfaces," sky and lake—but now becomes again, mirrored in the text directly below itself, in *Spiegel*. These mirrors, as wide as all night, stand—now at their line-end and its turning in turn—facing and opposed to each other (*gegeneinander*). As with each of the first words of the two preceding lines, *gegeneinander* names and enacts the linearity and bipolarity of the imagery: a corridor of rays, mirrors (mirroring the former), across from—both opposed and connected to—one another, in a back-and-forth of verses and light. As the line continues, the "I" comes to line up as well, with its "you." This happens first visually, textually, as *ich* and *dir* reflect one another above and below. Then it occurs in an alternate syntactical scansion of the line, as if its syntax would allow one to read through the comma at line's end, the phrase "ich bin [,] / hingestossen zu dir" thus repeating and reenacting the exchange of rays, the mirroring, the facing-one-another in, this time, the confronting and meeting of the poem's personae—as if, in this fourth repetition, the mirroring and facing would yield to contact (*hingestossen*) and as if the first strophe's exchange of discourse (*fragen-sagen*) would manifest itself in this contact. But the line's actual syntax has the "I" continue through and beyond its contact with the "you": what the "I" also is, is "of one / mind" (*eines / Sinnes*) "with this."

Our analysis must pause at this line-end (*mit diesem*), just as a reading would of necessity equivocate momentarily between the formal line-break and the enjambment of the phrase's syntax. The pause is built into the poem's articulation, for here something turns, changes, and is over. After the strophe's four first-words, in a kind of semantic anaphora, have mirrored the visual and spatial fixity and face-to-faceness they represent, and after even the claim of "ich bin / . . . eines / Sinnes" can be taken to repeat this condition a fifth time—in the sense that the "I," come up against the "you," affirms its sameness and solidarity with something, its seeing eye-to-eye—the turn across the two verses to "diesem / Vorbei" introduces the change of and the reversal to a non-alignable element.

This *Vorbei* is both spatial and temporal, at both its semantic and poetic levels. Spatially, something has (been) passed or gone by, with which the "I" affirms its oneness; poetically, the same spatiality is marked in the single-word position of *Vorbei* as the last line of the strophe: reach this point, the very word itself, and it has passed and gone. But the spatial dimensions have yet a further difference marked upon them. "Eines Sinnes," "of one mind" with the imagery and semantics of "hingestossen zu dir," "gegeneinander," and each word above these, shoots beyond itself, as the same phrase ("ich bin eines Sinnes") can mean being of one direction ("einer Richtung"). Without this directionality pointing beyond the very spatiality of *Vorbei*'s alignment with the dominant fixity and repetitions of the strophe,[18] "ich bin / . . . eines / Sinnes mit diesem / Vorbei" could freeze the *Vorbei* not as passed and gone, but as fixed in, now, a sixth first-word position of mirroring one another. Instead, in addition to its meaning as spatially passed, *Vorbei* also means and functions temporally, as past: *Vorbei ist vorbei*, the gone-past is past and gone. And so the senses of being "of one mind" or eye-to-eye with this *Vorbei* have directed themselves, extended themselves, to stretch the doubling of an image with its reflection around a corner or turn (the enjambment) of time: what one would be aligned with and still reflecting is past; one is eye-to-eye with what is not there, spatially or temporally. The past—semantically, this is all of the preceding strophe—is poetically past at this point of turning and punctually terminating the strophe. *Vorbei ist vorbei:* over means over.

But. A poem titled "Aber" is not going to be without its adversative counterturns, its hesitations, its qualifications. And a poem that has so densely aligned "I" with "you," and mirrors with their further spatial mirroring, is not going to allow its facile undoing by an opposing turn toward temporality, which "other"— temporality as the other of spatiality and of specular copresence in its mirroring—would thus directly and undialectically reinstate the same bipolar oppositionality and face-to-faceness (*gegeneinander*) that would ostensibly here be past and over (*vorbei*). "But:", the poem says ("Aber:", with the colon underscoring the opposing, adversative, countering character of the "But," and thereby also contrasting with the "Aber" of the title, without colon), and it will now alternately rush and pause between its phrases and the four colons that structure its remainder.

Aber: mein Herz
ging durch die Pause, es wünscht dir
das Aug, bildnah und zeitstark,
das mich verformt—:

(But: my heart / went through the pause, it wishes you /
the eye, image-near and time-strong, / that transforms
me—:)

The "I"'s "heart / [that] went through the pause"—the first past-tense verb of the poem—may be, representationally, the continuing amorous sentiment that has survived its claimed renunciation (the claim of *vorbei* as the two lovers meet—*hingestossen*—at lakeside at night);[19] it may also invoke the momentary failure, the flutter, the shock, and the risk of passing through a myocardial attack; it certainly also is, in its poetic register, the ongoing motion of the poem through the pause that is the gap between the strophes, between the "over" and the "but." But the word "pause" recalls as well the pause of the enjambment between the *diesem* and the *Vorbei* that appeared to change everything—from spatial fixity in multiple reflections to temporal transience, from presence to past. And in recalling the space and the second between "this" and "over," the "over" is not over, no longer or not yet over; it survives in this renaming just as it also, we recognize, remained present, not passing, in its locative pronominal indication by the "this."[20] A heart going through a pause is a reinstating of the duplicity of space and time, for it is *both* a heartbeat's instant and a spatial image—*through* which one might pass—of that instant: while still temporal (*Pause*), it renders spatial once again what had just, instantaneously, been punctually dissolved from spatial fixity to temporal passage (*Vorbei*).

The syntactically and semantically dense remainder of this strophe further complicates the coimplication of space and time at this point—or pause—in the poem. The heart that "wishes you / The eye" returns to the dominant visuality and spatiality of *Strahlengang* and *Spiegel*, but like most wishes, it wants something in return for the act. "Dir etwas wünschen" probably means "zu dir etwas wünschen," an intimate, amorous speech-act whereby one's wishes go out to a lover; given the flexibility of German grammar and its underdetermination here, the phrase may also (if less likely) mean "the eye wishes [something, i.e., the heart] to you." In either or both cases, the "wishing to you" wishes for something *from* its wishing *to*. What is wished to you is "the eye" (I adopt this reading), one of the deepest and most variously and surrealistically employed words in Celan's lexicon; and this eye would be at once characterized both spatially and temporally, "image-near" (*bildnah*) and "time-strong" (*zeitstark*), both of which compound adjectives double their characteristic qualities: so the image (spatial) is measured spatially (*nah*), and time's power of decision and reversal, its *kairotic* power, is strengthened. And this doubly empowered eye, as capable of measuring an image within an eyelash's nearness as an instant within an eye's blink (*Augenblick*), is, in its being the object of a wish, an object of force with respect to the wisher. (Such an exchange of what I may call the object-eye and the subject-eye, seen and seeing, may recall both Baudelaire's reversing *regard* in "A une passante" and Walter Benjamin's most succinct definition of *aura:* "to endow a phenomenon with the ability to look back at us in return." Celan was a famously expert reader of both Baudelaire and Benjamin.)[21] This eye has the power to form and deform, shape and misshape ("das mich verformt");[22] whereas the German prefix *ver*- is predominantly negative, the range of the verb *verformen* has to allow for neutral meanings as well, and is perhaps best understood as "transform"; only the intensity and context of its employment will allow us to decide whether this is good or bad, a positive shaping or a negative, too intense misshaping or deforming. From the invisibility of the heart, through the eye—both wished out or toward and now metamorphosing back—the "I" is made and undone: by an eye, an eye of space and time, of imagery and its passing. But this power and exchange is also wished upon a "you."

The colon at the end of this strophe marks another pause between strophes, but this time—uniquely in the poem—the colon after *verformt* is preceded by a dash.[23] "The eye . . . that transforms me—:" with both the connections and the separations effected by the dash, the colon, and the pause between strophes, what follows next must be at once *to* the "you"'s eye (a consequence of the wish, namely the power to see), and *from* that eye to the "me" (another consequence, namely the capacity of being seen). It will be self-evidently "image-near and time-strong."

> die Schwäne,
> in Genf, ich sah's nicht, flogen, es war
> als schwirrte, vom Nichts her, ein Wurfholz
> ins Ziel einer Seele:
>
> (the swans, / in Geneva, I didn't see them, flew, it was /
> as if were whirring, from out of nothingness, a
> boomerang / into the target of a soul:)

The swans are a visual image from familiar, indeed classical poetic precincts, representing the figure of the poet and, in their reputed death- or swan *song*, an association with poetry; they also evidently have biographical resonance here, of a likely experience of Celan aside the lake in Geneva.[24] They are instantly there, without preparation or transition, at the head of the strophe, and then in the world, "in Geneva." But for all this immediate "image-nearness," they are then just as immediately invisible, nonvisual, *not* to the eye: "ich sah's nicht." Unseen, the swans flew, and as flying objects, they are associated with the sound of whirring, whizzing. The representational detail may be exact to the experience of unseen swans heard flying, batting their wings and making the air whir, above the surface of a Swiss lake at night. But it also recalls this poem to the cluster of those about objects in flight, and also inserts it into the poetics of missed ends.

For the swans serve a comparison of flight toward what the poem has inscribed as its directions and regions: following a single direction and a single mind ("ich bin . . . eines Sinnes"), passing with the heart, and here aiming at a soul's target or goal (*Ziel*). Both the terms of this last strophe's first comparison and the detail of the object's flight are exacting in their demands upon the precision of the image. The swans' flight, since unseen, is—in the emerging comparison—as if "from nothingness," from what would be a void except that something is unmistakably coming *toward* one from out of it—"vom Nichts her." Invisible sound comes toward one—velocity's sound supplementing its invisibility—as if a *Wurfholz* were flying "into the goal/target of a soul." The qualification of the projectile as a *Wurfholz* deflects the object from its very achievement. The specificity of the *Wurfholz* would be lost, meaningless, if it *were* to strike its target here. For *Wurfholz* is correctly to be understood as a boomerang—as Böschenstein and Hamacher both do, for example—since otherwise, a *Wurfholz* is not thrown at all, but, in its meaning as a *Speer-* or *Wurfschleuder,* is used only to throw another object—a spear—more powerfully.[25] And in the poem "Ein Wurfholz," the familiar and specific characteristic of a boomerang is brought out by Celan: that it returns to its thrower ("so kommt es / geflogen, so kommts / wieder und heim" ["thus it comes / flown, thus it comes / back and home"], I, 258).[26] But the condition of its returning is that it first *miss* its target; only thus will the flight outward become, parabolically or circularly, the flight back. And so the directionality toward the goal (captured in the accusative "ins Ziel") is arrested and deflected, detoured, short of its achievement; the arc[27] from "from" to "into" ("vom Nichts her . . . ins Ziel einer Seele") turns around.

A pause between motions outward and back, predicated upon a gap between a projectile and the attainment of its goal, is here marked by another colon. (Colons conventionally point to what follows them; in Celan they read backwards as well.) This colon first marks a transformation by inversion of the image of the swans who have become a boomerang. There, that image had begun with the visual swans, then negated them as unseen, only to have them become the limit—the velocity, the *schwirren*—where sight becomes sheer sound in the figure of the whizzing boomerang, nearing—but missing—its target. Here, after the colon, the limit between sight and sound, and between nearing and missing a point of termination, would become transformed into "so much / time" as if it were a visual measure of a missing gap, where the semantic sense of "much" (*viel*) inverts, by stretching out, the rapidly closing instantaneity of "schwirrte . . . ein Wurfholz / ins Ziel," as the closing of space (distance) by the approaching projectile is inverted into the opening up of time. (It may be that this inversion of closing into opening, diminishment into expansion, is embodied in the alternate scansions of the word and meaning of *soviel* itself: "*só*viel Zeit," accenting the shorter, instantaneous *nunc stans,* "so*víel* Zeit," accenting the lengthening toward eternity.)

soviel
Zeit
denk mir, als Auge, jetzt zu:

(so much / time / think to me, as an eye, now:)

This (re)appearance of time, just as the visual image had become "image-near"—the very image of nearing—now becomes,
suspended and pausing as the single, readable word of its line, the
time of the poem, for, now back in the present, the "I" speaks, re-
quests, and says "now." It is worth recalling, as the formal device
does for us, the other single-word lines of the poem: "(Du," positing the addressee who in turn addresses, asks, thus positing the
minimal point of departure and structure of exchange for the
poem; and "Vorbei," representing both passage and, followed immediately by the strophes' gap and the "Pause," its adversative
("Aber:") overcoming. Here, the *Zeit* and the reappearance of the
present-tense, addressing "I" together have the effect of re-presenting the "you," nowhere linguistically present in the lines but
invoked—performed—by the address as an indeterminate imperative of pure intent. The "you" that had been wished "the eye" has
asked of it the thought or intentionality ("jemandem etwas zu-
denken," to intend someone to have something) of "so much time
. . . now." How much? At least as much, which means as little, as
separated the boomerang from its goal. This instant is supposed
to turn from thought or intention to something granted—performed (*zugedacht*, dedicated, bequeathed, willed, marked as intended)—by or as an "eye"; the "I" would here get back a return
on its wishing "you / the eye" in the preceding strophe. (The
phrase "als Auge" may also modify *Zeit*, and might also even, by
proximity of position, modify *mir*, but both these possibilities
seem less likely than the reading I am pursuing.) And thus
granted in thought *by* an eye, time would be thought granted as visual: as velocity, as a whizzing projectile, as an image, as that
which, "image-near and time-strong," shapes and misshapes. The
naming of such time "now" (*jetzt*) opens up "that much time" (*soviel Zeit*) between the two colons: an instantaneous gap becomes
a visually measured—metered, versed, readable—pause.

From a spatial—spatially nearing and closing (the accusative

ins)—gap, to its inversion into a tempo-textual—temporally lengthening and visually measuring, readable—pause, a pause requested
to be intended or granted by one "as an eye," and "now," in the
poem, textually visible and fixed as such: from this visible pause,
consequences must be drawn for the present-tense now of the
poem's ending.

dass ichs
schwirren hör, näher - nicht
neben mir, nicht,
wo du nicht sein kannst.

(that I / may hear it whiz, nearer—not / next to me,
not, / where you cannot be.)

The consequence "dass ichs / schwirren hör, näher" returns—
brings circling back—the boomerang as the audible, liminally visible figure of the collapsing of space (visibility, distance) by velocity into the narrowing instant of time, without the aim or goal
(*Ziel*) being reached. We are nearing, in other words, the poem's
double miss. The nearer it gets—all this the nearness of entry of
the initial single accusative prepositional contraction, *ins*—the
longer it stays; or, put another way, it cannot reach its goal, as an
image of a boomerang, except by missing it. *Näher,* nearer, is the
readable measure—no less readable than was *Näh'res* in "Unter ein
Bild"—of the gap[28] between a goal and a miss, between a narrowing instant (*ins*) and a widening gap (*jetzt . . . näher*).

If this appears in one guise as the poem's version of Zeno's
paradox, such that "nearer" never becomes the ultimate adja-
cency and tangency that is "next to" ("näher - nicht neben mir"),
it is also still the image of the boomerang becoming nearer qua
audible image, and stronger qua the readable (*schwirren* as *Schrift*)
measure of time. *Schwirren,* in other words, in being thus staged,
displays its very perceptibility as sheer readability. But the closer
it comes in *this* whirring, whizzing poetry, *now,* the more nearly it
will not hit—it will miss—its mark. Now no longer as the "now" of
the three-line, discursive pause of "soviel / Zeit / denk mir, als
Auge, jetzt zu," the poem's signal of the image flying and not hitting is the single readable and textual trait—the dash, a *Ver-*

hoffen—between *näher* and *nicht.* It is the trace of the word, the word entitling and entitled by the whole poem, that turns against and turns around, adversative and boomerang-like, reversing the line's directionality, splaying the "nearer" and the "next to" apart, making them miss each other, at the instant of their nearest approach: "näher, aber nicht neben mir," "nearer, but not next to me." As a boomerang, it may come "vom Nichts her," and in missing its goal, at once be *näher* and—already—reversing, reversed, to return whence it came, to not (*−nicht*). The threefold *nicht* will not end—will "not-end"—this poem's flight. Ever nearer, but not next "to me"—like Maurice Blanchot's description of something missing in Celan's text, not unlike in Zeno's paradox: "quelque chose en nous, hors de nous, qui a besoin que nous manquions à nous-mêmes pour passer la ligne que nous n'atteindrons pas" ("something in us, outside of us, that needs us to be missing to ourselves so that it might cross the line that we will never reach").[29] The repetition, then, of *nicht* ("nicht / neben mir, nicht"), more than an intensification of "nicht / neben mir," takes the whizzing of the boomerang "vom Nichts her," from being nearer the "soul" it would hit, to being *not* next to one, to being *not*—as if, boomerang-like, it had returned home to not. Which would be "wo du nicht sein kannst." As the boomerang elliptically gets nearer and then not nearer, the "you" that was addressed ("ich / sags dir") and then contacted ("hingestossen zu dir") also becomes not nearer or next to the "I," but rather a not-being-there. The projectile that draws nearer and nearer only to return afar—the trajectory of the poem's image—carries with and over it the attraction and rejection of the "you"'s place and being in the poem.[30]

As with an ellipse, the poem "Aber" has two foci: the boomerang's flight and the "you"'s fate, which represent both the poem's representational course or trajectory, and its possible address and reception. "Ich sags dir . . . wo du nicht sein kannst." ("I tell you . . . where you cannot be."). On the condition that it *miss* its goal, the boomerang is at all times, like the arc of a circle, turning and returning to its point of departure; thus, to be coming "nearer" is also to be returning to not and nothingness, whence it came. The poem's prolonged present of whizzing nearer—but not next—to one, seems to attract the "you" to the answer promised with "ich / sags dir," but it rejects the place of the "you" between "nearer" and "not / next." Drawing near means flinging afar; flinging from afar and drawing near and nearer means not arriving—a two-sided arcing-away of an ellipse, a double miss of an ellipsis. With each "focus," the poem begins with proximity, and the entry into contact—"ich / sags dir," "hingestossen zu dir," "als schwirrte . . . ein Wurfholz / ins Ziel einer Seele"—and moves back under the sign of "not": "nicht / neben mir, nicht, / wo du nicht sein kannst." The boomerang's flight to *and from* its goal maps the poem's trajectory to *and from* its addressee: the double miss.

In sequence, were one to begin at the instant of contact (*hingestossen, ins Ziel*) and move back from it, this poem's structure would have the tropological shape of a hysteron proteron that we read in "Unter ein Bild," "the last before the first": first contact, then the distance before the contact. But such sequentiality conforms neither to the particular conditions of the boomerang and its flight (it comes "vom Nichts her," whence it returns, before and instead of ending "ins Ziel"), nor to the doubleness of the poem's address. The "you" that asks ("Du / fragst ja") is also, as Beda Allemann observed, itself an interrogative, and it remains a goal (*Ziel*) of Celan's poetry.[31] "Du / fragst ja": you, the mark of a question, a question mark. The poem is addressed to a question mark, and all the time that it is projecting an answer, it is also rejecting the place of the question. This poem to a "you" is also "where you cannot be." To see and read *this*—from first line to last—is as exacting an act of vision and reflexivity as to see one's own eye measuring an approaching boomerang. One is "seeing" the visible become invisible—"ich sah's nicht"—and left reading the signs measuring the disappearance of the goal into an inscribed place of disappearance: *jetzt, näher, nicht, wo du nicht sein kannst—Schwirrschrift*. In the boomerang-like return of the *schwirren* in the present tense of the poem's ending, it neither returns to an "I" ("nicht / neben mir"), nor arrives at a "you," nor achieves any end (*Ziel*) of its trajectory except a flight into the script of its ending. To play out the image, one could say that the boomerang of *schwirren* returns not to the hand that throws it—another double miss—but to the hand that writes it.

The "you" addressed, and marked as a question mark, to whom a shaping and misshaping eye is wished, and who then is rejected through its power of bestowal: this is a reading eye that can see, there in the last three lines, but cannot reach or be at its end. Like the boomerang, it draws nearer to its goal in order to fly back whence it departed. In between a question and a rejection is the project, the projectile, the trajectory. At all times coming *and* going—not a sequential coming-and-then-going, or a near-and-then-back-afar—the "I" that answers and the eye that inquires each whiz toward one another. The phrase "dass ichs / schwirren hör" could even have the eye (*das Auge*) as the object of its contraction, like the eye that whirred in the poem "Soviel Gestirne." Reading Celan's poems of whizzing projectiles, is to read—elliptically, with double focus—poems' trajectories toward their readers, and readers' nearing to the poems, in which the sign of the contact is never seen except in the legible sign of invisible oscillation and deferred contact—*schwirren*. We recall that in "Unter ein Bild," the arrow flew from the soul—"Später Pfeil, der von der Seele schnellte / Stärkeres Schwirren." ("Later arrow, that sped from the soul / Stronger whizzing.")—but the reversibility remained that it was Van Gogh's vector across the painting, away from the viewer, the painting itself, from Van Gogh to the viewer, and the author/reader-viewer's vector across the gap before the painting, following that "first" vector toward the painting but also founding the possibility of the other two readings. In Celan's whizzing boomerang of script, away is toward: reading is toward and away from an end "where [it] cannot be."

The arch stands because all the stones
want to plunge at the same time.
—Heinrich von Kleist

From a rolling up at an end and an impossibly enfolded circling around to a beginning, to a projectile missing a goal and an end, to a plunge remaining—to the end—beneath a shipwreck, these steps cover a poetic distance both amazingly large and quite immediate and ready-to-hand in Celan's work. The route is in fact sketched across the stepping-stones of key words in his famous precursor-poem "Tübingen, Jänner": "the floating Hölderlin towers" ("schwimmende Hölderlintürme"), suddenly "buzzed by gulls in circling flight" ("möwen- / umschwirrt"), followed immediately by drowned figures and diving, submerging words—"Besuche ertrunkener Schreiner bei / diesen / tauchenden Worten" ("Visits of drowned joiners by / these / plunging words") (I, 226); the second half of the poem takes place, it could be said, figuratively under water, after drowning. But while "Tübingen, Jänner" may be counted among poems of shipwreck and drowning in a figurative and extended sense, a cluster of shipwreck-and-drowning poems exists in Celan's work in a tightly defined and readily surveyable form. We will glance at two by way of introduction to an analysis of a third longer and later one.

The graphic representation of going overboard a ship in "Schuttkahn" (I, 173)—the first half of the poem above, the second half below the waterline that is represented, midpoem, by fifteen dots across the page—is matched by its logical representation of a sequence that does not lead where it is headed. The rubbleship leading us to evening (*Abend*) at the "waterhour"—perhaps the rubbleship of biographical memory, of Celan's forced labor on a road-building crew in occupied Bukowina, of his parents' similar work (to their death) along the River Bug;[32] also unmistakably, an allusion to Oswald Spengler's *Der Untergang des Abendlands,* the ship carrying the historical rubble of the West at the hour of its decline—has "a dead / why" ("ein totes / Warum") at the stern's helm ("steht am Heck"). That, like the legend of the Flying Dutchman, this figure is dead but still steering, that, like Charon's captaincy of the ship of the dead (*Schutt* can also mean "ashes"), this figure is a servant of Death and steadily steering, gives one ambivalent confidence in its direction. But like the opening lines of "Aber"—"Du fragst / ja"—a question, *Warum,* calls for an answer: it directs, heads, steers toward a response. Or perhaps goes overboard, abandoning ship, for in the second strophe, below the waterline of ellipses that leaves out the event itself, the first word reports a lightened burden (*Geleichtert*).[33] As if under water, the breathing would have to be of an aquatic kind, and so the lung inflates itself like a jellyfish ("Die Lunge, die Qualle / bläht sich zur

Glocke"). But with the mention of the bell, an instrument of sound and tone, the strophe turns into what it also is: the second half of a poem responding to a question. In a classical scene of inspiration ("bläht sich") followed by ex-pression (*hellgeatmete*)— classical also in Celan as an example of *Atemwende,* "breath-turn," the figure used by him to describe poetry[34] and to name a volume of his poems—the poem issues its response:

> ein brauner
> Seelenfortsatz erreicht
> das hellgeatmete Nein.

(a brown / soul-appendage reaches / the brightly breathed no.)

The neologistic expression "soul-appendage" immediately recalls the physiological term of which it is itself a poetic extension: *Wurmfortsatz,* the appendix, which leads nowhere, as its other name—*Blinddarm,* "blind intestine"—also states. An extension or prolongation (*Fortsatz*) that would proceed—*Fortsatz* is the German for the Latin *processus*—nowhere, here achieves the expression of "no" (*Nein*). What kind of process is this? In its technical terminology, it is a non sequitur: "no" is not a logical answer to "why," or, put another way, the poeto-logic of this poem only extends the question "why" to and into the response that denies, without answering, the question. But then the question is dead, a nonstarter and a dead end from the start ("ein totes / Warum"), and perhaps the helmsman—the direction-giver or *gubernator*— it represents (also a Horatian figure for the poet) is simply thrown, rejected, overboard, as if in poetic mutiny. "Schuttkahn" is the aquatic counterpart to "Aber" (which appears six poems later in the volume *Sprachgitter*); it responds to a question with its negation, and represents the gap, the missing step, between question and answer as a logical nonstep and poetic ellipsis.

A question and a poem leading nowhere—or only to "no"— "Schuttkahn"'s primary image is explicitly echoed in a later rewriting: the long poem "Es ist alles anders" (I, 284) contains the phrase, "am Heck kein Warum." But the going overboard—jumping or being thrown—that is both implicit and elliptically missing in "Schuttkahn" is postponed to the end in the explicit shipwreck poem, "Mit erdwärts gesungenen Masten" (II, 20). Its inversion of dimensions, in which it is not a terrestrial ship that sinks toward water but heaven that sinks toward earth,

> Mit erdwärts gesungenen Masten
> fahren die Himmelwracks.

(With earthward-sung masts / sail the heaven-wrecks.)

recalls the inversions of the prose aphorisms of Celan's youthful *Gegenlicht*, and anticipates a later inversion—also of sinking wreckage—in "Von der sinkenden Walstirn": "der Himmel / stürzt sich / in die Harpune" ("heaven / hurls itself / into the harpoon") (III, 72). The apocalyptic image may, as Gadamer suggests, recall Caspar David Friedrich's painting of shipwreck, "The Wreck of the Hope."[35] But as a poem producing—poetically expressing—its own shipwreck, "Mit erdwärts gesungenen Masten" remains in the vein of "Schuttkahn." The first strophe states the poem's singing (and, punningly, sinking: *gesungenen/gesunkenen*) guidance of the shipwreck. The second names this sinking ship as the poem itself:

> In dieses Holzlied
> beisst du dich fest mit den Zähnen.

(In this wooden song / you bite on hard to yourself with your teeth.)

The "you" holding on—to the lines of the masts or the lines of the poem—by its very teeth[36] desperately resists its drowning, and is the last thing to be seen as the poem goes under:

> Du bist der liedfeste
> Wimpel.

(You are the song-fixed / Pennant.)

There are at least two ironies in the poem's attachment of a desperate addressee to its wreckage. The "you" who is the "song-fixed / pennant" (with a sense in *liedfest* of "song-faithful," "song-knowledgeable," as well as of a "song festival")[37] may not be, as in Gadamer's touchingly trusting interpretation that itself follows a passage from Benjamin, the last best sign for hope.[38] Although the pennant of a sinking ship might conventionally be the last thing to go under, it might—in this inverted shipwreck—be the first, for the *Masten* that would bear the *Wimpel* are pointed downward (*erdwärts*) from the start. So the poem leads its addressee into the deep head first, as it were. Furthermore, if a ship is going down from the start, one does not necessarily want to go down with the ship; jumping ship, rejecting it, may be the only way out. Here, on the contrary, the addressee is sinking with the ship-poem, and the poem names the addressee its pennant, its banner—its sign. To be fixed to this song as its sign is to be pointed downward, to be the one last word—*Wimpel*—before the bath of whiteness of the remaining page below. If the addressee is also the poem's reader, holding on to the lines of verse to the end, he cannot escape the poem's wreck but can only, like a small vessel portrayed on a pennant, become its very *mise-en-abîme*. "In dieses Holz-lied / beisst du" becomes "Du bist": biting these lines (*beisst*) means you become and you are (*bist*) the last sign of its voyage—synecdoche of its singing and sinking.

In "Schuttkahn" the moment of going overboard is missing, but marked as missing in the line-long ellipses; in "Mit erdwärts gesungenen Masten" the final plunge of the sinking ship is withheld but signed as due in the addressee's identification with its last, sinking word. "Von querab," Celan's most extended and elaborated poem of *naufrage* (II, 354), returns to "Aber"'s structure of an exchange between an "I" and a "you," and thus includes both a narrative of going overboard and under, and a pursuit, a doubling, a response. But here it is not a question that receives the answer "not," but a danger, a cry that receives—a reading.

At first the poem's opening is not a dramatic shipwreck but perhaps only a quotidian evening or nightfall aboard a sailing ship:

Von querab
komm ein, als die Nacht,
das Notsegel
bauscht sich,

(From aslant / come in, as the night, / the emergency
sail / billows,)

"Von querab" is not anybody's idiomatic German, but it appears in context to signify the changing of the tack or direction of a vessel—here, including a poetic vessel—from going diagonally with the direction of the wind (*querab*) to turning into it (*komm ein*).[39] "As the night" may be either a benign or an inspired simile (if inspired, recalling the opening of Hölderlin's "Brod und Wein"), suggesting how gently and yet thoroughly this maneuver can be effected, but this assumes that the phrase *is* a simile. The *als* may rather be a temporal "as," meaning "when," and *die Nacht* an apposition to the following *Notsegel*, in which case the phrase appears less benign and gentle, and more evocative of urgency, even emergency. In any case, it is the term and metaphor of the emergency sail—perhaps the last one left, if an imagined storm has already savaged the vessel—that cuts across the opening strophe and into the poem that plunges below. It is the cut that opens the entry for the addressee (the most familiar and intuitable sense of "komm ein") at the same time that it abruptly alters the direction of the ship, pushing it with its billowed sail, and cuts off its personae, perhaps pitching them overboard. *Segel*, etymologically recalling *Säge* (saw) and *Sichel* (sickle), is the opening cut—of time (*Sekunde*, from the Latin *secare*)[40]—that dismembers the poem it constitutes and launches. The opening two lines likewise provide the most directed prepositional puncture into any Celan poem's beginning. Colloquially unfamiliar and yet strangely comprehensible, the first four words lead one "from," "across," "down" (*ab*), and "in," with a directionality thereby established and sustained until the end.

In the poem, and on the vessel with the *Notsegel*, the "you" is instantly endangered and incised, crying out silently and slipping or pitching below.

> eingeschreint
> an Bord
> ist dein Schrei,
> du warst da, du bist unten,

> (enshrined / on board / is your cry, / you were there,
> you are below,)

Even if the cry is enshrined, encapsulated, it continues to cry out from within its shrine (*Schrei* within *einge s c h r e i nt*) and in each of its diphthong's repetitions (*eingeschreint . . . ist dein Schrei*) in this writing that has crying within it (*schreien* within *schreiben*). And even if the cry is cut off from its person, like a saint's finger in a reliquary, it continues to function synecdochally—like the reliquary's bones—for the persona from whom it is separated: it marks that "du warst da." But precisely as a cry cut off, or, still crying, a cry from which the persona has dropped off: "du bist unten."

From "coming in" to being "on board" the ship, the "you"— and the poem with it—drops "under":

> unterhalb bist du,
>
> ich geh, ich geh mit den Fingern
> von mir,
> dich zu sehn,
> mit den Fingern du Untre,
>
> die Armstrünke wuchern,
>
> (down below you are, // I go, I go with the fingers /
> from me, / to see you, / with the fingers, you down-
> there, // the arm-stalks multiply,)

There may be a deliberate and staged tracking of this descent from the perspective and speaking-standpoint of the speaker, from *unten* (below indicated from above) to *unterhalb* ("underneath," amidst the "under," still viewed from above) to *du Untre* (now identified as the under, with the speaker's coidentification with this level). But whether the words deliberately trace this descent (and whether the poem, with its several short and abrupt pauses in the descent, is altogether a mimesis of a sinking body, momentarily buoyed in its descent as its surface area changes angles) the words themselves are traced by an "I" who now appears at the precise middle—the underwater line, as it were—of the poem. The "I"'s introduction is an exchange with a sinking "you," and this occurs as subtly as does the "you"'s slowly twisting shape as it sinks. With the chiastic inversion of "du bist unten, / unterhalb bist du," a twisting change of place anticipates the exchange of "ich geh . . . / von mir / dich zu sehn . . . / . . . du Untre," at the center of which—the crossing—is (but for the accusative instead of the dative for "you") the minimal chiasmus: "von mir / dich zu." "I go from me you to . . . ," "I go to you under": I go under. The title of Hans Blumenberg's well-known little study of the topos of shipwreck is *Schiffbruch mit Zuschauer;* here we have "Schiffbruch mit zuschauendem Sinkenden," "Shipwreck with Sinking Audience."

The fingers also change from the grotesque to exchange with the fraternal. First, in the construction "ich geh mit den Fingern / von mir" (instead of "ich geh mit meinen Fingern"), the fingers not only figure a kind of blind reading of the world, advancing hesitantly on fingertips ("mit den Fingern . . . dich zu sehn"), but also ghastly fingers cut off, severed from their body, as if the "I" were carrying one hand's severed fingers in the other. But then the fingers also cross, as if in a fleeting, sinking handshake. The phrasing "ich geh mit den Fingern / von mir" gives itself over to "dich zu sehen, mit den Fingern, du Untre," so that the fingers literally cross from "me" to "you," as if the fingers had been passed, in a last handgrasp. That the fingers might touch, between "me" and "you," precisely amidst the powerful metaphor-cum-metonymy of "mit den Fingern . . . dich zu sehn," marks this point as one of tangible poetry. With the fleeting image of a possible handshake, Celan recalls a possible poetry: "Ich sehe keinen prinzipiellen Unterschied zwischen Händedruck und Gedicht." ("I see no difference in principle between a handshake and a poem.").[41] And with "seeing with fingers," he calls forth a possible seeing of its reading, from blind reading to a kind of braille reading.

For "Mit den Fingern zu gehen, dich zu sehen" invokes a *tasten*, a touching and feeling one's way along in the dark or the half-light, which is Celan's image for reading in what is perhaps his most ambitious poem, "Engführung." After landing amidst "Gras, auseinandergeschrieben" ("Grass, written apart"), and being directed "Lies nicht mehr – schau! / Schau nicht mehr – geh!" ("Read no more, look! / Look no more, go!") (I, 197), the poem's figure is represented as performing the following action: "ein Finger / tastet hinab und hinan, tastet / umher: Nahtstellen, fühlbar

. . . " ("a finger / feels up and down, feels / around: suture marks, palpable . . .") (I, 199).⁴² These *Nahtstellen* are lines of poetry—marks of sutures upon the scars, *Narben*, that figure several times in Celan's work. "Mit den Fingern . . . zu gehen" may also recall—distantly and ironically—Hölderlin's image at the end of "Patmos" (str. XV, ll. 1–4) for the close reading that might bring "Stilleuchtender Kraft aus heiliger Schrift" ("quietly lighting power out of holy Scripture"): "Zu lang, zu lang schon ist / Die Ehre der Himmlischen unsichtbar. / Denn fast die Fingern müssen sie / Uns führen . . ." ("Too long, too long already has / The honor of the heavenly ones been invisible. / For they must almost lead us / By the fingers . . .").

Indeed, in "Von querab," reading with the fingers leads to an encounter—and, indeed, via Scripture—yielding not an exchange of spirit (the Hölderlinian power behind light) for sacred text, but a ratio of fingers reading to armstumps multiplying: "die Armstrünke wuchern," ("the armstalks/stumps multiply,"). The fingers may have appeared strangely disembodied, as if one's hands could somehow go holding their own severed fingers ("ich geh mit den Fingern / von mir"), but the armstumps/stalks are doubly disembodied, from both torsos and fingers, and yet profusely full of growth. The relation of the *Armstrünke* to the descending fingers is of a cutting and severing that produces an exchange from wholes to parts. The descent of the poem, from the initial incision of the *Notsegel* and the scream of the "you" "enshrined / on board," turned to the seemingly disembodied fingers, now standing—as they sink—for the "you" and "I" altogether. As the "armstumps" are also "armstalks," they multiply, both in a proliferation of sheer numbers and in a luxuriant but grotesque new growth, sprouting plantlike like so many new fingers.

Here it is that the ironic recall of Scripture is heard: *wuchern* is Biblical, used by Luther to translate and to condemn "Jewish" usury (his "Schrift über die Wucher"), and it is also still today the technical term to describe a cancerous growth; the two senses—*die Wuchere*, the usurers, the cancers, as the Jews—were brought together in Hitler's *Mein Kampf* and Rosenberg's *Mythus des 20. Jahrhunderts*. At this grotesque and abused "scar" in the poem—a scar-line marking dismembered Jews, multiplying corpses, all in the name of the abuse heaped upon them by a German word and its extensions, its own grotesque growths—the telling and transforming relation of the armstumps to the fingers may be that the fingers, while detached, nonetheless can tell of the arms from which they were severed, and yet for which they synecdochally still signify: reading fingers, however cut off, still find and transmit a sense of the dismembered body politic. The *Strünke*, which included *verstümmelt* (mutilated, garbled) among their etymological roots—thus, however distantly, recalling the *mauscheln*, the "speaking like Moses" which meant "to speak incomprehensibly, to speak gibberish" when Germans said it of Yiddish-speaking Jews—may sink down lifelessly and at the same time sprout up with new, if deadly, growth, but they are in either case cut off from wholeness and articulation, like the single line floating in the poem. But the fingers, similarly severed, go to see and read: the synecdoche of the fingers supplements the loss of the arm, as reading becomes the poetic prosthesis for the garbled signs that the *Armstrünke* are. The ratio, neither direct nor inverse but synecdochal, has the cutting-off, the disarticulation, of the person—the cry from the person, the person from the ship, the fingers from the arms, and the arms from a body (politic)—become both the surface and the instrument of its own reading. The disarticulated—*Strünke, verstümmelt*—gets read by the parts cut loose and going under.[43]

Above this underwater scene, where armstalks may semifloat like aquatic plants and fingers go searching, one sign also stands for another, and both of them are similarly in a pattern of descent and detached singularity:

> das Leuchtfeuer denkt
> für den ein-
> sternigen Himmel,
>
> (the beacon/warning flare thinks / for the one- /
> starred heaven,)

That the beacon can think for the one-starred heaven tells both of the many-starred sky reduced to one (to the star of David, itself reduced millionsfold), and of the heaven descending, perhaps already descended, toward its substitutive, memorial sign, like the *Himmelwracks* that sank *erdwärts* into the song that sang this decline. For the beacon may wish to warn of danger, especially at a site already marked by and known for shipwreck; and so in some sense it always signals too late: it warns of shipwreck *after* shipwreck.[44] And after shipwreck, still signaling for rescue, a *Leuchtfeuer* can go up, this time meaning a flare, a burst of light in the sky—*einsternig*—that signals disaster, emergency (*Not*), a cry (*Schrei*) for help to anyone out there to see it and read its meaning. In this respect, the doubleness of the *Leuchtfeuer*—a signal sent from land to sea, hoping for its safe (and safeguarding) reception, and one sent from sea to anywhere, hoping for its saving, rescuing reception—resembles that other signal, a projectile that may, when launched from a ship, signify the seaworthiness of the vessel thus far, and alternately, when launched by a survivor on a deserted island, signify the shipwreck behind one and the hope for rescue—for a reception and a response—ahead. This is of course Celan's message in the bottle (*Flaschenpost*), his figure for the poem,[45] which like the double structure of the *Leuchtfeuer* comes before one possible disaster and after another.

A beacon warns against shipwreck where there has been danger; a flare calls from a shipwreck the moment after the disaster, but the moment before going under. In between danger, wreckage, rescue, and survival, the *Leuchtfeuer* would light two paths, each to safety, but one avoiding the wreck and the other illuminating it. In "Von querab," the disaster at sea—the emergency, the cut, the cry, the man overboard—has already occurred, and so the *Leuchtfeuer* provides whatever light it can as it substitutes for a reduced, unsaved chosen people and a reduced, nonsalvationary heaven. (So, too, Celan's *Flaschenpost* is sent after disaster, certainly not by an idle passenger on a pleasure cruise.) But a flare that goes up comes down, and its illumination dies with its fall. This far down the poem's descent, by declining light,

> mit dem Schwertkiel
> les ich dich auf.

> (with the sword-center keel/quill / I read/gather you up.)

The tempting representationality of this last image tests—
and fails—its possible presentation. A *Kielschwert*, a withdrawable
center-keel, may be withdrawn, lifted up, into the hull of a vessel,
but anyone gone overboard and sought below cannot be lifted up
to safety with it. Its inversion into *Schwertkiel* calls attention, in this
poem marked by cuts (*Schwert*, sword), to the word's separable and
reattachable parts. A whole word made of parts may have each
part stand for the possible relations of one to the other. From *Segel*
to *Schwert*, via the separated *Schrei* and the severed *Strünke*, the
poem has cut into and off from itself: it would be left littered with
dismembered parts, with only the gathering up of these remnants
remaining: "les ich dich auf." The only ascent (*auf*) after all the
descent—the prepositions *von, ab, ein, unten*—would, after all,
have the last word. The very instrument of the cutting is also the
means of collection: I cut you, I collect you. The fingers that "go
to see you" may hold a sword—and thus, retrospectively, the mu-
tilating sense of "die Armstrünke wuchern" reemerges—but if
they are also reading fingers, they are also simultaneously the "I"'s
writing fingers. The *Kiel* or quill "reads you up." *Ablesen*—as in the
Celan lines "Von der sinkenden Walstirn / les ich dich ab" ("From
the sinking whale-brow / I read you off") (III, 72)—may be a common verb for "reading off" from a gesture or a sign (as from a
brow), but *auflesen* is not incomprehensible, especially after the
explicit combination of gathering and reading in its use in
Celan's great poem "A la pointe acérée" (I, 251):

Auf-
gelesene
kleine, klaffende
Buchecker: schwärzliches
Offen, von
Fingergedanken befragt

(Up/Open- / gathered/read / little, gaping /
beechnuts: blackish / openness, by / fingerthoughts
questioned)

The gathered beechnuts are "read open" and display a book
(*Buch*) within them that may be probed with "fingerthoughts."

Here, a cut opens a poem, an addressee plunges within, and a quill writes, penultimately, of the reading it—named "I"—can give the plunging "you." Only if the poem cuts, if you cry, go overboard and under—only if there is cry-writing (*Schrei-schreiben*)—can the flare be lit and the guiding fingers write their way to your being read. Reading underwater, at the end of the incisions and inscriptions of wreckage, is the message in the bottle of this Celan poem. The response is written into the message: reading up from descent is carved into the pen's text that cuts down, across, into—that writes—itself. The reading that would identify—the reader that would identify *with*—the "I" that "reads up," is the same that, cyclically, repeatedly, cuts down across the page, enshrines a cry, and wields its sword to the dismembering end.

Between a sky-scroll rolling up and a world's images being enfolded within it, a poetic re-presentation of the visual becomes readable to the point of their disappearing departure altogether. Between the boomerang not hitting and the "I" not answering, in which gap of a resisting, hesitating "Aber" neither the projectile achieves its goal nor the poem its end, a "you" enters and exits. Between an entrance with a sail and an ending with a sword-keel-quill, a "you" goes overboard and underships, where the "I" awaits the trajectory it initiated. A roll that encircles reversibility and terminal indeterminacy—"Des untern? Obern?"—a loop that inscribes exclusion—"wo du nicht sein kannst"—and a plunge that recollects its dismemberment—"ich lese dich auf"—are three trajectories that span the spaces opened by ends that respond to beginnings that will not reach their ends. Eyes that cannot see for brightness or darkness, speed or water, and cannot help but hear, touch, shape, and read through such gaps—"Augen im Sterbegekluft" ("eyes in the kleft of dying") ("Schneebett," I, 168), "Sichttunnels, in / den Sprachnebel geblasen" ("sight-tunnels, blown / into the fog of language") ("Unter der Flut," II, 315)—are taught their lessons (*leçons*, readings) between the "I"'s and "you"'s of Celan's poems of vanishing seeing, missed flight, and shipwrecked sinking.

Afterword

Poetries of Inversion
and a Genre of Lyric

At one of the recent ends of the Western lyric, with Paul Celan, we have seen lyric poems absorb and transform motifs, themes, and structures of the nonlyric literary tradition. Apocalypse and the accompanying revelation or, as a fateful counterturn, its inscrutable enfolding; winged flight and its successful arrival at a goal or—another counterturn—its very success measured by a nonarrival, a miss, and then a double miss; shipwreck, drowning, and their survival or—the counterturn—coexistence with a watery after-death: these were the topoi and imagery, the structures and stakes, which Celan's lyric poems took and reworked from an entire literary thesaurus. Whether Biblical prophecy, or metamorphic narrative verse, or epic structures Christianized into stories of death and rebirth, this "stuff"—*Stoff*, material—of the Western literary tradition could be rewritten in Celan's lyrics to non-narrative ends and to lyric nonends.

Such transhistorical, interlingual, cross-generic appropriation and recasting of literary materials is not unique to Celan, nor to the lyric; intertextuality of this kind is rather the very stuff of Western literature—its tradition—*tout court.* What is more specifically a *lyric* constituent, I have been arguing, is the structure of inversion that characterizes the way a poem directs its reading, and the way its directions toward its ends relate to their consequences of nonends. Inverting reflection, with its uncanny recurrence in the specific tropological form of chiastic inversion, has been shown to instate and to empower—to structure and to operate—lyric poetry and its reading in the several dozen instances studied in this work.

It is not as if nonchiastic, noninverting lyric poems (short, nonepic verse texts) cannot be found, and probably found aplenty. But it is not by such empirical finding of evidence and counterevidence that questions of genre and generic definition are to be decided. At the end of these pages I shall have some speculative remarks to offer on the problem of the lyric genre and the forms of its possible existence and conceptualization. To make our way to such generic questioning, we would do well to ask of some other poetic texts whether their kinds of inversion, as both a tropological means for, and, perhaps, a structural limit to, the sort of knowledge provided by such literature, are qualitatively like or unlike the massively chiastic inversions of the lyrics examined in this book. We may thereby test the theoretical comprehensiveness as well as the self-limitation of an understanding of the lyric in terms of inversions at the ends of our understanding.

The poems we have studied have been self-evidently, even complacently "lyric" in the sense of their accepted universal (Western universal) designation as such. They have also been modern, in the sense of postmedieval. The two "counter"-cases I propose to look at here will differ once historically, and another time generically. Pindar's Pythian 8 ode is, of course, archaic, while passages from Dante's *Commedia* are embedded in a manifestly nonlyric, epically and confessionally narrative text. (The *Commedia*'s premodern or modern status is much more undecidable, but, for our purposes here, this question is irrelevant.) In what follows I look at these two texts with an eye toward patterns of statement-via-inversion and, specifically, toward their tropes and tropings. In this manner we will come to some sense of the measure and boundaries of the lyric poem.

Pindar's Pythian 8 ode is a victory or epinician ode, with its dominant mode of celebration, and as such it is one part of Pindar's large contribution to helping initiate the association of the lyric form of the ode with celebration, an association that has predominated in our tradition ever since. The poem, from 446 B.C., celebrates the Aiginetan Aristomenes' victory in wrestling at the Pythian games, but also—through a series of associations that are subtly analogical and boldly metaphorical by turns—the divinity Hesukhia, identified with the principle of tranquility or calm, and ultimately a principle and state of cosmic order as well. The poem begins:

> Calm [Hesukhia] of the tranquil kindly heart
> daughter of Justice
> with you the city prospers and grows tall.
> In debate and battle
> you hold the master keys.
> Receive this honored Pythian crown that Aristomenes
>   brings you.
> Gently you act and bear
> doing as you would be done by
> both at the perfect season.[1]

I do not intend to analyze the ode's complex association, often typical for Pindar, of the athletic, the political, and the mythical realms of endeavor and achievement, especially as this has so excellently been done by D. S. Carne-Ross. Rather, I shall point out and then inquire into the poem's establishing of an arc of praise and celebration that turns—within itself—against itself. After it introduces the many values in its opening lines—tranquility, kindness, justice, prosperity, honor, gentleness, perfection—amidst the imagery, faint but nonetheless explicit, of the upward direction of height and growth ("grows tall," "perfect season"), the poem turns in the opposite direction. Still addressing the divinity, but drawing out the analogy with the victorious wrestler, Pindar turns with the adversative-cum-conjunctive sense that is often common to Greek particles:

> But the man whose heart is rammed
> with rancorous hate, should he
> fall foul of you, harshly
> you front the attack and pitch
> Pride [hubris] in the deep.

Falling, and being flung, into depth answers responsively to the poem's opening of growth to height, and a few lines later, in a pairing that Carne-Ross renders parenthetic, a fall is again made to correspond, however adversatively, to a benefit:

> (What profits most is
> the gift we take freely granted from a homestead.
> But Too-Sure-of-Himself gets a tumble at your hands in
>   time.)

But if a fall answers a rise or the receipt of good fortune, the emerging structure of Pindar's poem also has a rising fortune following upon a fall. After the poem's mention of the divine defeat of two mythical menaces, the giant Porphyrion and the dragon Typhon, it introduces the beneficent sense of what *falls* from gods so that something good may *arise:*

> Thunder [Zeus] laid them low
> and the arrows of Apollo who of his good will
> received your son, Xenarkes, as he brought
> Delphi's crown of bay and a Dorian triumph song.

> She fell not far from the Graces,
> this island city [Aigina] where Justice lives,
> the valor of the sons of Aiakos
> holding her straitly.

The thunder, lightning, and arrows that fall from divinities on high, consequently laying low the monstrosities that were not to rise up, has a corresponding—part parallel, part inverted—counterpart in the "fall" of the city, as if a seed, "not far from the Graces," so that it might rise up nobly. But what fell from Zeus and

Apollo had to be high to begin with—quite literally like the arrows that rise in order the more powerfully to fall—and so Aigina's seed, too (hence the parallel), was of high to begin with: to begin its beneficent or fortunate fall.

Now it is clear that the structure or figure emerging in these first three strophes of Pindar's ode is that of a circle, with each arc of decline or assent receiving its response in a corresponding arc of assent or decline. The circle, thematically here one of mythic fatality and fortune, may have a partial formal correspondence in the ancient mode of composition (preponderantly oral) known as ring-composition, in which phrasings, motifs, and the statements that retell a familiar story recur in a poem in order to structure it circularly, that is, repetitively for the benefit both of its oral delivery and its aural reception. The circle, like the ring, not only joins an arc on one of its "sides" (parts) to a corresponding and opposite arc on another "side" ("opposite" in the sense of movement along a circle's circumference, or with respect to fixed coordinates of up and down); it also joins beginning to end, and thus end to beginning. In the line-and-a-half that immediately follows those just quoted, Pindar provides a remarkably beautiful statement of this: "teléan d' ĕkhei dóxan àp' àrkhãs," which Carne-Ross renders only, but equally beautifully and exactly, in Latin:[2] "[Aigina] perfectam habet gloriam ab initio." Carne-Ross's interpretive gloss brings out the grammatical point and precision of his having adopted Latin to translate the Greek: "[The phrase states] the simultaneous existence of origin, arkha, and end, telos. . . . Here, instead of treating origin and end as separate even though inseparable entities, Pindar fuses them by making 'end' an adjective modifying the island's original, originating glory. At the origin (when Zeus planted his seed in the island's ancestral heroine), Aigina's glory was already final, *perfecta*."[3] The joining of end and origin at a point—geographic and political (the city Aigina), temporal and mythic (its perfect founding)—is the achievement and the very mark of the structuring form of the circle, and this is our point so far. It should also be observed, however, with its relevance to come only when we turn to Dante, that the phrase in question is as well both syntactically and semantically an instance of the trope hysteron proteron, the last before the first.

The end and its condition of ultimately being achieved (*teléan, perfecta*) come *before* the origin or first beginning that semantically "begins" the sequence only at its end.

The circular structure and circulating thematics that the poem thus establishes, with its corresponding arcs of rise and fall and points of ending and beginning, cannot be pursued analytically in its every detail: the fifteen-strophe poem is too rich and complex for that task here. The myth that is told in the ode's second triad, for example (such a myth being a generic requisite—if not universally so—of the epinician ode), appears to resketch the structure in its thematics. Elliptically retelling parts of the second and successful assault on Thebes by the Epigonoi, after the failed first assault by the Seven against Thebes, the myth has victory following and compensating for loss in the image of a son (Alkman) succeeding, literally as successor, where a father (Amphiaraos) had failed—"Sire to son, innate / the noble temper shines"—but the myth also turns or arcs symmetrically against this celebratory aspect in telling of the first expedition's leader (Adrastos) having his son die—thus succeed militarily, but not generationally—in the second. Carne-Ross summarizes the myth's pattern as "victory with sorrow and loss for the victor," and sees it as of a piece with "the poem's thematic pattern that is unfolding before our eyes: rising/falling, victory/defeat, happy or victorious falls (Aigina's, not far from the Graces; the victor's, on the bodies of his opponents), and now this sorrowful victory."[4]

Such thematic material, as intricate and compelling as it is, cannot be traced further here. Rather, we need to attend to two other parts of the poem in order to bring the issue of its circular pattern to a focus upon the question of how it poetically operates its structure of circulation. The first is the passage in the fifth strophe where Pindar, as he frequently does,[5] associates one or more features of his poem with the themes and patterns (victory, speed, dazzling strength and beauty, deserved and continuing fame) it is celebrating; in our modern critical-theoretical language, we can identify this as the moment of self-reflexivity.

But this thing
which runs at my feet, your debt [*khréos*],

youngest of [Aigina's] glories/beauties,
let it go forward, child, winged by my art.

Carne-Ross calls this "one of the densest and most brilliant bits of
writing in Pindar," and helpfully brings out the double meaning
that allows Pindar to associate his poetic achievement with his pa-
tron/victor's athletic one. *Khréos* means debt, "the debt of song
which the poet owes the victor," and it runs at the poet's feet in the
sense of being at hand, pressing, urgent. But it also means business
or affair, thus, "this business of yours, your victory," and it runs "because victory, the glory of victory, is of all things transient and will
run away unless the poet secures, stays it with his song. Song arrests victory's transience and by making it winged—a figure Pindar uses several times—gives it a longer, even an immortal life."[6]

"Your debt" is "my song," but also "your victory" which, without becoming "my song," will run out, faster but less strong or enduring than song: we read in the circulating semiosis of the meaning of *khréos* a miniature circle—a version of what modern critical
language, to invoke it once again, calls a *mise-en-abîme*—of success
and its profit (the debt owed) threatening to become its own loss
lest the profit of that one (athletic) success be transformed into
the shape of the debt made good or successful (the present song).
But—and here is the real joining of the figure of circularity—the
last step, transformation into winged song, returns to the first,
the speed or transience of victory. Our interpreter, Carne-Ross,
catches this twist under the name of its trope: "This is paradoxical, though; a flying object is gone even more quickly than one
that merely runs. A paradox indeed, one the poet had been at
grips with all his life, the relation between transience and permanence which is at the heart of the victory celebration, marriage of
a momentary glitter and an enduring text."[7] With the mention of
"an enduring text," we need now not so much to stay with the
term of paradox as to look at the moment elsewhere in the text
where this turn—from victory to song, transience to permanence,
via the very continuity of movement from fleeting to flying—re-
curs in an amplitude at once thematic and poetic.

This begins in the middle strophe of the poem's fourth triad
that corresponds symmetrically to the middle strophe of the sec-

ond triad where the lines just quoted appear. The thematic continuity is established by the explicit motif of parentage and child, the formal continuity by the implicit imagery of an arc:

> I pray, that heaven's envy may not mar,
> Xenarkes [Aristomenes's father], your family's good
> fortune.

Pindar's association and incipient transformation of Aristomenes' victory into his, Pindar's, song brought forth the term "child," and here he returns to the father-son theme. And if Pindar's song's "winged" form recalled the arc, the rise and fall, of Apollo's arrows from the third strophe of the ode—and Apollo the archer is also called "far-throwing" (èkatabóle) in the tenth strophe—here the implicit arc is that too much good fortune can lead to divine envy, wrath, and the consequence of taking a fall and being left with too little. A few lines later, Pindar makes this arc of rising followed by falling explicit once again, and the same verb of throwing (bállōn) makes the association with Apollo's arrows explicit as well: "God tosses this man up and that man down."[8]

My point is, first, that the circularity of theme (the victory/defeat, rise/fall theme), via the self-reflexivity of the theme having been made the image of the poetic form (the song's winged flight), and vice versa, issues as and informs the poem's formally and structurally symmetrical (circular) return, here in the fourth triad, to the imagery of rise and fall. But how can the poem escape its fate or doom of recirculating into fall, and how can our understanding escape or exceed a seemingly tautological one in which theme mirrors form which remirrors theme? This leads to the ode's astonishing last triad, and to our occasion for understanding a tropological dimension (or at least a troping) operative within an otherwise too blandly circular and symmetrical sense of its form.

Having returned to addressing Aristomenes and his wrestling victories at the end of the fourth triad, the poem begins its fifth triad with a characteristic arc that concludes or comes down with the force of a wrestler leaping in order to bring others down: "What a high grim fall it was! / you came down on those four bodies" where Carne-Ross's elegant segue from "high" to "fall" instates the arc that concludes with "down."[9] But as if the surface of the text still vibrates with the fourfold fall as a wrestling ring might, the strophe continues with the fateful consequences of the downward turn of the losers—in Carne-Ross's excellently colloquial rendering, "No sweet return for them / mother waiting, lilt of laughter at every corner. / No, it's slink down back lanes, / dodge their mocking eyes"—to conclude with an apothegm of deep decline: "Defeat bites deep," or Lattimore's "all stricken with their sad fortune," and Hölderlin's "durch das / Schicksal belehrt."

To have a victory ode take this deep turn to the losers' fateful fall may be intrinsic to the celebration;[10] it may also—and this is my point about the poem's poetics—indicate the momentum of every arc in the poem's circular structure: nothing can rise but for falling. The poem will nonetheless (Pindar is getting paid for this) end with hope, not lamentation: "Mother [Aigina], beloved, bring this city safely / home on freedom's voyage. In the name of Zeus, / Lord Aiakos, Peleus, brave Telamon, Achilles." In order to come to rest with an upbeat motion—itself a paradox—with the hopeful rather than the fateful, the poem and the shape of its circulation have to turn against themselves.

They do this in the most exacting, intratextual, or self-reflexive figures that the poem has yet displayed. A figure of a man flying high, as we would colloquially say, on the thrill of his victory is, after the second triad's self-reflexive figure of the poem's winged flight, the very image of the poem depicting, in its upbeat manner, this upward flight: theme is form and form theme, or, after I. A. Richards' model of metaphor, tenor is vehicle and vehicle tenor.

> Who wins some new fine thing,
> for the glory of it he flies
> lifted, hope-winged
> at the crest of man's estate.
> Wealth—what is wealth to this?

But for all the upward arcing of these remarkable lines—"flies / lifted, hope-winged / at the crest"[11]—*and as the very consequence* of their form, a fall must come, and it is introduced, once again with poetic form reflecting theme and vice versa, with a rapidity that does not even await a new line and that instantiates the rapid change of fortune the lines speak of:

> Mortal delight
> shoots up so fast and falls as quick to ground,
> shattered by averse dispose.

This shoots-and-falls—Lattimore has it as "delight is exalted, and thus again it drops," Hölderlin as "Das Erfreuliche wächst, so / Aber auch fällt es"—is the extension and enactment and consequence of the "flies / lifted" of the previous lines' flight. But what are we to make of the "shattered by averse dispose"? Is thematic shattering or breakage at all "reflected" or enacted in its poetic likeness?

Yes and no, in the sense that Pindar's poem strains here with and against the force of its formal and thematic arcing-into-otherness, so that a fall must follow rising for the poem to continue its success and self-succession and not break off, but the fall must itself also break or give way to another rise. The transition, transformation, and reversal of up into down (and back into up) is the very turning of the entire poem—its master troping, we might say—but in so doing the poem never—yet—turns against itself. Or, more precisely, we can now say that the poem's turn against itself—against simple, upwardly lifting, celebratory song—*is* its turning of and with itself. Its trope is apotropaic.

Carne-Ross calls the last two words of the lines last quoted "deliberately enigmatic in the Greek," and adds that his "averse dispose" "trie[s] to leave them inscrutable."[12] On the contrary, his literal rendering of the Greek *àpotrópō gnōma* may, at least halfway, lend insight rather than inscrutability.[13] The circular "master troping" of the poem is one of constant progress-as-reversal (victory as loss, rise as fall, etc.) without that reversal becoming a thought-stopping contradiction: the turning (*trepein*) turns with and against itself without simply becoming contrary, opposite, or—an ultimate reversal—a stoppage or blockage of motion. The momentary crash or shattering of the arc of flight in the fall here is, as an image but also as a verbal infratext appearing from out of the text and its troping, the *inversion* of all that the text does into all that at once resists it (a-verse, *apotrópō*) and that it resists—its own aversion to its turning and returning against itself.

Which is to suggest that the hidden but here surfacing self-inversion within the poem's circular troping would be most properly itself when it turns against even itself: when the apotropaic force within the troping becomes apotropaic of and to itself. That a turning-against or aversion can turn against itself—be self-averse—is the surprising and singular feature of Pythian 8, so that this lyric is both on a constant track of inversion—every direction taken and given reverses itself—and never, ultimately, crosses itself up since its arcing always turns again against its turning-against. To speak in visual figures, it is a circle that never twists itself into a figure eight.

This is demonstrated in the poem's concluding strophe, both thematically and verbally. The crash that brought flight to its fall, and brought out the averse/adversative force within all the poem's turning—the turning-away within the turning—bounces, as it were, with continued consequentiality, not unlike the "high grim fall" that lingered over the next five lines of ignominy. Here, the transience of "shoots up so fast and falls as quick" is first reemphasized, followed by an answer to the question of man that likewise underscores the transience of a fading dream and the insubstantiality of an obscure shadow:

> ephámeroi: tí dé tis; tí d' oŭ tis; skiãs ŏnar
> ánthrōpos.

> (Creatures of a day. What is he, what is he not? Dream of
> a shadow, / man.)

But in the caesura in the middle of the line (*tí dé tis; // tí d' oŭ tis*), the precise balancing moment or spot within the turning between opposites ("What is he, what is he not?"), we can spot the poem's recovery from the negativity of exposed adversity, a recovery of its continued turning by way of the very agency of the adversative. From asking affirmatively to asking negatively, and apparently, or momentarily, accenting the negative ("Dream of a shadow, / man"), the poem turns—is already turning—to the explicit adversative of the next line-and-a-half, with its beautifully affirmative and light-shedding, shadow-dispelling statement:

àll' ŏtan aĭgla diósdotos ĕlthē,
lampròn phéggos ĕpestin àdrōn kaì meílikhos aiōn.

(But when the radiance granted by Zeus comes, / a
bright light rests on men and life is sweet.)

It is these lines, as bright and generous as any in Western poetry ("the greatest perhaps in Greek," Carne-Ross says[14]), that through their adversative's turning with, and therefore against, the "averse" (àpotrópō) tendency within the poem's arcing, then allow the poem's conclusion to be upbeat, hopeful, celebratory.

ᛊ

The themes of Pythian 8 were paradoxical: that joy in victory should be matched with sorrow, rise with fall. Through the poem's passages into self-reflexivity, we were able to see that its form and structure, in their circular arcing, were no less "paradoxical" or self-opposing: any arc's turning was incipiently and ineluctably a turning-away or -against. But the threat of bottoming-out with "averse dispose" itself turns against its turning-against: the adversative, so common and powerful in Pindar (and, as we saw in Hölderlin's "Andenken," so successfully adapted by Pindar's greatest poetic heir), circles around and reverses the turning-down. Pindar's ode is inverting everywhere, but nowhere is it twisted or crossed. The poem remains, thematically and poetically, a circulation along the arc of its winged flight, where even the necessary fall recalls and reflects—reverts to—its height. Another aspect of this understanding is the observation that, to my knowledge, the troping of this poem is without the trope of chiasmus.

Dante's *Commedia* is widely and justly known as a magnificent structure of inversions—we glanced at some of these already in the Leopardi chapter, the inversion of narrative death by drowning into Christian and poetic resurrection, for example—and as we turn now to examine some of its specifically tropological passages of inversion, we can bypass much thematic summary and representation. Let us just recall that, whether in its spatial inversions (down in Hell leads to its reversal into the up of the mountain of Purgatory, and left-and-right directions are also significantly reversed) or its temporal ones (the narrative is the condition of possibility for its telling, but the telling is the constitution of the narrative), Dante's poem almost constantly keeps the structures and performances of inversion before the eyes and mind of its reader. Being in two times, two directions, two states at once—then/now, down/up, sinner/saved, and so on—is thus as much the condition of the reader as it is the story of the construction of the character and author Dante and the poem's construction of that story.

One of the ways the *Commedia* keeps this megastructure of inversion before its reader's eyes (one among many, including, for example, the present-tense addresses to the reader about the import of "past" narrative events, a technique I also alluded to in the Leopardi chapter) is through its deployment of fine, specific, often quite brief tropes of reversal: brilliant but small individually, they add up to a distinctive feature of the weave or intratext of the megastructure. The three canticles, it is well known, have a representational strategy predominant to each, which in each case corresponds to that particular realm of the afterlife construed physically as well as facultatively: *Inferno*'s strategy is mimesis, corresponding to Hell's fictive subterranean earthiness and to the sense that the dead souls are the *forma perfectior* of their once living bodies; *Purgatorio*'s strategy is poetic fantasy, corresponding to Mount Purgatory's conspicuously invented status and to the faculty of imagination or *fantasia;* and *Paradiso*'s strategy is sheer intellection, corresponding to both Dante and Beatrice's space-traveling and the divine realm itself being nothing more or less than acts of God's mind. But this level of correlation between discursive strategy and facultative or metaphysical characteristic, as essential as it is to understanding the poem, is not what I mean by Dante's deployment of specific kinds of tropes. Nonetheless, to pose first the question of the poem's tropes by their appearance or absence in certain canticles can be a heuristically productive way to introduce our inquiry into Dante's tropes of inversion.

If in a certain sense all of the *Commedia*, from the first canto of *Inferno* onward, is structured as a hysteron proteron—the last before the first—this sense is only a conceptual one, and not a materially tropological one. That is, that death comes before (re)birth, and that Dante-pilgrim has completed the voyage before Dante-poet undertakes to begin its representation (whence the voice that can speak of the end before even beginning: "ma per trattar del ben ch'i' vi trovai, / dirò . . . [But, to treat of the good that I found in it, / I will tell . . .]," *Inf.* I, 8, 9[15]), are preconditions for the poem's sense that are not themselves tropologically embedded in the same "form" that they constitute. The famous unprecedented survival of death by drowning in *Inferno* I, that we already glanced at in the Leopardi chapter, conceptually crosses a state of living with the impossibility of being left alive,

> così l'animo mio, ch'ancor fuggiva,
>> si volse a retro a rimirar lo passo
>> che non lasciò già mai persona viva. (I, 25–27)

> (So my mind that was still fleeing / turned back to gaze
> upon the pass / that never left anyone alive.)

but does so with an admirably balanced, uncrossed parallel construction: "l'animo mio . . . si volse a retro a rimirar lo passo" is syntactically paralleled by "lo passo . . . non lasciò già mai persona viva." (Only the doubled directionality of still fleeing, "ancor fuggiva," and turning back, "si volse a retro," instantiates a sense of crossing like a twisted torso and neck.) Indeed, one looks in vain, to my knowledge, for a single instance of the trope of hysteron proteron in the entire *Inferno*.

It is in *Paradiso*, rather, that one encounters the first hysteron proteron and ultimately one finds it there no less than five times.[16] This trope, with its considerable counterintuitive daring, is there once used in a highly posed and static image of a hierarchy that, in its representation of a reversal of a temporal and historical sequence, finally reestablishes a rectified order of divine salvation: it is the image of Mary above Eve, her healing coming after the latter's original sin, but here, in the image, coming first:

> "La piaga che Maria richiuse e unse,
>> quella ch'è tanto bella da' suoi piedi
>> è colei che l'aperse e che la punse." (XXXII, 4–6)

("The wound that Mary closed and anointed, / that one who is so beautiful at her feet / is she who opened it and pierced it.")

The hysteron proteron here is typically striking in its reversal of temporal order while also somewhat blunted or muted in its deployment in a static, almost iconographic image. Each of the other instances of the trope in *Paradiso*, however, may be said to be blunted in a different way: they are instances of its familiar, even banal employment, which is simply to indicate great speed, as in our colloquial banal use of the trope when we say, "I was asleep before my head hit the pillow." The first of Dante's uses of this trope, which is also his most classical, may stand for the other three as well:

e forse in tanto in quanto un quadrel posa
e vola e da la noce si dischiava,
giunto mi vidi ove mirabil cosa
mi torse il viso a sé. (II, 23–26)

(And perhaps in that time that a bolt strikes, / flies, and from the catch is released, / I saw myself arrived where a wondrous thing / drew my sight to it.)

The perfect parallel between the illustrative (or similic) speed of a bolt striking, flying through the air, and being released from the crossbow, and the represented speed of Dante-pilgrim arriving at the sphere of the moon before his sight is drawn to it, cannot be gainsaid in its poetic mastery. But in its statement it means about as much as "very fast indeed."[17]

The appearance of hysteron proteron in *Paradiso* to mean great or hyperbolic speed is curiously balancing of its entire absence from *Inferno*, the canticle which, with its strategy of exaggerated "realism" corresponding to the doctrine that afterlife in Hell is more really real than life on earth, may properly be called hyperbolic. Two comparisons of *Inferno*'s depictions of great speed with that of the hysteron proteron just glanced at in *Paradiso* are instructive of what the trope of hysteron proteron does and does not perform in Dante's *Commedia*. Virgil recalls, for example, how he responded to Beatrice when she asked him to leave Limbo and help Dante:

"tanto m'aggrada il tuo comandamento,
   che l'ubidir, se già foss, m'è tardi." (II, 79, 80)

("Your command so pleases me, / that had I obeyed
already it would be late.")

This is not the hysteron proteron it might have been for the second line remains in the conditional (the act remains unrepresented), but it *is* hyperbolic: it means Virgil cannot obey Beatrice fast enough. And in Dante's political invective against his city of Florence, forecasting a deserved retribution,

E se già fosse, non saria per tempo. (XXVI, 10)

(And if it were already come, it would not be too soon.)

this is not a hysteron proteron's putting of fulfillment before premature anticipation, but mere hyperbole: Florence cannot get its comeuppance soon enough. Hysteron proteron in *Paradiso* does the hyperbolic work that hyperbole alone does in *Inferno*. What, then, is the difference, and what may be learned from this with respect to Dante's poetic inversions and their lyric or nonlyric employments and modes?

The figure of inversion that is materially (verbally) forceful but semantically limited in *Paradiso*'s several uses of hysteron proteron may appear somewhat underwhelming because both the principle and the action of reversal have become, by the poem's third part, as common and saturating as they have. But this should not dull us to earlier moments where tropes of inversion are powerfully novel, and remain so after many rereadings. Two of these, each still representing great speed, may lead us to the special efficacy as well as the self-limitation of Dante's art of poetic inversion. In *Inferno*, when Dante wants to describe how quickly Phlegyas and his boat come across the marshy Styx to him (that is, his character) and Virgil, he employs the classical image of the flying arrow that his best instance of hysteron proteron also alluded to:

Corda non pinse mai da sé saetta
   che sì corresse via per l'aere snella,
   com' io vidi una nave piccioletta
venir per l'acqua verso noi. (VIII, 13–16)

(Bowstring never drove arrow from itself / that coursed
so swiftly through the air / as a little bark I saw / come
towards us then through the water.)

The hyperbole of speed ("faster than a speeding bullet," our cartoon cliché might have it) is foregrounded, but if this is all we notice, we notice little indeed. The figure is also what is called a
change-of-point-of-view simile, in which the speed of the arrow's
flight *from* a bow (*da sé*), as from a distant shore, is compared to
the speed of the bark coming *toward* (*verso*) the point of observation. In other words, the perspective needs to be, and is, reversed,
in order to see departure as arrival; and perhaps the fact that in
this figure a far point, the shore toward which the characters are
traveling, is thereby brought into comparison with a near one at
which they still stand, allows for some resemblance between this
trope and hysteron proteron, since it may be said to invert later
(future) and earlier (or present). But the real force of reversal
here is not merely that of perspective or point-of-view, but the chiastic inversion that constitutes the figure itself:

... pinse ... saetta
      ×
... nave ... / venir

(... drove ... arrow
      ×
... bark ... / come)

A trope of hyperbole, conveying the great speed that is one of the
dramatic effects of the *Commedia* in its *Inferno* as well as, certainly,
in its *Paradiso* (notably less so in *Purgatorio*, where one scarcely rushes
God's merciful plan of purgation), is here also a simile or comparison that reverses the point of view—to little effect that is immediately obvious, perhaps, but in a step that nonetheless contributes
to inculcating the practice of reversal that is the poem's pattern
throughout. But it is also a third trope as well, a formal and material (verbal) chiasmus that has inversions of syntactic order (motion—object moving × object moving—motion) crossing and re-
crossing around the manifest inversion of represented perspectives.
Later in *Inferno* we observe a similar tropological complex, in-

volving strange motion and extraordinary speed (and once again the flying arrows) entangled with reversed perspectives and chiastic inversion. At the end of canto XVII, as the mythic monster Geryon is carrying Dante-pilgrim and Virgil down to the Malebolge—one of the most inventive sequences of the poem—Dante employs in an extended simile one of the many instances of falcon-and-falconer imagery used in the poem:

> Come 'l falcon . . .
>
> . . . / . . . /
>
> discende lasso onde si move isnello,
>> per cento rote, e da lunge si pone
>> dal suo maestro, disdegnoso e fello;
> così ne puose al fondo Gerïone
>> al piè al piè de la stagliata rocca,
>> e, discarcate le nostre persone,
> si dileguò come da corda cocca. (XVII, 127–136)

> (As the falcon that has been long on the wing / . . . / . . . / descends weary, with many a wheeling, / to where it set out swiftly [English inverts the order of these last two phrases], and alights far / from its master, disdainful and sullen: / so did Geryon set us down at the bottom / at the very foot of the jagged rock, / and, disburdened of our persons, / vanished like an arrow from the string.)

One of the highly and immediately effective achievements of this extended simile is surely the comparison of Geryon's reluctant transport service with the sulking, dissatisfied descent of a falcon to his falconer after an unsuccessful hunt. It is also, however faintly, another change-of-point-of-view simile, for the perspective from which the falcon's descent is depicted is presumably the human one, from the ground looking up, while Dante, imagined with Virgil on Geryon's back, can only depict their descent from the flight downward: they—and we the readers with them—are with Geryon, being "set down." But there is another reversal at play as well, and noticing this one leads to the figure's embedded chiasmus. Whereas the falcon comes down and "alights" (*si pone*) in his return, Geryon came down and departed or "vanished" (*si dileguò*) in order to return, with the by-now familiar speed of "an arrow from the string." The change of perspective has introduced, in fact, a change of consequence: return-down inverted into arrival-to-return-up.

From this curious reversal not only of point of view but of motions and directions (the falcon's returning down compared to Geryon's downward circling that then inverts into a return up), we may now notice a partially doubled chiasmus at work in this tropological nexus:

discende . . . / . . . si pone
           ×
. . . ne puose . . . // si dileguò

(. . . descends . . . / . . . alights
           ×
. . . set us down . . . // vanished)

but also:

. . . si move isnello / . . . si pone
           ×
. . . ne puose . . . // si dileguò

(. . . set out swiftly / . . . alights
           ×
. . . set us down . . . // vanished).

In the comparison, the falcon's descent and alighting are inverted into Geryon's alighting and ascent, and also the falcon's initial setting-off and now its landing are likewise inverted into Geryon's first landing and then setting off.

I have already recalled the *Commedia*'s massive or "mega-" structure of inversion, and I have also alluded to the role that discrete instances of the inversion of perspectives play in directing the reader of the poem to the altered attitudes, and their consequences, which Dante-pilgrim and, with him, the reader must learn to acquire and accept in the course of the literary voyage. There is, furthermore, specific good sense for a reversal not only of perspective, but also of motion, to be embedded in a complex simile of the falcon and its falconer. The earthbound perspective of the falconer has both his lure and the falcon's ultimate goal of return always on the terrestrial surface itself. Dante-pilgrim has to learn to relinquish this perspective—to be lured and to return *upward*, not downward—and he undergoes this reversal by submitting to another, prior one: he goes down, through Hell, in order to go up. If going down really means (or comes to mean) going up, then the falcon's descent here prefiguratively figures this very inversion.[18] But in its comparison to Geryon, the falcon's descent is inverted in a perverse way, as it were, for here Geryon's return as an ascent back up—itself the inversion of the falcon's descent—is a literal ascent but an allegorical (or spiritual) entrapment in the depths of Hell. Dante and Virgil descend literally to have this way inverted into spiritual ascent, while Geryon ascends literally (after his forced service as a taxi of descent) to remain forever, by inversion, in a posture and place of descent and fall.

Is there, however, any obviously good or compelling thematic sense to the poem's having the kind of chiastic crossings and double crossings we have been noticing? Inversions of directions down and up, and of motions away and toward, are explicitly and repeatedly deployed within the Christian thematics of death and resurrection, damnation and salvation, life as exile and an afterlife as a return home, and so on. A partially doubled chiasmus such as we have just seen, inverting descent and ascent and taking off and setting down, is—more than any change-of-point-of-view simile—either a signal of the temptation of the gratuitously decorative (some would say baroque, even twisted), or an actual poetic tendency toward blockage or stoppage of the poem's narrative argument as well as the clarity and efficiency of its comprehension. The *Commedia*'s argument and its comprehension, it is well known, are both instances of narrative *conversion*.[19] If I now turn to two instances of tropes of inversion, one in *Purgatorio* and one in *Paradiso*, which are remarkably like the two just examined from *Inferno*, it is so that we can appreciate the difference between inversions that tend toward chiastic knots, as it were, and those that are, chiastically or not, effective tropes of conversion. A final look at another instance of chiasmus in the poem will then allow us to conclude this survey, detailed but hasty, of tropological inversions in Dante's *Commedia.*

A single, massive reversal of perspective informs an only apparently "naturalistic" and terrestrially familiar image toward the end of *Purgatorio:*

E già per li splendori antelucani,
　　che tanto a' pellegrin surgon più grati,
　　quanto, tornando, albergan men lontani,
le tenebre fuggian da tuti lati
　　e 'l sonno mio con esse; ond' io leva'mi,
　　veggendo i gran maestri già levati. (XXVII, 109–114)

(And now before the splendors that precede the dawn, /
and rise the more welcome to pilgrims / as, returning,
they lodge less far from home, / the shades of night fled
away on every side, / and my sleep with them; whereupon
I rose, / seeing the great masters already risen.)

The radical change of point of view is one between earthly pilgrims returning to their homes and families after a pilgrimage to a holy site, and Dante-pilgrim returning but still on his way to an original, spiritual home with God, far above earth in Paradise. "Returning home" in the image's similic vehicle means for Dante-pilgrim, by inversion, "leaving one's earthly home," and at the same time, by conversion, it means "returning home" in the heightened, spiritual sense of the poem's allegory. "Returning" (*tornando*) from the pilgrimage site in the image likewise means by inversion "not yet there" (Dante is still on the way) and at once, by conversion, it means "re-turning," turning back from a state of exile and converting to a true citizenship in the city of God. The double sense of the poem's image—literally inverted, allegorically converted—is also at work in the beautiful efficacy of the detail of "the splendors before the dawn" ("li splendori antelucani"), for the splendors welcoming the pilgrims who are after their holy visit but not yet all the way back from it are still splendors before (*ante*), and so "after" is still, by inversion, "before," just as, in Dante's conversion, he is still before his oral confession in the presence of Beatrice at the end of *Purgatorio,* and before his physical conversion or return to Paradise and God thereafter.

For all this tropological inversion in the image in the service of the allegorical conversion in the poem's narrative, the lines themselves are purely unchiastic and, in fact, constitute parallel upon parallel. The inverse ratio of "more welcome . . . less far from home," for example, has no inverted counterpart; rather, it invites the parallel (because still inverse) ratiocination of the alternative "less welcome . . . more far from home," and the two phrases, "più grati" and "men lontani," are not only grammatically parallel; they are also graphically parallel, one above, one beneath the other at the two lines' ends. The motions in the six lines are parallel throughout. In the image itself, the splendors rise and the pilgrims do, too, to continue returning, and then, in the turn to the comparison, the shades of night move on as well for Dante-pilgrim, his sleep does as well ("le tenebre fuggian da tutti lati, / e 'l sonno mio con esse" is a parallel construction that does not even need the repetition of the verb "flee"), and, in a final, this time explicit parallel, he rises and sees "the great masters already risen" ("leva'mi" and "levati" phonetically parallel and also graphically parallel one above and beneath the other at their lines' ends).

Our second instance of a trope of inversion that is also a trope of conversion is briefer yet more daring than the last. Beatrice addresses Dante-pilgrim as he is ascending from earth toward the first heavenly sphere at the beginning of *Paradiso:*

"Tu non se' in terra, sì come tu credi;
    ma folgore, fuggendo il proprio sito,
    non corse come tu ch'ad esso riedi." (I, 91–93)

("You are not on earth, as you believe; / but lightning, fleeing its proper site, / never darted so [fast] as you to yours are returning.")

The initial impression conveyed by Beatrice's comparison is of hyperbolic speed: you, Dante, are flying as fast as a lightning bolt. (The hyperbole of speed is then completed, as it were, in the hysteron proteron of the next canto: "perhaps in that time that a bolt strikes, / flies, and from the catch is released, / I saw myself arrived where a wondrous thing / drew my sight to it.") But within the hyperbole is a stunning reversal of direction: lightning flees down as you, Dante, return up. The second half of this reversed comparison instantly explains itself in accordance with the poem's entire thematics of inversion and conversion: Dante-pilgrim's voyage of inversion converts him from loss and exile below, on earth, to a return to God above. This sequentiality to the figure's operation—from hyperbolic speed, via reversal of direction, to the thematics of conversion—masks, however, the structure of inversion within it, which is a double chiasmus:

(lightning) fuggendo il proprio sito
            ×
(you) ad esso riedi;

but also:

Tu non se' in terra
        ×
tu . . . ad esso [proprio sito] riedi.

What we may call the first chiasmus here embodies and transacts the real efficacy of the figure's reversal of direction: lightning "fleeing its proper site," syntactically inverted into "to yours (e.g., to your, Dante's, proper site) returning," inverts direction but also an earthbound sense of what is proper. What is the "proper site" for man is *not* where he would be seen as quotidianly as lightning is in the sky. And this, then, is the force of what we may call the second chiasmus in the figure: Dante-pilgrim's "you are not on earth" (heretofore his "proper site"), syntactically inverted into "to your (proper site) are returning." The returning to the proper site in Paradise is empowered, in the chiastic inversion, by the negation of Dante-pilgrim's former state ("you are not") and knowledge ("not . . . as you believe"), and it retrospectively recasts the former site—earth—as improper.

This doubly chiastic inverting—its twisting and troping of there and here, down and up, fleeing and returning—is not only entirely in the service of the *conversion* of Dante-pilgrim, being dramatically effected in space and space-voyaging between the top of

Purgatory and the entry into the celestial spheres. The complex trope in fact reveals a semantic conversion—an overcoming of a once sufficient, now false sense, in a higher and truer one—in its very literalism about the lightning. For the "proper site" of lightning was believed to be the sphere of fire, between the earth and the moon,[20] while in the fiction of the poem, Beatrice and Dante are at this very instant traveling from the top of earth (Mount Purgatory) to the sphere of the moon. Thus, the trope enacts, *in its very functioning and reading,* the change of point of view such that what was normally above man (lightning in the sky) is now below, while Dante, previously below the region of lightning, is now, in the inversion effected by the trope itself, arriving above it.

Chiasmus, here in its form of syntactic inversions, can operate in accord with the poem's poetics of conversion as effectively as, in our previous example, a reversal of perspective could have built within it a series of parallels that know no inversion at all. There are surely other moments in the *Commedia* where chiasmus is similarly functional.[21] But in concluding this brief survey of the poem's tropes of inversion, we should look at one more chiasmus that is at once beautiful, harmless, even gratuitous, yet also signaling its duplicitous poetic power within the *Commedia:* powerful when employed for and with the narrative's poetics of conversion, but seductively self-involved and arresting in its autonomy when emerging on its own. This chiasmus occurs in the little and touching presentation that Pia gives in her address to Dante, as the third of three souls he listens to early in *Purgatorio:*

"Deh, quando tu sarai tornato al mondo
    e riposato de la lunga via,"
        seguitò 'l terzo spirito al secondo,
"ricorditi di me, che son la Pia;
    Siena mi fè, disfecemi Maremma:
    salsi colui che 'nnanellata pria
disposando m'avea con la sua gemma." (V, 130–136)

("Pray, when you have returned to the world / and have rested from your long journey," / followed the third spirit upon the second, / "remember me, who am la Pia. / Siena made me, unmake me did Maremma, / as he knows who with his ring / had plighted me to him in wedlock.")

The thematic and doctrinal significance of Pia in the poem is obscure, and seems to correspond to the small and delicate stature of her appearance in the poem at all. But her miniature address and self-presentation, the one proleptic and the other retrospective, may, in its mere seven lines, be said to display the entire shape of the *Commedia*. Dante is always twice-turning in the poem, once to return to God and then, saved, to return to earth, and here Pia addresses him in the long view of the full arc of "the long journey." Having proleptically completed that journey, Dante is asked to do what, indeed, he is doing throughout the fiction of the poem from the first canto of *Inferno* onward: remember. But for all the doubled circularity of the first four lines of Pia's address—Dante still returning to God, but in order to return to earth and men; and he is bidden to remember in the future as he is always already remembering in the fiction of the poem—what is perhaps more striking still is the passage's linear sequentiality: you will have returned to the world; then you will have rested; so the third spirit followed the second; then remember me. And, in perhaps a fifth sequential step following upon these four, Pia begins to supply the memory, her story: "Siena made me." But at just this point the linearity is interrupted and inverted by the delicate one-line chiasmus: "Siena mi fé, disfecemi Maremma," where the Maremma prison in which her husband had her incarcerated (evidently so he could marry again) undoes or unmakes in death the person whom her native city is said to have made. As instantly as this chiasmus appears, the next two lines pass on in the continuing and then abruptly concluded narrative memory of Pia's life, marriage, betrayal, and death.

The chiastic inversion of the one line has either nothing but decorative significance, or all the proto-sense of the entire poem's reversals of life into death, death into higher and more real (after)life. It is tropologically, verbally-materially real, but perhaps entirely overcome or bypassed in the six other lines that surround it in their linear and circular accounts, as it is certainly overcome and overwhelmed by all else that is the *Commedia*, the very poem of narrative inversions and conversions. In its one-line minimalism, this chiasmus may be the lyric moment within the poem's massively epic, narrative, autobiographically converting constructions of sense.

？♣

To view Pia's chiasmus as quintessentially "lyric" is admittedly to repeat Benedetto Croce's gesture of sifting out pure *poèsia* from among *non-poèsia*.[22] Even as the gesture acknowledges this affinity, it may signal an inflection. Chiasmi are not only or essentially lyric, or poetic. They are there in language as in literature, in life as in language. Like all inversions, their interest and importance is in the direction and consequences of their force.

These last pages' excursion through Pindar's ode and passages of Dante's poem allows us to bracket and book-end with a differential, limiting understanding the itinerary of this book's chapters, with its readings of lyric poems as the inversions of their ends into endings, returns, and rebeginnings. In the cases of the lyric, the structure of chiasmus—both the material trope, constructed of and lodged in the poems' language, and the more speculative shape of crossing and inverting patterns of reading and understanding—was found to be a preponderant and perhaps determining figure. But now we may compare with our modern lyrics from Shakespeare to Celan an archaic lyric without chiasmus and a vernacular poem full of tropes and structures of inversion, including chiastic ones, that is not lyric but rather resolutely narrative on the grandest scale. The circularly arcing shape of Pindar's Pythian 8 ode in its thematics as well as its self-reflexivity is inverting not by crossing, but by aversion and adversative—by a turning against or away from its turning (*apotrópōs*) that ultimately turns against or away from its own turning against and away; by the adversative movement and countermovement of the verses. The narratively and spiritually and cosmologically reversing structure of Dante's *Commedia* inverts as many of its elements and coordinates as it does—life and death, down and up, then and now, exile and home, radical fiction and the uncompromising claims of truth—not without chiasmus but with and for the decisive pattern of *conversion*, and in no direction so much as the linear, future orientation of converting the example of one man's story into a narrative of universal exemplarity.

We may generalize about Pindar's ode as a celebratory circulating between rise and fall, fall and rise, that nonetheless—self-resistingly—does not want to end with yet another declining portion of its arc; we recall its beautiful penultimate image of divine light upon men, and its closing affectionate and hopeful call. In a poem that repeatedly displays the shadow of loss within the light of celebration, this artful ending with celebration from out of shadow may be visualized as something like the fillip that, with measured excess, darts—apotropaically—out of and against a fatal circularity. (Graphically, this shape would look like a capital Q.) It may be that lyrics that do not invert chiastically invert otherwise—asymmetrically, paradoxically, astonishingly. Thus Pindar's ode's celebration can celebrate victory *and* defeat, and can self-reflexively celebrate both celebration *and* lament. The lyric tradition of odes and elegies would in this view constitute the symmetrical and balanced pairing of the always excessive measures that invert or spill over—as celebration beyond others' lament and lament that is celebrated, respectively—the otherwise circular and figure-eight patterns of its inversions.

The apparently simple and dartingly fast trope of hysteron proteron in Dante's *Commedia* is a minimal paradigm of that poem's inversions of last and first, end and origin. Conceived as a loop (the poem begins by recalling its end, and it ends by returning Dante-pilgrim to earth so that he might become Dante-poet and begin the poem), the circulating structure of the poem's character and story and coordinates is recurrently effected or operated by specific, material figures of inversion that reverse direction and perspective, including chiastically. But as we saw with the small but perhaps equally paradigmatic instance of Pia's address and self-presentation, the chiasmus can become most visible when visibly functioning least, gratuitously poetic because semantically trivial. It may be that the narrative loop of the entire *Commedia* aspires to a straightening-out between beginning and end such that all inversions, twists, and chiasmi within it, while not disappearing, would enter into the text's linearity like the weave of a rope. At the farthest remove from the crisscrossed edifice and artifice that is the *Commedia,* there would appear, then, something like flat, unproblematic narrative, where one begins at the beginning and ends at the end, without being troubled by any knowledge that one also had to be at the end before the beginning, and return to the beginning at the end. Pia's chiasmus would be the meek and delicate mark and reminder of inversions that display all linear narrative as conversion narrative.

Lyric, it seems, shapes and reshapes itself between the limit-cases represented by Pindar's ode and Dante's poem at their own virtual limits: between pure circularity, with inversion a geometric principle of symmetry, and pure linearity, with inversion flattening toward invisible regularity. In this understanding the limits of lyric are neither historically discrete nor generically pure, for other kinds (or shapes) of literature are contemporary with Pindar, and lyrics are written by Dante inside as well as outside his *Commedia.* Rather, lyric as the space and temporality of inversions between circles and straight lines, admittedly an abstraction of, a drawing-away from the materiality of texts, is a conceptual scheme that nonetheless remains tethered to the minimal point of tropes of inversion.

It may be that all literary artifacts are, like human customs according to Lévi-Strauss, instances of a limited number of sets of options and combinations, and these sets would be genres.[23] They have only virtual and conceptual reality—one can no more see a genre than one can touch one—and yet this is not to say that they are ever without imagistic shapes, whether these are circles and lines, or imitations of actions, or voices heard and overheard. I imagine literary genres as permanently tethered, within a discursive field, to one or several of its potentials or resources. They may, being flexible, assume many shapes and serve many purposes in their actual textual instances—the texts we call lyrics, or tragedies, or novels—but being elastic rather than malleable, they return by a counterforce to their tethered point of self-identification. Some may fray, wear, snap, and finally have their remnants scattered beyond retrieval or recognition. Others seem, almost counterintuitively, to gain in elasticity the farther and more daringly they are misshapen. If lyric is tethered to its points of inversion, then it must not only undergo misshaping to the limit that it will be said to have no generic shape of any kind; it must also return from an end or the ends of its genre to rebegin by reinversion. Every lyric of this genre would have been, and will rebecome, a generic lyric. All directions and consequences of lyric poetry are materially empowered, whereas the power of its virtual and conceptual genre is a radical of construction, a condition established and reestablished between texts and the consequences of their directions. A genre of lyric is the radical of constructing poetry's reading as the inversion of ends, along with their correspondent comprehensions, into the recurrent understandings of endings.

Notes

Introduction

1. Northrop Frye, *Anatomy of Criticism: Four Essays* (Princeton: Princeton U.P., 1957), 273: "We should therefore get a clearer impression of the lyric if we translated *ta mele* as 'poems to be chanted,' for chanting, or what Yeats called cantillation, is an emphasis on words as words." W. R. Johnson, *The Idea of Lyric: Lyric Modes in Ancient and Modern Poetry* (Berkeley: U. of California P., 1982), 27, 28: "In Greek lyric, however, the music existed for the sake of the words—melody, rhythm, voice, dancing, lyre, and *aulos* ('oboe') all conspired to reinforce and emphasize separate syllables and to augment the clarity of the sung words. What mattered was the performance of the poem, and what mattered in the performance was that the words of the song should be as clearly intelligible as was possible. . . . In Greek lyric as it was performed and written to be performed, there were no slurred words, no vocal or instrumental virtuosities; rather, the word, magnified, illlumined, and framed by melody, instrument, and, sometimes, by dance. In sum, music intensified the words that the poet and his audience shared; it did not substitute for them or suborn them as decoration. In this sense, what we must bear in mind is that this was not

257

so much a musical poetry (in our sense of the word *musical*) as a performed poetry, a poetry with music."

2. Paul de Man, *The Rhetoric of Romanticism* (New York: Columbia U.P., 1984), 261: "What we call the lyric, the instance of represented voice, conveniently spells out the rhetorical and thematic characteristics that make it the paradigm of a complementary relationship between grammar, trope, and theme. The set of characteristics includes . . . specular symmetry along an axis of assertion and negation (to which correspond the generic mirror-images of the ode, as celebration, and the elegy, as mourning), the grammatical transformation of the declarative into the vocative modes of question, exclamation, address, hypothesis, etc., the tropological transformation of analogy into apostrophe or the equivalent, more general transformation . . . of trope into anthropomorphism. The lyric is not a genre, but one name among several to designate the defensive motion of understanding, the possibility of a future hermeneutics."

3. John Stuart Mill, "Thoughts on Poetry and Its Varieties," cited in Frye, 5; T. S. Eliot, "The Three Voices of Poetry," in *On Poetry and Poets* (London: Faber and Faber, 1957), 89–102; Frye, 249; and Johnson, 1–23.

4. Eliot, 89, 92, 96, 97.

5. Frye, 249, 250, 271.

6. Eliot, 100.

7. Johnson, 3.

8. Ibid., 5.

9. Ibid., 23.

10. Frye, 246, 247.

11. Ibid., 280. Another suggestive reformulation of this is p. 300: "The idea of the riddle is descriptive containment: the subject is not described but circumscribed, a circle of words drawn around it." Although the notion of circularity is recognizably Fryean, my further remarks in this introduction turn his "circle of words" into a structure of inversion.

12. Johnson, 6, 19, 21, 22.

13. Helen Vendler, "*Tintern Abbey:* Two Assaults," in *Bucknell Review: Wordsworth in Context,* ed. Pauline Fletcher and John Murphy (Lewisburg, Pa.: Bucknell U.P., 1992), 173–90; 184. Subsequent page references given in the body of text. See also her elegant formulation on the reader in Keats's "To Autumn" in her *The Odes of John Keats* (Cambridge, Mass.: Harvard U.P., 1983), 246: "The poet is so unconscious of his reader that we have only the choice of becoming him in his apostrophe and losing our own identity. . . . If we see at all, it is through the eyes of Keats that we see, not through our own."

14. See Johnson, 25–29, and D. S. Carne-Ross, *Pindar* (New Haven: Yale U.P., 1985), 2, 13, 14, 64, 65.

15. Barbara Herrnstein Smith, *Poetic Closure: A Study of How Poems End* (Chicago: U. of Chicago P., 1968), viii. See pp. 234, 235 for her reticence about any simple literary-historical schematization of the vagaries

of poetic ending. I also have no reason to believe that Herrnstein Smith would today conceive of the problems of poetic ending and its understanding as she did more than twenty-five years ago.

16. De Man, 261.

17. Paul Celan, "Der Meridian," in *Gesammelte Werke* in fünf Bänden, ed. Beda Allemann and Stefan Reichert with assistance from Rolf Bücher (Frankfurt: Suhrkamp, 1983), 3:199.

18. See Frye, 281: "All poetic imagery seems to be founded on metaphor, but in the lyric, where the associative process is strongest and the ready-made descriptive phrases of ordinary prose furthest away, the unexpected or violent metaphor that is called catachresis has a peculiar importance." For de Man on prosopopeia and anthropomorphism, see *The Rhetoric of Romanticism*, esp. 67–92 and 239–62.

19. William Empson, *Seven Types of Ambiguity* (1930), 2nd ed. (New York: New Directions, 1947).

20. Paul de Man, "Tropes (Rilke)," in *Allegories of Reading: Figural Language in Rousseau, Nietzsche, Rilke, and Proust* (New Haven: Yale U.P., 1979), 20–56; p. 38: "The determining figure of Rilke's poetry is that of chiasmus, the crossing that reverses the attributes of words and of things. The poems are composed of entities, objects and subjects, who themselves behave like words, which 'play' at language according to the rules of rhetoric as one plays ball according to the rules of the game." The chapter first appeared in French in 1971 as the introduction to a French edition of Rilke. On Joel Fineman's *Shakespeare's Perjured Eye: The Invention of Poetic Subjectivity in the Sonnets* (Berkeley: U. of California P., 1986), see my discussion in chapter 1.

21. For some insightful remarks on repetition in poetry, see Herrnstein Smith, 38 ff.

22. On three or four occasions in this study I refer to the imagery of loops interlaced and knotted, a figure eight (on its side, the mathematical symbol for infinity), and a Möbius strip, but this is only meant to be illustrative of a tropological structure I am explaining, and not to claim mathematical or specifically topological explanatory value. The Christian motif of death and resurrection, in which the new life is an inversion of the old one, explains only some of the thematics of several of the poems studied here. For some general and very probing remarks on inversion in Western philosophy and literature, see the opening pages of Werner Hamacher, "Die Sekunde der Inversion: Bewegungen einer Figur durch Celans Gedichte," in *Paul Celan*, ed. Werner Hamacher and Winfried Menninghaus (Frankfurt: Suhrkamp, 1988), 81–126, esp. 81–87.

Chapter 1. Shakespeare's Sonnets

1. Barbara Herrnstein Smith, *Poetic Closure: A Study of How Poems End* (Chicago: U. of Chicago P., 1968), vii.

2. Ibid., 51. See also her introductory statement (viii), that "closure—the sense of finality, stability, and integrity—is an effect that depends primarily upon the reader's experience of the structure of the entire poem."

3. *Shakespeare's Sonnets*, ed. with analytic commentary by Stephen Booth (New Haven: Yale U.P., 1977). I cite the sonnets from this edition.

4. Helen Vendler, "Shakespeare's Sonnets: The Uses of Synecdoche," in Shakespeare, *The Sonnets*, ed. William Burto (New York: Penguin-Signet Classics, 1988), 233–40, on synecdoche in sonnet 128, and "Introduction," to Shakespeare, *The Sonnets and Narrative Poems* (New York: Knopf-Everyman's Library, 1992), vii–xxviii, on form, voice, and irony in sonnets 60, 129, and 152.

5. Joel Fineman, *Shakespeare's Perjured Eye: The Invention of Poetic Subjectivity in the Sonnets* (Berkeley: U. of California P., 1986).

6. Fineman signals this already in his introduction (47), when after several pages of the grandest world-historical claims, he writes: "This is to make Shakespeare's name denominate a very general and a very broad event in the history of literature and in the history of ideas. In what follows I am, frankly, more concerned with specific literary attributes of Shakespeare's sonnets, and with the relation of these to the plays, than I am with this broad history. For this reason, at least in what follows, literary history and the history of ideas are significant only to the extent that in his sonnets Shakespeare seems to regret that he repeats them with a difference." In Fineman's own case, any regret that he repeats history with a difference is mock.

7. Fineman, 15: "It is this visionary subject, fully present to his object, to himself, and to the speech he speaks, that Shakespeare rewrites by revising the visual poetics of the poetry of praise. Very briefly, I argue that in his sonnets Shakespeare substitutes for this ideal and idealizing characterization of visionary language—'To hear with eyes belongs to love's fine wit' (23)—a different account that characterizes language as something corruptingly linguistic rather than something ideally specular, as something duplicitously verbal as opposed to something singly visual. The result is a poetics of a double tongue rather than a poetics of a unified and unifying eye, a language of suspicious word rather than a language of true vision. . . . In so doing he develops, or he comes upon, a genuinely new poetic subjectivity that I call, using the themes of Shakespeare's sonnets, the subject of a 'perjur'd eye' (152)." See also his concluding representation, 297–301.

8. An initial and trenchant criticism of Fineman's argument as a historical restabilization of the destabilization in and of poetic language he attributes to Shakespeare's sonnets may be found in the opening pages of E. S. Burt's "Hallucinatory History: Hugo's *Révolution*," *MLN* 105:5 (1990): 965–68, although Burt may have chosen to underemphasize the paradoxically mocking or mock character of Fineman's history.

9. This is especially the case in the second half of his second chapter (110–29) and notes (342–48) on Sidney and Spenser, Robert Fludd and Dante, Petrarch and Donne, and medieval philosophy.

10. See Fineman, 44–47, and for a simultaneous version of the same claim, Adena Rosmarin, "Hermeneutics versus Erotics: Shakespeare's *Sonnets* and Interpretive History," *PMLA* 100:1 (1985): 30: "By expecting the future readers they find, the sonnets prefigure our retrospective confirmation of their excellence."

11. I. A. Richards, "How Does a Poem Know When It Is Finished?" (1963), quoted in Herrnstein Smith, 96, 97.

12. Northrop Frye, *Anatomy of Criticism: Four Essays* (Princeton: Princeton U.P., 1957), 271.

13. Several recent attempts at developing a speech-act or performatives-based model of the lyric suggest that the issue of understanding nonetheless reposes itself in narrative terms; see Ross Chambers, "An Address in the Country: Mallarmé and the Kinds of Literary Context," *French Forum* 11:2 (1986): 199–215; and Steven Winspur, "Text Acts: Recasting Performatives with Wittgenstein and Derrida," in *Redrawing the Lines: Analytic Philosophy, Deconstruction, and Literary Theory*, ed. Reed Way Dasenbrock (Minneapolis: U. of Minnesota P., 1989), 169–88. On lyric poetry and the image, see Andrew Welsh, *Roots of the Lyric* (Princeton: Princeton U.P., 1979), esp. 79–99.

14. Booth, 500, 501, and 545, reports that "many commentators have hoped that it is not by Shakespeare," but while acknowledging our uncertainty, he defends both its thematic and rhetorical affinity with other sonnets and its place in the sequence ("the topic of damnation and salvation that is the common denominator of 144 and 146"). Vendler, "Introduction," xviii and xx, calls it "not a true sonnet," apparently because of its tetrameters in lieu of pentameters, and associates it with the "nonsonnet" 126, which of course has only twelve lines. (Sonnet 99, the third odd one, has fifteen lines.)

15. Booth, 500, has caught this feature of the sonnet exactly: "The effect it describes—that of being surprised by a sentence that signals one direction and then takes another—is an effect that Shakespeare is very fond of actually achieving in his reader; what the speaker tells us happened to him as he listened to his lady is what actually happens to a reader time after time as he reads these sonnets"; he identifies sonnets 13, 15, 35, 75, and 79 as similarly structured.

16. Referring to sonnet 62 and its turn from octave to sestet at a line-beginning adversative "but," Fineman, 53, observes that "the sestets of Shakespeare's sonnets characteristically turn upon the octave in just this poignant counterpointing way."

17. Booth's annotation, 501, that day following night is in Shakespeare's deployment of the proverb emblematic of both inevitability and hope, is nicely apropos of these lines' juncture where the inevitability of an end coexists with the still-hopeful, unattained character of that end.

18. That it is also, as Booth, 501, notes (crediting Andrew Gurr's "Shakespeare's First Poem: Sonnet 145," *Essays in Criticism* 21 [1971]:

221–26), a line that puns on Shakespeare's wife's name "Hathaway," and that leads in the next line to a further pun on her first name—"Anne saved my life"—strikes me not as puerile but as a further mark of the closing couplet's lyric density.

19. Richards' examples were William Empson's "Legal Fiction" ("Your dark central core / Wavers a candle's shadow, at the end") and his own "By the Pool" ("Here is an end"); cited by Herrnstein Smith, 174.

20. Booth, 181, 182; and Fineman, 145, 150, 159, 219, 270.

21. Vendler, "Introduction," xxiv, has succinctly observed how lines 5–7 alone represent "a condensed set of six time-frames."

22. Booth, 183.

23. Fineman, 236–38, for this quote and the remainder of his discussion of sonnet 43.

24. Ibid., 238; the term and structure of "cross-coupling"—a chiastic doubling that "redouble[s] with a difference the complementary similarities of a figurality based on likeness"—is introduced on pp. 37–42 and used *passim* in *Shakespeare's Perjured Eye*.

25. Booth, 203.

26. Ibid.

27. Ibid., 198.

28. Ibid., 204.

29. Booth (ibid.) notes here his note to lines 2 and 4 of sonnet 97, p. 314: "Question marks and exclamation points ('admiration points') are easily mixed up in a printer's font, and many Renaissance texts interchange them. Here, however, the Q punctuation was dictated by the Renaissance practice of sometimes retaining interrogatory punctuation in sentences which, like these, are exclamations structured like questions." Exclamations structured like questions may still, if only and especially rhetorically, be questions.

30. Fineman, 238, at the end of his commentary on sonnet 43, generalizes in just such language: "We grow accustomed to a kind of rhetorical mirroring of traditional visual imagery of unity, a mirroring that pervades the poems in the sequence, and that establishes a distinctive and discriminating screen or film or lens through which both the poet's compliments and his complements are regularly filtered."

31. Shakespeare's "till" here functions as does his word "still" throughout the sonnet sequence, a feature I allude to and extend in my chapter on Keats.

32. Fineman, 239.

Chapter 2. Leopardi's "L'Infinito"

1. After the classic studies by Francesco de Sanctis, *Studio su Giacomo Leopardi*, ed. Raeffaele Bonari (Naples: Alberto Morano, 1925) and Benedetto Croce, *Poesia e non-poesia* (Bari: Laterza, 1946), the most im-

pressive are Sebastiano Timpanaro's massive *La filologia di Giacomo Leopardi* (Florence: Le Monnier, 1955) and Piero Bigongiari, *Leopardi* (Florence: La Nuova Italia, 1976).

2. I have found the best general discussion of Leopardi in English to be D. S. Carne-Ross's wide-ranging chapter in his *Instaurations: Essays in and out of Literature, Pindar to Pound* (Berkeley: U. of California P., 1979), 167–92, but he does not, alas, treat "L'Infinito." The most intensive English-language interpretation of "L'Infinito," focusing on its status and workings as a European romantic sublime poem, is Margaret Brose, "Leopardi's 'L'Infinito' and the Language of the Romantic Sublime," *Poetics Today* 4:1 (1983): 47–71. See also Renato Poggioli's brief but sensitive commentary on the poem in *The Poem Itself*, ed. Stanley Burnshaw (New York: Holt, Rinehart, Winston, 1960), 276, 277. Verse translations exist by Kate Flores and John Heath-Stubbs, and prose translations by Margaret Brose, George Kay, and Renato Poggioli. Their guidance is notable because it often leads one to read the poem more closely by first leading one astray, dialectically providing its errancy on behalf of insight. I am also grateful to Anthony Oldcorn and his "Leopardi e Robert Lowell," in *La Traduzione del testo poetico,* ed. Franco Buffoni (Milan: Guerini et Associati, 1989), 355–59, for bringing Lowell's "imitation" to my attention, although it is useless as an aid—even a negative one—for understanding Leopardi.

3. Cited from Giacomo Leopardi, *Canti,* ed. Niccolò Gallo and Cesare Gàrboli (Turin: Einaudi, 1962).

4. Translation by Brose, 47, with slight modifications.

5. The setting has been much studied. Poggioli, 276, notes: "We should know something about [Monte Tabor's] location, which is in the immediate surroundings of the poet's home town. Recanati, like other places in the Marche, lies on a slope between the Adriatic Sea below and the peaks of the Apennines in the distance. Thus the hill should command an unobstructed view of the sea alone. But, at least in the spot where the poet liked to sit and muse—rather than to stand and gaze—the hill is not a lookout, since a hedgerow prevents the beholder from enjoying the full vista enclosed within 'the farthest horizon' (*ultimo orizzonte*) and the skyline."

6. This recognition must come against the grain of each of the three freestanding translations by Flores, Heath-Stubbs, and Kay, as each drops the *quella* of "di là da quella," rendering the phrase merely as "beyond" or "yonder." Poggioli and Brose, in the translations accompanying their interpretations, get it right.

7. Brose, 50–57, 62, 63, 65, 66, 68, and 69, gives the most sustained commentary on the sublime in the poem, whereas Poggioli, 277, is especially appreciative of its character as an idyll—"idyllic it is in its self-possession and calm"—and of the "per poco"'s achievement as "understatement."

8. Poggioli, 277, referring just to "the ephemeral whisper of the

wind passing by," and Brose, 65, moving from "the wind rustling through *these* plants" to "the voice of the wind," each curiously miss or downplay the reinteriorization of far to near that brings about the poetic "voice" here.

9. The precise terms of the comparison escape the three freestanding translations of the poem, each of which *reverses* the terms of the comparison "quello / infinito silenzio a questa voce"—each comparing instead "this" *to* "that"—while once again Poggioli and Brose get it right.

10. Oldcorn, 355, is correct to call the poem "assolutamente paratattico" and to specify that "[è] soprattutto nella seconda parte della poesia che ci troviamo davanti ad un sostenuto gioco di contrapposizioni," but I cannot follow him when he further qualifies this as "una specie di oscillazione ipnotico-sonnambulistica."

11. Cf. Poggioli's remarkably benign ("idyllic") paraphrase, 277: "Eternity and time merge anew in an infinity which the poet suggests—again in terms of space—through the image of a sea into which his thought and his whole being now willingly lose themselves in quest of peace."

12. Brose, 63, 64.

13. Cited from Dante Alighieri, *The Divine Comedy*, trans., with a commentary, Charles S. Singleton (Princeton: Princeton U.P., 1970–75); I sometimes modify the translation. I am grateful to John Freccero for first suggesting the "vo comparando"'s allusion to and contrast with Dante's "vo significando."

14. I owe to Allen Mandelbaum the suggestion that Leopardi's powerful foregrounding of the comparison in "vo comparando" may also allude to another passage in Dante, which Mandelbaum believes to be the first self-reflexive naming of simile in Western poetry:

> Dal centro al cerchio, e sì dal cerchio al centro
>   movesi l'acqua in un ritondo vaso,
>   secondo ch'è percosso fuori o dentro:
> ne la mia mente fé sùbito caso
>   questo ch'io dico, sì come si tacque
>   la glorïosa vita di Tommaso,
> per la similitudine che nacque
>   del suo parlare e di quel di Beatrice (*Par.* XIV, 1–8)

> (From the center to the rim, and so from the rim to the center, / moves the water in a round vessel, / according as it is struck from without or within: / into my mind fell suddenly / this which I say, as became silent / the glorious life of Thomas, / because of the likeness which was born / of his speech and of that of Beatrice)

The reversibility of outside and inside (circumference and center) in Dante's image that gives rise to the very simile would indeed seem to be recalled in the "loopings" of Leopardi's demonstratives and their regions. That the first line of the Dante passage is also a chiasmus underscores the correctness of Brose's insight below.

15. Brose structures her entire interpretation of "L'Infinito" around her claims for metalepsis in the poem and in Leopardi's poetics more largely. Here, she calls the "mi sovvien" "a metaleptic reappropriation of an affective presence" (63), in line with her broader understanding that "in terms of the Leopardian corpus, metalepsis would describe the underlying poetic strategy by means of which the affective (always *other*) can be activated within the presence of the text; the substitution of an absent plenitude for a present void" (60). Her interpretation is insightful and widely persuasive, and her metalepsis may be another name for what I call a "poetic loop," although I find her tropological and psychological-cognitive mix of metalepses from Quintilian to Chaim Perelman and Harold Bloom unwieldy.

16. Poggioli, 277; Brose, 62–64; Oldcorn, 355.

17. Brose, 61. She also calls *fu*'s tense the "aorist."

18. In addition to her extended (perhaps overextended) interpretation of metalepsis in "L'Infinito"—see my n. 15 above—Brose, 65–67, brilliantly finds the specific trope of chiasmus to be also structuring the poem in various ways. She notes the "phonetic chiasmus between the first and last lines":

c*a*ro   c*ol*le
      ×
d*ol*ce   m*a*re

and persuasively finds similar chiastic reversals of sound, of "the progression of first-person pronomial indicators"

mi fu   mi fingo
      ×
mi sovvien   m'è

and of the relations between the poet and "the figurative capacity of his thought." She goes so far as to suggest "a central axis" for this "chiastic pattern" and to find it in the poem's formal middle—"the affective center of *L'Infinito*, 'ove per poco / I cor non si spaura' (ll. 7–8)." I shall elsewhere in this book have great respect for the determinants of formal middles of poems, but I have argued above why the lines from "E come il vento . . ." to "Vo comparando . . ." must be regarded as the poem's "central axis" or point of chiastic interlacing and inversion, while Brose's argument about the sublime in "L'Infinito" leads her to privilege an "affective center."

19. John Freccero, *Dante: The Poetics of Conversion*, ed. Rachel Jacoff (Cambridge, Mass.: Harvard U.P., 1986).

20. It seems unhelpful to characterize the opening lines as "childhood reveries," Brose, 61.

21. Oldcorn, 355, 356, notes that "Per la sua estensione (quindici versi), questa poesia sfiora, superandola, la canonica misura lirica del sonetto, ma, abbandonando insieme la tradizionale corrispondenza fra misura sintattica e misura metrica e la rima, si pone come una nuova sfida alle chiusure petrarchesche," although I cannot agree that Petrarch's poetic example, including in his sonnets, stands for any closure. There is one fifteen-line sonnet by Shakespeare—no. 99—and other English Renaissance instances of the variant form; see *Shakespeare's Sonnets*, ed., with an analytic commentary, Stephen Booth (New Haven: Yale U.P., 1977), 321.

Chapter 3. Coleridge's "Kubla Khan"

1. Cf. Thomas McFarland, *Romanticism and the Forms of Ruin: Wordsworth, Coleridge, and Modalities of Fragmentation* (Princeton: Princeton U.P., 1981), 3, himself quoting Lucien Goldmann on Pascal's *Pensées* as "achieved by . . . inachievement."

2. I disagree here with the assertion by Marjorie Levinson, *The Romantic Fragment Poem: A Critique of a Form* (Chapel Hill: U. of North Carolina P., 1986), 11: "The English fragment is thus constituted a poetic form by the reader's perception of that work as an element in an epochal set. Or, one poetic fragment does not make a fragment poem; ten do." Even if no other fragment poems existed, and even if we had no reason to believe (as we perhaps do not) that Coleridge intended to add anything more to "Kubla Khan" as we have it, we would still have to read the poem in terms of its word and image of "fragment."

3. Cf. William Hazlitt, *The Examiner* (2 June 1816) and Thomas Moore, *The Edinburgh Review* (September 1816), in Coleridge, *The Ancient Mariner and Other Poems: A Casebook*, ed. A. Jones and W. Tydeman (London: Macmillan, 1973), 62, 65, and 74–76.

4. Cf. Leigh Hunt, *The Examiner* (21 October 1821), in *A Casebook*, 81; and John Bowring, *The Westminster Review* (January 1830), in *Coleridge: The Critical Heritage*, ed. J. Jackson (New York: Barnes and Noble, 1970), 550.

5. J. L. Lowes, *The Road to Xanadu: A Study in the Ways of the Imagination* (Boston: Houghton Mifflin, 1927).

6. E. S. Shaffer, *'Kubla Khan' and The Fall of Jerusalem: The Mythological School in Biblical Criticism and Secular Literature, 1770–1880* (Cambridge, England: Cambridge U.P., 1975), 18 ff.

7. George Watson, *Coleridge the Poet* (London: Routledge and Kegan Paul, 1966), 119.

8. This is a good part of the spirit and the achievement of McFarland's *Romanticism and the Forms of Ruin.*

9. Citations of "Kubla Khan" are from *The Complete Poetical Works of Samuel Taylor Coleridge*, ed. E. H. Coleridge (London: Oxford U.P., 1912), 1:295–98.

10. This judgment, if systematically argued (for this is not the place), would yield a critique of McFarland's book, but also of Levinson's *The Romantic Fragment Poem* and especially its chapter on "Kubla Khan," 97–114, where the reading is specifically ideological.

11. This is precisely the meaning of "half-intermitted burst": the divisions further empower themselves through a splitting or halving of the middle, thus, "half-intermitted." I thank Arden Reed for having called my attention to this.

12. Cf. Wordsworth's famous simile for imagination as a self-concealing origin, "like the mighty flood of Nile / Poured from his fount of Abyssinian clouds / To fertilise the whole Egyptian plain" (*The Prelude* 1850, VI, ll. 614–16).

13. Cf. Hölderlin's Homburger-fragment known as "Urtheil und Seyn," *Sämtliche Werke*–Grosse Stuttgarter Ausgabe, ed. Friedrich Beissner (Stuttgart: W. Kohlhammer, 1961), 4:216, 217, where he understands judgment (*Urteil*) as the original partition (*Ur-teilung*) between being and consciousness.

Chapter 4. Reading Keats

1. An incomplete listing of the Shakespeare sonnets that deploy the range and tension of the ambiguities of the word "still" would include nos. 5, 7, 24, 54, 63, 65, 74, 76, 81, 105, 119, 136, 153, and others still. Helen Vendler, *The Odes of John Keats* (Cambridge, Mass.: Harvard U.P., 1983), 243 and 322, n., in her discussion of Keats's "To Autumn" also notes Spenser's use of "still" in his "Mutability Cantos": "Great Nature, ever young, yet full of eld; / Still moving, yet unmoving from her sted"; and "[air] flit[s] still, and with sub*till* influence / Of his thin spirit all creatures . . . maintaine[s] / In state of life" (my emphasis).

2. In her discussion of "To Autumn," 234, 237, 238, 249, 264, and esp. 276 and 278, Vendler has apposite remarks about Shakespeare's sonnets behind Keats's great ode, but she does not mention Shakespeare's use of "still." My own brief analyses of passages from the odes in this chapter have different emphases than, and diverge at points from, her readings, but my debt to her study is nonetheless great.

3. I quote from *The Poems of John Keats*, ed. Jack Stillinger (Cambridge, Mass.: Harvard U.P., 1978). Subsequent citations of Keats's poems are from this same edition, identified by line number(s); in the case of the long poems, the roman numeral indicates the book or canto; the arabic numeral, the line number(s).

4. I cannot agree with Vendler's assertion, 200: "The pathetic fallacy—that the rest of nature suffers with Saturn—is in this passage lightly refused." She is right when she then adds: "In the later *Fall of Hyperion*, the pathetic fallacy is explicitly rejected." But the lines she adduces as evidence—"Still buds the tree, and still the sea-shores murmur. / There is

no death in all the universe, / No smell of death" (I, 422–24)—nonetheless have a vicious irony within them and their use of "still," as well as in the continuation of the line where Vendler breaks off her quotation: "—there shall be death."

5. On this topic, see Vendler's extraordinary concise and correct formulation at the end of her study of the progress of the odes, 292, 293: "Philosophically speaking, the most interesting of Keats's conclusions, as he comes to the end of his sequence, is his view that art is both absolutely dependent on, and at the same time absolutely sacrificial of, nature."

6. Paul de Man made a similar observation about the interference of activity and its nonending in his reading of the title "The Fall of Hyperion," in "The Resistance to Theory," now in *The Resistance to Theory* (Minneapolis: U. of Minnesota P., 1986), 16.

7. My disrespect for the quality of the poetry relegates my commentary on "Bright star!" to a footnote, which I place here for its semantic similarity to "still they were the same." The unfortunate sestet of the sonnet—

> No—yet still steadfast, still unchangeable,
>   Pillowed upon my fair love's ripening breast,
> To feel for ever its soft swell and fall,
>   Awake for ever in a sweet unrest,
> Still, still to hear her tender-taken breath,
> And so live ever—or else swoon to death.

—states (and overstates) the same semantic movement from "still" as the not-yet-over, the "for ever," to its undoing in the stilling of the too insistent and yet too silent, stilled "hear[ing of] her tender-taken breath." For in what is the sestet's redeeming poetry, the repetition "Still, still to hear" brings out the word's silencing effect (allowing us also perhaps to hear the female persona's breath fatally "taken" as well), and so the either/or of the last line tips more insidiously to its last word than just through the weak "or else swoon."

8. Paul de Man, "Introduction" to *The Selected Poetry of Keats*, ed. Paul de Man (New York: Signet Classic-New American Library, 1966), 11.

9. The intensely precise and justly praising reading of "To Autumn" by Vendler makes the most persuasive case yet for how the poem can be both as exceptional as it is and yet also issuing from the project of all the preceding odes. Her attention, 261, 262, to the "twitter" of the swallows in the famous last line is the significant step toward integrating our understanding with Keats's integration of poetic art and natural sound in this ode:

> The glance that rises to the skies in the last line (the swallows twitter "in," not "from," the skies) has lifted itself away from the panorama of the land and its missing riches, and is purged of self-referential pathos and nostalgia for the past. The ode has floated free of its occasion, and ends poised in the sound of

song, sufficient unto itself. . . . A completed poem . . . is nothing but a thin thread of sound, rising and falling in obedience to its governing rhythms. Though it possesses, seemingly, all the expressive power of human speech, the music of poetry is in fact not ordinary speech but rather sound lifted and sinking as the metrical law governing it rises and falls. . . . It is for this reason that Keats's "perfected" word for poetic utterance, for which he has been seeking throughout the last stanza (trying, in sequence, "songs," "music," "wail," "mourn," "bleat," "sing," and "whistle"—and even, perhaps, "touch" and "bloom"), is "twitter," a verb which preserves the association of a neutral fluttering sound, rising and falling, though within the smallest of gamuts.

On the nonpathetic and "neutral" character of poetic utterance, see my remarks on Hölderlin's *klirren* in the next chapter. See also Richard Macksey, "'To Autumn' and the Music of Mortality: 'Pure Rhetoric of a Language without Words,'" in *Romanticism and Language,* ed. Arden Reed (Ithaca: Cornell U.P., 1984), 263–308; on the utterance of the last stanza, 304–7.

10. For a different reading of the marking of nature in the third stanza—as humanized, that is, cultivated, throughout—see Vendler, 245 and 254.

11. I observe nonetheless that, in a poem about writing, where writing is to be taken *au pied de la lettre,* "This living hand" recalls the word "still" in its words "silence" and "chill," and decomposes the word into its own key words and letters "it," "is," and "I."

12. Lawrence Lipking, *The Life of the Poet: Beginning and Ending Poetic Careers* (Chicago: U. of Chicago P., 1981), 181. The remaining quotes from Lipking are from 182.

13. Cf., for a corresponding sense of the poetic conversion of death into a new life, the lines very nearly at the "end"—the breaking off—of *Hyperion* (corresponding, that is, by the inversion of the end of one Hyperion-poem into the beginning of the other):

Most like the struggle at the gate of death;
Or liker still to one who should take leave
Of pale immortal death, and with a pang
As hot as death's is chill, with fierce convulse
Die into life . . . (III, 126–30)

The word "still" and the turn from "chill" to "hot" make this passage as intertextually pertinent to my discussion of "This living hand" as does the (re)turn of death to life.

14. Roman Jakobson, "Linguistics and Poetics," in *Style in Language,* ed. Thomas Sebeok (Cambridge, Mass.: MIT P., 1960), 358: "The poetic function projects the principle of equivalence from the axis of selection into the axis of combination."

Chapter 5. Three Hölderlin Poems

1. Examples range from Paul de Man's scattered essays on Hölderlin during some seventeen years (1955–72), to more recent work such as Andrzej Warminski, *Readings in Interpretation: Hölderlin, Hegel, Heidegger* (Minneapolis: U. of Minnesota P., 1987) and Anselm Haverkamp, *Laub voll Trauer: Hölderlins späte Allegorie* (Munich: Wilhelm Fink, 1991). But de Man's interest in a comprehensive study of Hölderlin and romanticism foundered, so that today his essays are not widely recognized as a far-reaching interpretation of Hölderlin equal to that of his half-book on Rousseau (the second half of *Allegories of Reading*), his several influential essays on Wordsworth, or even his intriguing introductory and passing pages on Keats. Only two of these essays appeared in German and they have had little resonance upon German scholarship. Significantly, Warminski and Haverkamp are both professors of English in America with an understandably small audience among discipline-bound German Hölderlin scholars.

2. Friedrich Hölderlin, *Sämtliche Werke*–Frankfurter Ausgabe, ed. D. E. Sattler et al. (Frankfurt: Roter Stern, 1975 ff.). Richard Sieburth's translation, *Hymns and Fragments of Friedrich Hölderlin* (Princeton: Princeton U.P., 1984), is the first to base itself in part on the Frankfurter Ausgabe, and while it cannot reproduce the facsimiles and the many variant versions that the German edition can, its choice of texts, as well as its emphasis on the draft versions and the fragments, gives the English-language reader at least an impression of what this new German edition will mean for reading Hölderlin, something the decorousness and polish of the Michael Hamburger translation, *Poems and Fragments* (London: Routledge & Kegan Paul, 1966), and the Christopher Middleton translation, *Selected Poems* (Chicago: U. of Chicago P., 1972), cannot do.

3. Alessandro Pellegrini, *Friedrich Hölderlin, Sein Bild in der Forschung* (Berlin: Walter de Gruyter, 1965).

4. Martin Heidegger, "Wie wenn am Feiertage" (1941), *Erläuterungen zu Hölderlins Dichtung*, 4th expanded ed. (Frankfurt: Vittorio Klostermann, 1971), 51, 52; my emphases.

5. Peter Szondi, "Der andere Pfeil: Zur Entstehungsgeschichte des hymnischen Spätstils" (1963), *Hölderlin-Studien*, 2nd ed. (Frankfurt: Suhrkamp, 1970), 40, 41; my emphases. I henceforth cite this essay in the body of my text by page number(s) only. The typescripts of Szondi's lectures on Hölderlin, posthumously published in *Einführung in die literarische Hermeneutik*, ed. Jean Bollack and Helen Stierlin (Frankfurt: Suhrkamp, 1975), contain a more extended and nuanced discussion of the poem's opening that nonetheless does not change my point here; see 222–43.

6. Friedrich Hölderlin, *Sämtliche Werke*–Grosse Stuttgarter Ausgabe, ed. Friedrich Beissner (Stuttgart: W. Kohlhammer, 1951), 2, 118–20. I preserve Hölderlin's orthography, and henceforth cite "Wie wenn am

Feiertage" without further reference, citing other writings of his in the body of my text by volume and page numbers only (with a slash and a "2" after the volume number—e.g., 2/2—to indicate Beissner's apparatus). Translations are my own, for the sake of literalness, although I have consulted with profit those by Hamburger, Middleton, and Sieburth (see n. 2).

7. See Szondi, 42, and also Rainer Nägele, *Text, Geschichte und Subjektivität in Hölderlins Dichtung: "Unessbarer Schrift gleich"* (Stuttgart: Metzler, 1985), 181, 182, for an incisive discussion of the dispute between Heidegger's and Szondi's interpretations of the opening of the poem.

8. Szondi, "Über philologische Erkenntnis" (1962), *Hölderlin-Studien*, 15–21.

9. Paul de Man, "The Rhetoric of Temporality" (1969), *Blindness and Insight: Essays in the Rhetoric of Contemporary Criticism*, 2nd rev. ed. (Minneapolis: U. of Minnesota P., 1983), 190.

10. See "Über die Verfahrungsweise des poetischen Geistes" and the other fragments presenting the theory of the triadic "Wechsel der Töne," in Hölderlin, 4, 241–65, 228–32, and 266–72.

11. Heidegger, 61, 62.

12. De Man, "Les exégèses de Hölderlin par Martin Heidegger," *Critique* 100/101 (1955): 813, 814.

13. Heidegger, 72 and 76; see also 71: "the sacred is, through the stillness [*Stille*] of the protecting poet, transformed into the mildness [*Milde*] of the mediable and mediating word."

14. De Man, "Les exégèses," 812, and Nägele, 184.

15. Cf. Hölderlin's "Patmos," 2, 171, for a similar passage combining the physical and the interpretive images of a hand: "Zu lang, zu lang schon ist / Die Ehre der Himmlischen unsichtbar. / Denn fast die Finger müssen sie / Uns führen und schmählich / Entreisst das Herz uns eine Gewalt."

16. This is one aspect of what has, since Hellingrath, been recognized as the Pindaric form of Hölderlin's late poetry; cf. Beissner's commentary, 2, 677, 678, and Heidegger, 68, and Szondi, 37–39.

17. Cf. Szondi, 42, 43, and the more recent study by Bernhard Böschenstein, *Frucht des Gewitters: Hölderlins Dionysos als Gott der Revolution* (Frankfurt: Insel, 1989).

18. The chiasmus, spread over strophes 4 to 9, is schematically:

Wenn hohes er [ein Mann, der Dichter] entwarf		wenn er [der Gott] nahet
	X	
Ich [der Dichter] sei genaht		sie [die Himmlischen] werfen mich tief unter

19. For evidence of Hölderlin's textual knowledge of Goethe's poems in the latter's *Schriften* of 1789, see the allusions to and citations of

Goethe's poems in the versions of *Hyperion* ("Wonne der Wehmut," 3, 462, and "Prometheus," 3, 517) and in his letters (probable allusions to "Das Göttliche" and "Zueignung" in the letters of 24 January 1801 and from the end of February 1801, 6, 412, 416, and 6/2, 1057, 1063, and above all the citation of "Grenzen der Menschheit" in the letter to Böhlendorff of 4 December 1801, 6, 427, and 6/2, 1078).

20. Johann Wolfgang von Goethe, *Werke*–Hamburger Ausgabe, ed. Erich Trunz (Hamburg: Christian Wegner, 1948), I, 103.

21. Goethe, I, 102. On Hölderlin's use of an image of the boat rocking on the lake (in the third version of "Mnemosyne," 2, 197) in its relation to Rousseau, see de Man, "L'image de Rousseau dans la poésie de Hölderlin," *Deutsche Beiträge zur geistigen Überlieferung* 5 (1965): 178, 183.

22. For an extravagant image in Hölderlin that similarly pretends to receive heights into depths and to give them back out again, but actually displays them as only upon the surface, see "Heidelberg," 2, 14: "und es bebte / Aus den Wellen ihr [die Gestade] lieblich Bild."

23. Cf. also the use of the words *Schein* and *Schatten* as terms of poetological reflection in Hölderlin's theoretical writings (4, 155, 231, 237, 266–67), and in his letter, written from Homburg, to Neuffer of 12 November 1798 (6, 289, 290).

24. In not being any more animal than human in its imaging of poetic utterance, it thus seems to go beyond Keats's swallows' "twittering," praised by Helen Vendler and discussed in the previous chapter.

25. De Man, "Les exégèses," 813.

26. What I, with Szondi, am here calling the "elegiac mode" would obviously include the odes as well, as in the image from "Heidelberg" cited in n. 22 above.

27. This in disagreement with Heidegger's interpretation of *Gesetz* in "Wie wenn am Feiertage," 62: "Die 'Natur' ist die alles vermittelnde Mittelbarkeit, ist 'das Gesetz.'"

28. Heidegger, "Hölderlin und das Wesen der Dichtung" (1937), *Erläuterungen*, 37.

29. Quoted in Beissner's note to the Grosse Stuttgarter Ausgabe, 2/2, 802.

30. Heidegger, "Andenken" (1943), in *Erläuterungen*, 79–151. For Beissner's remark, see 2/2, 802.

31. Jochen Schmidt, *Hölderlins letzte Hymnen: "Andenken" und "Mnemosyne"* (Tübingen: Max Niemeyer, 1970), 1–50; cited in the body of my chapter by page number(s). See also the orthodox readings by Cyrus Hamlin, "Die Poetik des Gedächtnisses," *Hölderlin-Jahrbuch* 24 (1984/85): 119–38, and Wolfgang Binder, "Hölderlin: Andenken," *Turm-Vorträge* 1985–86, ed. Uvo Hölscher (Tübingen: Hölderlin-Gesellschaft, 1986), 5–30.

32. Dieter Henrich, *Der Gang des Andenkens: Beobachtungen und Gedanken zu Hölderlins Gedicht* (Stuttgart: Klett-Cotta, 1986). I am in-

debted also to a discussion with the French translator of Hölderlin, Jean-Pierre Lefebvre, for details about "Andenken" and the topography and history of Bordeaux that go in the same direction as Henrich's reading. See his "Auch die Stege sind Holzwege," in *Hölderlin vu de France,* ed. Bernhard Böschenstein and Jacques le Rider (Tübingen: Narr, 1987), 53–76.

33. Anselm Haverkamp, *Laub voll Trauer,* 71–92; cited in the body of my chapter by page number(s).

34. Corresponding to the parody of the "Patmos" lines—Wilhelm Busch's "Wer Sorgen hat, hat auch Likör" ("Whoever has troubles, has liquor, too")—is Erich Fried's parody of "Andenken": "Was bleibt, geht stiften" ("What remains, goes founding"). Both cited in Haverkamp, 78.

35. After many years its best analysis and discussion remains Peter Szondi's "Überwindung des Klassizismus," in *Hölderlin-Studien.* See also Schmidt's brief version of the theory, 4–11. For a brief presentation of it in English, see Sieburth's discussion in his introduction to his translations, 11–16.

36. A similar unilinear and comprehensive claim for the poem's arrival at its end may be found in Schmidt, 30, 31: "The tone of remembrance intensifies itself to that of an inner sight and a deeply self-emersed meditation, which in the last verse's gnomic utterance achieves its goal with a decisively comprehensive and conclusive gesture." Unexpectedly then—and in an error that is to be accounted for by Schmidt's insistence on bringing "Andenken" together with Hölderlin's early *Hyperion* and his letters to Schiller—he later qualifies such conclusive claims by making the ending and achievement of "Andenken" only asymptotic: "The verse 'Was bleibet aber, stiften die Dichter' projects a poetic ideal, the unattainability of which lies grounded in the necessarily infinite progression of consciousness, and it may therefore be thought only in infinite approximation" (40).

37. In addition to Henrich, 92, 93, see Lefebvre, "Auch die Stege sind Holzwege," and Adolf Beck, "Kleine Zufallsfunde," *Hölderlin-Jahrbuch* (1953): 68, cited in Schmidt, 18.

38. John Freccero, "The Figtree and the Laurel: Petrarch's Poetics," *Diacritics* 5 (1975): 34–40.

39. See Micah 4:4, "But they shall sit everyman under his vine and under his figtree; and none shall make them afraid: for the mouth of the Lord of hosts hath spoken it."; and John 1:48–50, "[Jesus:] Before that Philip called thee [Nathanael], when thou wast under the figtree, I saw thee . . . [Nathanael:] Thou art the Son of God . . . [Jesus:] Thou believest because I told thee that I saw thee under the figtree. Thou shalt see yet greater things than that."

40. Heidegger, *Erläuterungen,* 151.

41. See, for example, "Der Rhein," with its fifteen strophes divided into five triads, each triad's strophes having fifteen, sixteen, and four-

teen lines in sequence, until the penultimate strophe begins "Doch einigen eilt / Diss schnell vorüber . . . " ("For some, however, this / hurries quickly by . . . ") and has only fifteen lines, while the ultimate strophe ends "wenn alles gemischt / Ist ordnungslos und wiederkehrt / Uralte Verwirrung" ("when everything is mixed up / without order and there returns / primeval confusion") and with only twelve lines (2, 148). See also "Brod und Wein," equally symmetrically constructed with its nine eighteen-line strophes in groups of three, each strophe divided into three sections of three elegiac distichs apiece—except for its seventh strophe, which is the one with the famous line about "Dichter in dürftiger Zeit" ("poets in a needy time") and which lacks a distich (2, 94). These unmistakable—and entirely unmistaken—formal signals are only some of the radical innovations that make Hölderlin a contemporary of Mallarmé and Celan.

42. On Hölderlin's use of caesura (*Zäsur*) in this extended sense, see his "Anmerkungen zum Oedipus" (5, 195–97) and "Anmerkungen zur Antigonä" (5, 265), and also Philippe Lacoue-Labarthe, "The Caesura of the Speculative," *Glyph* 4 (Baltimore: Johns Hopkins U.P., 1978), 57–84.

43. When a version of this interpretation was presented at the University of Lausanne, a supportive audience made its contribution to the continuing parody of the "gnomic" last line: "Was bleibet aber, schneiden die Dichter" ("What remains however, the poets cut") and "Was bleibet aber, stiften die Schneider" ("What remains however, the tailors found").

44. It has been known at least since Rolf Zuberbühler, *Hölderlins Erneuerung der Sprache aus ihren etymologischen Ursprüngen* (Berlin: Walter de Gruyter, 1969), 109, that one sense of Hölderlin's *stiften* is *versteifen*, to stiffen, and that this stiffening or fixing of poets' words is what is also called for famously at the end of "Patmos": "dass gepfleget werde / Der veste Buchstab, und Bestehendes gut / Gedeutet. Dem folgt deutscher Gesang" ("that the fixed letter / May be cared for, and what exists be well / Interpreted. This, German song observes") (2, 172). I am arguing here that in the middle of the poem, one cannot find the lines founded and stiffened, but only read them as unimaginably flexing back and forth, or inverting.

45. At the limit between the phenomenality of perception and the fixity of material inscription, the lines in the poem's middle are marked chiastically. Bernhard Böschenstein, *Frucht des Gewitters,* 147, has noted that in their words' initial letters, they repeat the *s*'s and *g*'s of the encoded name of Hölderlin's former and recently deceased lover Susette Gontard, without remarking that these repetitions precisely constitute a double chiasmus: "Nicht ist es gut, / *S*eellos von *s*terblichen / *G*edanken zu *s*eyn. Doch *g*ut / Ist ein *G*espräch und zu *s*agen," that is, $g \ldots s \ldots \times s \ldots g \ldots s \ldots g \ldots \times g \ldots s \ldots$.

46. The tautological gloss is what Schmidt, 22, provides: "The 'mortal thoughts' are those that are not directed toward the essential and re-

maining, toward the immortal: unpoetic thoughts, transient like the hub-bub of the day that they concern themselves with, indeed, equivalent to de-souling 'care' [entseelenden 'Sorge']." This one-sided reading is recalled when, in his interpretation of the end of the poem, he reintroduces the "soulless" as what the poem simply rejects: "This awareness, that brings itself about in reflection, of the tendency toward remaining that is already in the two other highest forms of life [love and deeds] is what further inspires [*beseelt*] the poet, *in as much as he rejects the 'soulless,'* to what is proper to his task as poet, to the founding of what remains" (40, my emphasis).

Chapter 6. Baudelaire's "A une passante"

1. Walter Benjamin, "Über einige Motive bei Baudelaire," in *Gesammelte Schriften*, ed. Rolf Tiedemann and Hermann Schweppenhäuser (Frankfurt: Suhrkamp, 1974), I, 607, 608. Henceforth cited in the body of my text by page number only. Translations are my own.

2. For an example of close readings from abroad, see Paul de Man on "Correspondances" and "Obsession" in his "Anthropomorphism and Trope in the Lyric," in *The Rhetoric of Romanticism* (New York: Columbia U.P., 1984), 239–62. For French writers shedding light on Baudelaire's poems, there are of course many remarks by Proust, Valéry, and others, but see best, perhaps, Mallarmé's poems such as "Les Fenêtres" and the *Tombeau* sonnet on Baudelaire, in *Oeuvres complètes*, ed. Henri Mondor and G. Jean-Aubry (Paris: Gallimard, 1945).

3. Charles Baudelaire, *Oeuvres complètes*, ed. Claude Pichois (Paris: Gallimard, 1975), I, 92, 93. All other Baudelaire poems are also cited from this edition. The translation is my own.

4. For an account of these two manuscripts, and the genesis of the latter out of the former in response to Horkheimer and Adorno's critique of Benjamin's work, see my "Benjamin, Baudelaire, and the Allegory of History," in *Allegories of History: Literary Historiography after Hegel* (Baltimore: Johns Hopkins U.P., 1992), 206–8.

5. See, for the interpretive extension of Benjamin and Baudelaire toward revolutionary contexts, the interesting, excessive, and finally massively failed work by Wolfgang Fietkau, *Schwanengesang auf 1848—Ein Rendezvous am Louvre: Baudelaire, Marx, Proudhon und Victor Hugo* (Hamburg: Rowohlt, 1978).

6. Thus, "d*ou*leur majest*ueu*se" inverted in "fast*ueu*se / S*ou*levant," "*ou*rlet; / . . . stat*ue*" inverted in "b*u*vais . . . / . . . *où* . . . *ou*ragan," reinverted then in "d*ou*ceur . . . *tue*." I am very grateful to Claude Reichler for pointing this out, as well as the feature of masculine and feminine rhymes in the two quatrains.

7. Baudelaire, *Oeuvres complètes*, 1022.

8. On a poem directing itself to "une passante" becoming the poem "A une passante," it is worth noting that the previous Pléiade edition had

its editor, Yves-Gérard Le Dantec, entitling the poem "Une passante," *Oeuvres complétes* (Paris: Gallimard, 1954), 88, the current edition entitling it with the more common "A une passante," with neither editor remarking on the choice and change of title.

9. On the "Eau, quand donc pleuvras-tu?" of "Le Cygne" as an apostrophe to apostrophe, see Jonathan Culler, "Apostrophe," *Diacritics* 7:4 (1977): 64, 65; and on the poetic and interpretive implications of the "sans eau"/"Ovide" play in the same poem, see my *Allegories of History*, 219–24 and 323, 324, n. 24.

10. On anthropomorphism as giving ("the *taking* of something for something else that can then be assumed to be *given*," 241), see his "Anthropomorphism and Trope in the Lyric," cited in n. 2. On prosopopeia as giving-and-taking face, see above all his "Autobiography as De-Facement," *The Rhetoric*, 67–81, but also "Wordsworth and the Victorians," *The Rhetoric*, pp. 89–92, and "Shelley Disfigured," *The Rhetoric*, 119–22.

Chapter 7. Three Wallace Stevens Poems

1. Harold Bloom, *Poetry and Repression: Revisionism from Blake to Stevens* (New Haven: Yale U.P., 1976), 267–93, and *Wallace Stevens: The Poems of Our Climate* (Ithaca, N.Y.: Cornell U.P., 1977).

2. Helen Vendler, "Stevens and Keats' 'To Autumn,'" in *Wallace Stevens: A Celebration*, ed. Frank Doggett and Robert Buttel (Princeton: Princeton U.P., 1980), 171–95, and *Wallace Stevens: Words Chosen out of Desire* (Cambridge, Mass.: Harvard U.P., 1986), 45–50. See also the suggestions contained in Richard Macksey, "'To Autumn' and the Music of Mortality: 'Pure Rhetoric of a Language without Words,'" in *Romanticism and Language*, ed. Arden Reed (Ithaca, N.Y.: Cornell U.P., 1984), 263–308.

3. I mean by this suggestion that Stevens' posture of impersonality, his motif of what I would call absolute bookishness, and his practice of splaying apart and plaiting back together words' sounds and their meanings all may be seen to derive from Mallarmé. I do not, in this association, understand Mallarmé as the agonized and sterile exile portrayed in the opening pages of W. R. Johnson's *The Idea of Lyric: Lyric Modes in Ancient and Modern Poetry* (Berkeley: U. of California P., 1982), esp. 8–12, and I also acknowledge that the association runs against the grain of Vendler's emphasis on Stevens' personality of *desire* in her *Wallace Stevens*.

4. The thought of reading Stevens with Shakespeare's sonnets in mind came from some asides in Vendler's *Wallace Stevens*, and from recalling lectures by and conversations with Angus Fletcher.

5. On "die unscheinbaren Worte," see Rainer Maria Rilke, "Die armen Worte, die im Alltag darben," in *Sämtliche Werke*, ed. Ernst Zinn (Frankfurt: Insel, 1955), I, 148.

6. I think of "Autumn Refrain," the poem that both takes itself and its speaker away from Keats—"The yellow moon of words about the

nightingale / In measureless measures, not a bird for me / But the name of a bird and the name of a nameless air / I have never—shall never hear"—and, in the middle of the very line just quoted, gives both back to Keats with all the ambivalence and ambiguity of his word "still": "And yet beneath / The stillness that comes to me out of this, beneath / The stillness of everything gone, and being still, / Being and sitting still, something resides, / Some skreaking and skrittering residuum / . . . And the stillness is in the key, all of it is, / The stillness is all in the key of that desolate sound." And see also, with reference to Keats's Saturn in his Hyperion poems, the second stanza of "Examination of the Hero in a Time of War": "the God whom we serve is able, / Still, still to deliver us, still magic, / Still moving yet motionless in smoke, still / One with us, in heaved-up noise, still / Captain."

7. Stevens' poems are cited from Wallace Stevens, *The Palm at the End of the Mind: Selected Poems and a Play,* ed. Holly Stevens (New York: Vintage, 1972). For an interpretation that reads Stevens' career as an unfolding *away from* "The Snow Man"—a negative version, in other words, of the kinds of understanding of poetry I discussed in my opening paragraphs to this chapter—see Alfred Corn, "Wallace Stevens and the Poetics of Ineffability," in *Ineffability: Naming the Unnamable from Dante to Beckett,* ed. Peter S. Hawkins and Anne Howland Schotter (New York: AMS Press, 1984), 179–87. The insensitivity of the reading of "The Snow Man," the unilinear and monothematic reading of the career, and the religious piety of the argumentation are all equally out of touch with Stevens' artistry.

8. See Stéphane Mallarmé, "Le tombeau d'Edgar Poe," in *Oeuvres complètes,* ed. Henri Mondor and G. Jean-Aubry (Paris: Gallimard, 1945), 70, and Walter Benjamin, "Die Aufgabe des Übersetzers," in *Gesammelte Schriften,* ed. Rolf Tiedemann et al. (Frankfurt: Suhrkamp, 1972 f.), IV/1, 13 ff.; English in *Illuminations,* ed. Hannah Arendt (New York: Schocken, 1969), 74 ff.

9. Cf. Stevens' contrast in "An Old Man Asleep" between "the self"'s possessive pronoun "your" and "the earth"'s definite article: "The redness of your reddish chestnut trees, / The river motion, the drowsy motion of the river R."

10. By keeping the second stanza one line shorter than the first, Stevens cuts off the visual mirroring—itself chiastic: "the mind is not part of the weather" × "the air [= the weather] is clear of everything [= the mind not part of]"—of the two parts at this point, and also thereby avoids a fourteen-line poem when this one, in its thirteenth line, will already powerfully recall two of Shakespeare's sonnets.

11. With reference to the excellent essay by Christiaan L. Hart Nibbrig, "Totschreiben. Erste Notizen zu einer Poetik der letzten Dinge," *Akzente* 5 (1987): 387–402, I would also say that this limit is death.

12. G. W. F. Hegel, *Vorlesungen über die Ästhetik* I, in *Werke,* ed. Eva Moldenhauer and Karl Markus Michel (Frankfurt: Suhrkamp, 1970), XIII, 173.

Chapter 8. Three Celan Poems

1. Celan texts are cited by volume (roman numeral) and page (arabic numeral) from Paul Celan, *Gesammelte Werke* in fünf Bänden, ed. Beda Allemann and Stefan Reichert with assistance from Rolf Bücher (Frankfurt: Suhrkamp, 1983). All translations are my own, although I have consulted with respect and profit *Poems of Paul Celan*, trans. Michael Hamburger (New York: Persea Books, 1988), *Speech-Grille and Selected Poems*, trans. Joachim Neugroschel (New York: E. P. Dutton, 1971), and *Last Poems*, trans. Katharine Washburn and Margret Guillemin (San Francisco: North Point Press, 1986).

2. For another, engaging commentary on "Unter ein Bild" that nonetheless makes no use of either its emblem structure or its apocalyptic one, see Christiaan L. Hart Nibbrig, "'Wenn Bilder den Mund und Texte die Augen aufmachen . . .' Zwischen Wort und Bild: Übersetzungsprobleme," in *Mit den Augen geschrieben: Von gedichteten und erzählten Bildern* (Dichtung und Sprache, Bd. 10), ed. Lea Ritter-Santini (Munich: Hanser, 1991), 170–95; on "Unter ein Bild," 188–91. "Unter ein Bild" is not Celan's only ekphrastic poem—see, for example, "Einkanter" (II, 392), on a Rembrandt etching—but it is to my knowledge his only emblematically structured ekphrasis, and so I treat it here in isolation from the others.

3. I owe to discussion with Jim Porter and Yopie Prins the insight that the word *Rabenüberschwärmte*, with its *über* but especially with its *schwärmte* (as in *Schwärmerei*, enthusiasm), suggests the experience of the sublime, which similarly plays on a one-dimensional sense of the liminal, the two-dimensional sense of being lifted up and above and being brought low at the same time, and the three-dimensional imagery of great volumes of water such as cataracts and ocean waves.

4. Apart from this tropological *structure* of hysteron proteron that I read in "Unter ein Bild," the only technically exact instance of the *trope* of hysteron proteron that I am aware of in Celan's work is in his youthful poem "Ein Rosenkelch," in *Das Frühwerk*, ed. Barbara Wiedemann (Frankfurt: Suhrkamp, 1989), 142: "Trifft mich kein Pfeil und keiner mehr spannt hier den Bogen" ("No arrow hits me and no one more here draws the bow"). Here, as is also implied in "Unter ein Bild," the trope adopts the favored classical model of the arrow striking before it leaves the bow; for a vernacular version of this classical trope, see Dante, *Paradiso* II, 23 ff.: "e forse in tanto in quanto un quadrel posa / e vola e da la noce si dischiava, / giunto mi vidi ove mirabil cosa / mi torse il viso a sé."

5. Stéphane Mallarmé, *Oeuvres complètes*, ed. Henri Mondor and G. Jean-Aubry (Paris: Gallimard, 1945), 378. And we recall here Celan asking in "Der Meridian" (III, 193), "sollen wir . . . Mallarmé konsequent zu Ende denken?"

6. One exception would be Wallace Stevens' "The Reader" (1935),

which forms an eerie pendant to Celan's rare and great apocalyptic-salvationary poem, "Einmal, / da hörte ich ihn" (II, 107).

7. See Celan, "Der Meridian" (III, 195): "Wer auf dem Kopf geht, . . . der hat den Himmel als Abgrund unter sich."

8. I refer to *Paradiso*, from cantos XVIII–XX, in which all the action and representations are in the face of the "sky-writing" of the heavens as a text for Dante-pilgrim, to the point and end where God appears as a book enfolded upon itself (XXXIII, 86).

9. Among many others, Peter Szondi argued persuasively against the wishful claims for "parallel passages" in the interpretation of poetry, first in general (his specific examples were from Hölderlin) in "Über philologische Erkenntnis" (1962), *Hölderlin-Studien*, 2nd ed. (Frankfurt: Suhrkamp, 1970), 15–21, and then in regard to Celan in "Durch die Enge geführt," *Celan-Studien* (Frankfurt: Suhrkamp, 1972), 48 ff. On the imagery of skin sutured and rescarred, see the lines from "Engführung" quoted below in the text.

10. Hans-Georg Gadamer, *Wer bin Ich und wer bist Du? Kommentar zu Celans "Atemkristall,"* 2nd rev. ed. (Frankfurt: Suhrkamp, 1986), 149.

11. Werner Hamacher, "Die Sekunde der Inversion: Bewegungen einer Figur durch Celans Gedichte," in *Paul Celan*, ed. Werner Hamacher and Winfried Menninghaus (Frankfurt: Suhrkamp, 1988), 112.

12. In addition to the traditional associations of flight and poetry from Greek and Latin antiquity to Dante and beyond, there is a subtradition within German poetry itself that includes Goethe's "Harzreise im Winter," Eichendorff's "Es ist als hätte der Himmel," and Heine's "Auf den Flügel meines Gesanges."

13. Celan's poetology, like that of most poets, is written into his very poems, but it is also contained in his major statement of his poetics, "Der Meridian," his speech on the occasion of his reception of the Georg-Büchner Prize in 1960. I do not intend to comment on this extraordinary text here, the density and artistry of which—comparable to Hölderlin's poetological writings—would demand a separate and extended treatment, except to note in it the poetological model of the bifocal, out-and-back figure of the elliptical exchange between poet and audience that veers away from each in turn ("Umwege von dir zu dir" ["detours from you to you"], III, 201). See as well, in his other, briefer statement of his poetics, the remarks on the award of the Bremen Literature Prize in 1958, the figure of the chancy project of a poetic projectile that leaves the poet for an unknown addressee, word of the receipt of which might nonetheless get back to one—the message in the bottle: "Das Gedicht kann, da es ja eine Erscheinungsform der Sprache und damit seinem Wesen nach dialogisch ist, eine Flaschenpost sein, aufgegeben in dem—gewiss nicht immer hoffnungsstarken—Glauben, sie könnte irgendwo und irgendwann an Land gespült werden, an Herzland vielleicht. Gedichte sind auch in dieser Weise unterwegs: sie halten auf etwas zu" ("The poem may

be, since it is a manifestation of language and thereby, in its essence, dialogical, a message in the bottle, given up and out in the—admittedly not always strongly hopeful—belief, it could wash up on land somewhere, sometime, on heart's land perhaps. Poems are, in this way as well, underway: they go toward something") (III, 186).

14. Hamacher, 112–17.

15. Celan frequently places an entire strophe in parentheses, but this is the only instance where the *first* strophe is so bracketed. It is thus the symmetrical counterpart to "Engführung"—they appeared in the same volume of verse, *Sprachgitter* (1959)—the last strophe of which is in parentheses (I, 204).

16. I owe this genial suggestion, as well as many insights into the poem "Aber," to a conversation with Christiaan Hart Nibbrig.

17. Bernhard Böschenstein, "Genève et son lac: Trois témoignages de la poésie allemande," in *Littérature Histoire Linguistique: Recueil d'études offert à Bernard Gagnebin* (Lausanne: L'Age d'Homme, 1973), 94. Celan's "Aber" enters into the line of German poems crucially employing the imagery of reflected images on the surfaces of lakes, including, as we have seen, Goethe's "Auf dem See" and Hölderlin's "Hälfte des Lebens."

18. This auxiliary sense of the phrase "eines Sinnes zu sein"—to hold to one direction—both awakens and is reinforced by the sense of another verbal construction close to the poem's "mit diesem Vorbei zu sein": *vorbeigehen*, meaning "to miss," as a shot or projectile misses its mark.

19. Böschenstein, 94.

20. Celan was a careful reader of Hegel's *Phänomenologie des Geistes*, and this play between the fixity and the transience of "this" (*diesem, dieses*) recasts the point of the *Phänomenologie's* first chapter on "sense-certainty" (*sinnliche Gewissheit*).

21. Walter Benjamin, "Über einige Motive bei Baudelaire," in *Gesammelte Schriften*, ed. Rolf Tiedemann and Hermann Schweppenhäuser (Frankfurt: Suhrkamp, 1974), I, 646, 647.

22. See Böschenstein's paraphrase, where he speaks of the "regard de l'autre qui transformera le moi en une image accessible dans le temps présent de la pensée amoureuse intense" (94).

23. Hamacher, 91, associates the dash—*Gedankenstrich*, "stroke of thought" in German—in Celan with his later use of the word *Verhoffen*, the pause wherein an animal in the wild stands still and senses what the air, its scents and sounds, forebode.

24. Beda Allemann reported in conversation his experience of hearing swans flying, unseen, at night, above the Lake of Zurich, beating the air with their wings, and suggested it might be a similar experience at Geneva that Celan renders here.

25. Joachim Neugroschel, in his translation of "Aber" in his *Speech-Grille and Selected Poems*, 133, the rigor of which I admire, inexplicably mistranslates *Wurfholz* as "javelin."

26. See also Celan's simile of language: "wie die Sprache, / wirf sie weg, wirf sie weg, / dann hast du sie wieder . . . " ("like language / throw it away, throw it away, / then you get it back . . . ") ("Es ist alles anders," I, 285).

27. The lake at Geneva, Lac Léman, is also known to its residents as *l'arc Léman* because of its conspicuously arced shape.

28. On the readable measure of a gap, see also Jacques Derrida's analysis of circumcision in the course of his reading of Celan's poem "Schibboleth," in *Schibboleth* (Paris: Galilée, 1986).

29. Maurice Blanchot, *Le dernier à parler* (Montpellier: Fata Morgana, 1984), 9.

30. Christiaan Hart Nibbrig has perceptively remarked in conversation that the "thereness" of the "you" in the poem is here precisely marked as missing in the missing word "there" (*dort*): a German reader would expect to find "nicht / neben mir, nicht dort, / wo du nicht sein kannst."

31. Beda Allemann, "Paul Celans Sprachgebrauch," in *Argumentum e Silentio*, ed. Amy D. Colin (Berlin: de Gruyter, 1987), 10: "Die Sprache ist für [Celan] . . . ein *Prozess*, mit dem man unterwegs ist und der auf etwas hinzielt. Das Ziel ist . . . das Andere—oder auch der Andere . . . jenes imaginäre *Gegenüber* Mandelstamms . . . verborgen hinter dem . . . *Du* . . . [dass] bei Celan ein Fragewort [ist]."

32. See Israel Chalfen, *Paul Celan: Eine Biographie seiner Jugend* (Frankfurt: Suhrkamp, 1979), 118–26.

33. The word has as well a specific nautical meaning (a *Leichter* is a barge used in unloading a larger ship, *leichtern* and the past participle *geleichtert* to so unload or be unloaded). *Leiche*, corpse, may also be signified within the word.

34. "Dichtung: das kann eine Atemwende bedeuten. Wer weiss, vielleicht legt die Dichtung den Weg—auch den Weg der Kunst—um einer solchen Atemwende willen zurück?" ("Poetry: that can mean a breath-turn. Who knows, maybe poetry will blaze back a path—also the path of art—for the sake of such a breath-turn?"), in "Der Meridian," III, 195.

35. Gadamer, *Wer bin Ich*, 63.

36. Cf. the image in "Mit den Sackgassen" (II, 358): "dieses / Brot kauen, mit / Schreibzähnen."

37. *Liedfest* invokes the German adjective, *bibelfest*, meaning familiar with, knowledgeable about the Bible, while the association of song (*Lied*) with festival (*Fest*) is found repeatedly in Hölderlin.

38. Gadamer, *Wer bin Ich*, 64, writes: "Wie der Wimpel eines untergehenden Schiffes als letztes noch aus dem Wasser ragt, so ist der Dichter mit seinem Lied als letzter eine Verkündung und eine Verheissung von Leben, ein letztes Hochhalten des Hoffens" ("Just as the pennant of a sinking ship is the last thing to still stick out of the water, so is the poet with his song, as the last man, a proclamation and a promise of life, a last holding-high of hope"). Benjamin wrote of himself to Gershom

Scholem as "like one who keeps afloat on a shipwreck by climbing to the top of a mast that is already crumbling. But from there he has a chance to give a signal leading to his rescue" (*Briefe,* ed. T. W. Adorno and Gershom Scholem [Frankfurt: Suhrkamp, 1966], 17 April 1931, 532). Celan's poem was published in 1965, before the edition of Benjamin's letters appeared, so it is unlikely he knew the passage, although likely that Gadamer has it in mind in his interpretation.

39. *Einkommen* is also already textual, as it can mean to write on behalf of something or someone ("um etwas einkommen").

40. On *Sekunde* as the cut of time in Celan, see Hamacher, "Die Sekunde der Inversion," 98, 99, and *passim.*

41. Celan, letter to Hans Bender, 18 May 1960, III, 177.

42. See also the phrases "von / Fingergedanken befragt" ("questioned / by finger-thoughts") ("A la pointe acérée," I, 251) and "ertastbar mit Fühl- / wörtern" ("touchable with feel- / words") ("Ich kann dich noch sehn," II, 275).

43. There may also be an allusion here to the artist's function at the beginning of Hamann's *Aesthetica in nuce:* to gather together *disjecta membra.*

44. Cf. Blanchot, *Le dernier à parler,* 13: "comme si avait déjà eu lieu la destruction de soi pour qu'autrui soit preservé" ("as if the destruction of oneself had already taken place so that the other might be saved").

45. See the comparison quoted in n. 13 above.

Afterword

1. It is with admiration and gratitude that for the translation of Pindar I am adapting the version, albeit incomplete, provided by D. S. Carne-Ross in his study *Pindar* (New Haven: Yale U.P., 1985), 169–84. Supplementing this version are those by Friedrich Hölderlin in volume 5 of the Grosse Stuttgarter Ausgabe, *Sämtliche Werke,* ed. Friedrich Beissner (Stuttgart: W. Kohlhammer, 1951ff.), and by Richmond Lattimore, in *The Odes of Pindar,* 2nd ed. (Chicago: U. of Chicago P., 1976).

2. Lattimore's English translation, "[Aigina] keeps / glory perfect from the beginning," is semantically identical, while Hölderlin's German one, "Vollen- / deten aber hat Glanz von Anfang," is even syntactically identical.

3. Carne-Ross, 175, 176.

4. Ibid., 179.

5. See, among several examples, Nemean 7, and also the famous openings of Olympian 1, 4, and 9.

6. Carne-Ross, 177.

7. Ibid.

8. Lattimore's and Hölderlin's translations of Apollo's epithet and the lines about one man going up, another down, each capture the par-

allelism of the throwing (*bállein*) with the flight of Apollo's arrows: "But you, archer of the far cast," and "God's luck is the giver, / that casts one man now aloft, and yet another beneath his hand"; and "Du aber, Fernhintreffender," and "Ein Dämon aber gibt es, / Anderswoher andere von oben herunter treffend, / Einen andern aber under der Hände," where Hölderlin's *treffen* has the sense of *werfen*.

9. Lattimore's move from "above" to "threw" ("And above four bodies you threw / your weight and your rage") and Hölderlin's phrase "gestürzt von oben" ("Auf vier aber bist du gestürzt von oben, / Auf Körper, übles / Gedenkend") similarly reproduce Pindar's arc.

10. Carne-Ross, 182: "Some have found the picture of the vanquished opponents cruel, but to Pindar's Greek sense of things it would have seemed the most natural way to convey the ecstasy of the victor, even if this poem has not required him to couple victory and defeat in the most emphatic way possible. In Greek you best describe A by setting it up against Z."

11. Hölderlin's "Herrlichst auf / Aus grosser Hoffnung fliegt / Auf geflügelten Lüften / Habend grössere" brilliantly captures in its alliterations and the intensification of the comparative the heightening uplift at work here.

12. Carne-Ross, 183.

13. Lattimore's "shaken by a backward doom" and Hölderlin's "von irrem / Rate geschüttelt" are perhaps more truly opaque.

14. Carne-Ross, 183.

15. The text of the *Commedia* and its translation are taken from Dante Alighieri, *The Divine Comedy*, trans., with a commentary, Charles S. Singleton (Princeton: Princeton U.P., 1970–75). Occasionally I slightly modify Singleton's English word order.

16. *Par.* II, 23–26; XVII, 73–75; XXII, 109, 110; XXXII, 4–6; and XXXIII, 16–18.

17. Another of the hysteron proteron tropes in *Paradiso* equally effectively and succinctly conveys the impression of great speed: "tu non avresti in tanto tratto e messo / nel foco il dito in quant' io vidi" ("you would not have drawn out and put / your finger into the fire so quickly as I saw") (XXII, 109, 110).

18. The poem's working-out of the inversion of the figure of the falcon and its lure may be spotted in a seemingly small metaphor in *Purgatorio:* Virgil enjoins Dante-pilgrim to lift up his head in spirited ascent with the words, "li occhi rivolgi al logoro che gira / lo rege etterno con le rote magne" ("turn your eyes to the lure which the eternal King / spins with the mighty spheres") (XIX, 62, 63). If, in earthbound practice, the falconer spins the lure down below to draw down the circling falcon, here—by inversion—the divine falconer spins the lure above, where the falcon had been, and the falcon, standing for man, is still below, to be drawn up.

19. See John Freccero, *Dante: The Poetics of Conversion*, ed. Rachel Jacoff (Cambridge: Harvard U.P., 1986).

20. John D. Sinclair, *The Divine Comedy of Dante Alighieri, III: Paradiso* (New York: Oxford U.P., 1981), 26, n. 11.

21. Canto XIV of *Paradiso* has been called the canto of chiasmus because of its plethora of instances of the trope, but I find many of them (e.g., "Dal centro al cerchio, e sì dal cerchio al centro," l. 1, or "Quell' uno e due e tre che sempre vive / e regna sempre in tre e 'n due e'n uno," ll. 28, 29) to be rather light formalisms, while the intellectual content of the canto's chiastic statement exceeds the bounds of this brief afterword.

22. Of Pia, Croce writes, "Her words are so delicate that they seem to be rather sighed than said, and they accompany as with music the utterance of that poor and gentle name"; cited by Sinclair in *The Divine Comedy of Dante Alighieri, II: Purgatorio* (New York: Oxford U.P., 1981), 78.

23. Claude Lévi-Strauss, *Tristes Tropiques*, trans. John and Doreen Weightman (New York: Atheneum, 1978), 178: "The customs of a community, taken as a whole, always have a particular style and are reducible to systems. I am of the opinion that the number of such systems is not unlimited and that—in their games, dreams or wild imaginings—human societies, like individuals, never create absolutely, but merely choose certain combinations from an ideal repertoire that it should be possible to define."

Index

Library of Congress Cataloging-in-Publication Data

Bahti, Timothy, 1952–
    Ends of the lyric : direction and consequence in Western poetry /
Timothy Bahti.
        p.   cm.
    Includes index.
    ISBN 0-8018-5192-0 (alk. paper) — ISBN 0-8018-5193-9 (pbk. :
alk. paper)
    1. Poetics.   2. Closure (Rhetoric)   I. Title.
PN1042.B24   1996
809.1'4—dc20   95-22341
                                                                    CIP